"The very best, the most sensible, the most practical, the most honest book on this matter of getting up good dinners, and living in a decent, Christian way, that has yet found its way in our household."—WATCHMAN AND REFLECTOR.

COMMON SENSE
IN THE HOUSEHOLD.
A MANUAL OF PRACTICAL HOUSEWIFERY.
By MARION HARLAND.

New Edition. One volume, 12mo, cloth, . . Price, $1.75

KITCHEN EDITION, IN OIL-CLOTH COVERS, AT SAME PRICE.

This edition is printed from new electrotype plates and bound in a new pattern cloth binding, and also in the favorite "Kitchen Edition" style.

The popularity of this book has increased steadily for the last ten years, and the sale has reached the extraordinary number of

Over 100,000 Copies.

Many housekeepers will gladly welcome their old friend in a new dress, and renew their copies worn by constant use; or, as the author herself expresses it, "I hope my fellow-workers will find their old kitchen companion in fresh dress, yet more serviceable than before, and that their daughters may, at the close of a second decade, demand new stereotype plates for still another and like this a progressive edition."

With the new edition of "*Common Sense*," the Publishers will issue, in uniform style:

THE DINNER YEAR BOOK.
One volume, 12mo, 720 pp., cloth, or "Kitchen Edition," without colored plates......$1.75.

BREAKFAST, LUNCHEON, AND TEA.
One volume, 12mo. Cloth, or "Kitchen Edition,".......$1.75.

Note.—The Dinner Year Book, with six colored plates, illustrating twenty-eight subjects, handsomely bound in cloth, will be continued in print at the regular price, $2.25.

⁂ For sale by all booksellers, or sent, post-paid, upon receipt of price, by

CHARLES SCRIBNER'S SONS, PUBLISHERS,
743 AND 745 BROADWAY, NEW YORK.

A NEW EDITION

Uniform with the re-issue of "Common Sense in the Household"

THE DINNER YEAR-BOOK.

By MARION HARLAND,

Author of "Common Sense in the Household," "Breakfast, Luncheon, and Tea," etc., etc.

One vol., 12mo, 720 pages, ... Price, $1.75

Kitchen Edition in Oil-Cloth Covers at same Price.

The Dinner Year-Book is, in its name, happily descriptive of its purposes and character. It occupies a place which, amid all the publications upon cookery—and their name is Legion—**has never yet been occupied.**

The author truly says that there have been *dinner-giving* books published, that is books of *menus* for company dinings, "Little Dinners," for especial occasions, etc., etc.; but that she has never yet met with a **practical directory** of this important meal **for every day in the year.** In this volume she has furnished the programme in all its details, and has superintended the preparation of each dish, proceeding even to the proper manner of serving it at the table. **The book has been prepared for the family, for the home of ordinary means, and it has hit the happy line where elegance and economy meet.**

The most numerous testimonials to the value of Marion Harland's "Common Sense" books, which the publishers have received, both in newspaper notices and in private communications, are to the effect—always expressed with some astonishment—that **the directions of these receipts, actually followed, produce the promised result.** We can prophesy the same for the new volume.

The purchaser will find that he has bought what the name purports—*The Dinner Year-Book*—a practical guide for the purchase of the material and preparation, serving, etc., of the ordinary home dinner for every day of the year. To these are added **twelve company dinners,** one for each month, from which a selection can be made—according to the time of the year—equal to any occasion which will be presented to the housekeeper.

This book, however, is not valuable merely as a directory for dinners appropriate to various seasons. It contains **the largest number of receipts** for soups, fish, meat, vegetables, entrees of all descriptions, and desserts, **ever offered to the American public.** The material for this work has been collected with great care, both at home and abroad, representing the diligent labor of many months.

Note.—The original Edition of The Dinner Year Book, with six colored plates, illustrating twenty-eight subjects, handsomely bound in cloth, will be continued in print at the regular price, $2.25.

*** *For sale by all booksellers, or will be sent, post or express charges paid, upon receipt of the price, by*

CHARLES SCRIBNER'S SONS, Publishers,

743 and 745 Broadway, New York.

THE COTTAGE KITCHEN

COMMON SENSE IN THE HOUSEHOLD SERIES.

THE COTTAGE KITCHEN

A COLLECTION

OF

PRACTICAL AND INEXPENSIVE RECEIPTS

BY

MARION HARLAND

NEW YORK
CHARLES SCRIBNER'S SONS
1883

HARVARD COLLEGE LIBRARY
BEQUEST OF
MRS. CHESTER N. GREENOUGH
SEPTEMBER 20, 1926

COPYRIGHT, 1888, BY
CHARLES SCRIBNER'S SONS

TROW'S
PRINTING AND BOOKBINDING COMPANY
201-213 *East Twelfth St.*
NEW YORK

INDEX OF GENERAL SUBJECTS.

	PAGE		PAGE
Beverages	238	Jellies, fruit	196
Blanc mange	226	Meats	36
Bread	148	Muffins	157
Cake	203	Pic-nic dishes	245
Corn-bread	157	Pickles	197
Custards	216	Porridges	137
Cheese-dishes	145	Poultry	73
Eggs	78	Puddings	166
Griddle-cakes	157	Salads	84
Fish	89	Sauces for puddings	183
Fruits, stewed and baked	193	Soups	9
Jams and marmalade	194	Vegetables	108
Jellies and blanc mange	226		

FAMILIAR TALKS.

	PAGE		PAGE
Country-boarding	67	Maid-of-all-work	141
Dish-washing	251	Meats	36
Flies	221	Soup and Stock-pot	9
"Kitchenly-kind"	186	Table manners	97

FAMILIAR TALK.

"It is only the really poor and the rich who can afford to marry and go to housekeeping now-a-days," is a saying that is no longer flippant, but so pertinent that wise humanitarians look grave with the hearing thereof.

To the factory-girl or the seamstress who has been used to "go out to work," a flat in a tenement house furnished with her own chattels, is *home*. She esteems it a privilege to be allowed to reign over the kingdom of three or four rooms, to take care of the cheap new furniture, and prepare three meals a day for herself and the husband who, perhaps, takes his dinner in a pail when he goes forth to his daily labor. The routine of homely tasks arranged by herself is a light cross compared with the stern necessity of rising before sunrise on winter mornings, breasting evening storms, and toiling for ten hours of broiling summer days under the eye of an overlooker in a temperature where sickly girls faint every hour, and the most robust sigh, "Would God it were night!" She is her own employer, forewoman, and operative, and rejoices in her independence.

The rich—and less free—house-mistress pulls upon her husband's purse or her private fortune to maintain a handsome establishment, and yields plaintive assent when the nominal master of the abode rails at "the concern" as a "servants' boarding-house."

Young men belonging to the great middle class—to wit, clerks in banks, stores, and offices, small tradesmen, lawyers, doctors, and clergymen, who are beginning the practice of their professions—with salaries varying from $600 to $1,200 per annum, cannot think of such luxuries as homes, wives, and families of their very own for years to come.

I was a listener, some days ago, to a serious discussion of what we assume as a self-evident truth, the speakers being two lawyers of distinction, men who treated the question with frankness, without sneering at the "extravagant notions of modern women."

"The girls of this generation must marry middle-aged widowers, or remain single until the flower of youth has gone," was the summing up. "You and I married on $1,000 a year, and thought ourselves well off. Our daughters must have double that sum. Every clergyman and public register will tell you that the number of marriages is alarmingly on the decrease. Housekeepers cry out that the rise of salaries has not kept pace with the increased prices of provisions. The student of social economy puts the two facts together as cause and effect, and asks himself 'what the end will be?'"

When to this statement we subjoin the truth that within the last quarter of a century Cookery as an Art has become a fashionable study, that as such it has kindergartens, normal schools, professors, and itinerant lecturers, the problem is complicated. Must our girls practise the new branch merely as an accomplishment? Is the knowledge for which we have paid fancy (and fabulous) prices but another aspect of the "æsthetic craze," to be ranked in another decade with the passing rage for illuminated flat-irons and decorated rolling-pins?

In the hope of shedding one ray of practical Common

Sense through the fog that enwraps this subject, I have set myself to work to prepare a compendium of receipts that are economical, yet wholesome and palatable. I have kept steadily before me the end of adapting these to the use of young housekeepers, and the mighty mass of people of moderate means who crave something more tempting to eye and taste than the dry or coarse rations flung upon hundreds of tables with little more regard to the decencies of domestic life than is observed in supplying stall and sty.

As in nine cases out of ten, the first indication of the failure of physical powers is in the weakened digestive organs, so it may be affirmed that scarcity of means shows itself soonest and most decidedly in the kitchen. Coarser materials take the place of delicacies; sameness succeeds to tempting variety; and she is a woman of exceptional spirit, as well as cleverness, who does not grow more indifferent each day in the execution of duties that have become homely and hard.

The same rule obtains in households where limited resources and strict economy have always prevailed. Unfriendly criticism strikes most quickly and surely at the poor man who "sets a good table."

Fanny Kemble writes of her mother's talent for cookery: "It amounted to genius, and might have made her a preeminent *cordon bleu*, if she had not been the wife of a poor professional gentleman, whose moderate means were so skilfully turned to account in her provision for his modest table, that he was accused by ill-natured people of indulging in the expensive luxury of a French cook. I would joyfully many a time in America have exchanged all my boarding-school smatterings for her knowledge how to produce a wholesome and palatable dinner."

I shall feel far more than repaid for the trouble it has

cost me to prepare "The Cottage Kitchen" if it shall introduce into the rude plenty of one farm-house, or the monotonous fare served in the mechanic's "flat," savoriness which is wholesome in a succession of dishes that shall cheat poverty of some of its severity.

"If I had the materials I could cook as well as anybody," is the lament of her who cannot afford choice cuts, early vegetables, and forced fruit.

To nourish her family she fries tough meat into leather and strings, boils potatoes into wateriness, and soaks cabbage with grease. To tickle their palates she expends muscle and labor in the composition of "family pie-crust," and fills the same with half-sweetened dried apples.

I have been a summer boarder in farm-houses where they "calculated to raise nearly everything for the table;" have been permitted to sit in the neat kitchen of the mechanic's wife, and chat with her while she made ready "his" dinner; have gone on errands of business and mercy into far humbler abodes, yet where provisions were sufficient as to quantity, if common as to quality. Noting silently the processes of preparing food in all of these, I have made up my mind that the unsatisfactory results are attributable mainly to two faults on the part of the housewife.

First: an ignorant indifferentism on the subject of dainty cookery as a rule. Her family fare as well as their neighbors. They are no better educated in this respect than herself, or suppose that poor people must be content with poor living. She has to get up three meals a day, three hundred and sixty-five days in the year. The business is tiresome, because trite and uninteresting. She groans over baking, boiling, and frying, almost as dolorously as over the cleansing of pots, pans, and kettles. It is a flow that goes on forever without the sudden sally, the

FAMILIAR TALK. 5

sparkle and the dally of the brook. She never asks herself whether her husband may not weary of driving nails or laying brick, of ploughing, sowing, and reaping. That is his life-labor. She would despise him if he were as apathetic in the performance, loathed it as drearily as she does kitchen-work. If she is ambitious, she is apt to wish aloud that she had a trade or profession. Her web of life is a hit-or-miss carpet, and the knots have a way of coming out on the right, which is the wrong side. She is always discouraged, chronically fatigued, and given to declarations that a tread-mill is a bower of pleasure compared with the existence of the woman who does her own work. She would hardly discern exaggeration, and certainly see no burlesque in the humorously pathetic last words of the old woman, who was

"Going
Where washing ain't done, nor churning, nor sewing,
And everything else will be just to my wishes;
For where they don't eat there's no washing of dishes.
Don't mourn for me now, nor mourn for me never,
For I'm going to do nothing for ever and ever."

Far be it from me to deny that there are many and sharp crooks in the lot of our tired wife. Said a patient voice to the pastor who spoke of the praises of heaven, the advance from glory to glory—"Some time perhaps I'll understand it all. Just now I'd like to pray God to let me lie still in my grave for a couple of hundred years or so. Just to get rested out, you know!"

The fardel of human existence and toil *is* bound more tightly upon some shoulders than upon others. Yet the question to be pressed home to our housewife's consciousness and conscience is, whether she appreciates the truth that Home is her sphere since the Master has put her there and hedged her in by loves and duties, and house-keeping her trade, her profession, her mission.

Fault the second, I write down as mismanagement of time and forces.

The preparation of each meal is postponed until there is just time to get it ready between the commencement of the business and the hour of serving. Instead of forecasting breakfast in all its details, and so far as possible laying materials ready to her hand, time and nervous power are wasted when both are scant, in thinking, "What can we have?" and in collecting ingredients. The toilet is hurried that the work may be seized by the first handle that offers itself. Kindlings were not prepared, nor oatmeal put in soak at bedtime. The beef and potatoes that could have been wrought into croquettes, which would have been firm and fit for frying by morning, remain as they were left at dinner-time—the one a shapeless chunk, the other a pile of slaty-blue bullets. Clearly the only resort is that bane of the national kitchen, the frying-pan. The worried woman would cook coffee and biscuit in it, if she dared. "There is wit goes to the boiling of eggs," says the ancient adage. Calm judgment and foresight; a wise weighing of resources and capabilities are as much needed in kind, if not in degree, in the management of a kitchen as of an empire. She who feeds judiciously the bodies of that portion of the present generation given into her charge sets her mark upon her age and the next as truly as does he who writes an epic that is worthy to live, or she who delights the world with a "Middlemarch."

Thus stands the case, then! Every woman should face the fact—and consider it intelligently—that she chose her mission in accepting the hand of a man who, she knew, could afford to keep neither cook nor chamber-maid. *And* —having selected it of her own free will—she is bound by honor and conscience to make the best of it and of herself. Instead of wearying mind and spirit by stooping to her work, let her bring her work up to her level.

They have a way in the Western settlements of using bored logs for drain-pipes and conduits. When one of these gets choked with mud a big eel is put in at one end, which is at once plugged up. The eel, if he is tolerably enterprising, finding there is not room for turning his body, nor possibility of backing out, wriggles steadily onward until he emerges into the light. It may be a hundred or a thousand yards away from the starting-point.

It cannot be gainsaid that some women are created without taste for housewifery, nor that many of their sex are born deaf, others blind, and a few dumb. The success of these unfortunates in clearing away or working through the obstacles that clog their progress depends upon a sort of eel-like pertinacity of purpose their more gifted fellows should honor as it deserves to be honored.

I make no apology for describing minutely the proper method of preparing the plain dishes which every raw cook fancies everybody must understand how to get up. What our cottage housekeeper needs most is the just conception in cookery as in graver concerns—of the importance of common things. She is apt to slur over such weighty matters of the law of dietetics and health as bread-making and potato-boiling, and rush with mistaken ambition after "fancy-dishes." Hers is a zeal without knowledge as truly as that of the art-student who dives at once into color without the preliminary drill of charcoal and cubes. When this principle is reduced to practice, the term " good plain cook " will be a title of honor, instead of disparagement.

As to the lack of time for the day's work, the overlapping and "telescoping" duties that wring from the scared woman cries of horror and anguish, as she surveys the wrecked train of hours,—may I append to this introductory chapter a bit of sound, every-day wisdom I have quoted elsewhere and more than once, with tongue and pen?

The sweet-natured, clear-headed woman who talks to us behind "Mary Blake's" mask says:

"We have *all the time there is.* Our mental and moral status is determined by what we do with it."

Suffer one more quotation, four lines by Longfellow, which I tacked up in my buttery years ago, where my eye must fall upon them while mixing, beating, rolling, chopping, and what Mrs. Prentiss calls a "host of other *ings*" are going on.

"All common things, each day's events,
 That with the hour begin and end,
Our pleasures and our discontents
 Are rounds by which we may ascend."

SOUPS AND THE STOCK-POT.

AFTER setting down the heading of this chapter, an amused misgiving stole over me as to the probability that one in ten of the housewives for whom I write this series would know the meaning of that last and compound word. That the stock-pot, or jar, or crock, by whatever name known in various sections of our country, is not an established institution in the average American household, may account for the infrequent appearance of any kind of soup upon our tables, and the even rarer offering of really good broth or *potage*.

This important preliminary course of the family dinner and beginning of the serious business of the hour at company banquets is held in light esteem by no known civilized — or semi-civilized — nation except our own. The Frenchman will live, dance, and enjoy life upon a bit of black bread and onion soup, made savory by a bone for which he has paid a *sou*. The Italian shreds cabbage and dog-fennel into his broth with the lavishness of the theological student of old who heaved into the pot a lapful of poisonous wild things (*Query*: mushrooms?). The black broth of the Spartans is a classic legacy, and hungry Esau was no match for the artful junior — and Jew — who stirred the red lentile pottage before his eyes.

Our native housewife does not depreciate soups as she

does certain "fancy dishes" because they are difficult to prepare, and adorn rather than provide her board. She honestly classifies them as "slops" that go for nothing in her bill-of-fare. I have seen crockery cupboards in respectable, comfortable families, where one might look in vain for a single soup-plate. I know other and wealthier households where soup is not served for months together, even for dinner-company. There is more than one reason for this notorious disregard of an article of food decreed by so many other peoples and ages to be excellent. In New England the lack of the cheerful hospitality that delights soul and body in the Middle and Southern States is due, beyond doubt, to the fact that fewer servants are kept for domestic work in the first-named section than in the latter. Yankee thrift rebels at the thought of having "extra help" for purposes so unremunerative as entertaining strangers, and "company" becomes more and more a hardship to be avoided by every practicable and decent means. So, our notable housekeeper who washes her own dishes grows into the habit of counting the cost of whatever involves another stroke of mop or towel. With the labor-saving instinct in the industrious woman's mind goes the desire to save time. Soup is another course—therefore ten minutes more—in a meal that already takes at least half an hour out of the heart of the day. The change of plates exactly doubles the "bother" of service.

"You can't—fix it as you will—set soup, meat, and pudding on all at once."

Giving due place and weight to all these considerations, it is yet true that the main cause of the exclusion of soup from the tables of our middle and lower classes is that, not knowing how to make it, the product of their rare experiments in this line has discouraged the manufacturer and disgusted those for whom it was poured out. Dish-water is not soup, nor does the greasy paste which is its alternate better deserve the name.

"I observe that you insist upon the use of the soup-strainer in your receipts for soup-making," writes a correspondent. "Now, *my* John says you are wrong in this. He cannot relish anything of the kind unless the meat, vegetables, etc., are left in it, and the liquid pretty well thickened with flour or corn starch. Yet he is very fond of soup."

I answered: "My dear madam, your John may be fond of stews. He is not a soup-lover."

There are those who give the preference to broths, thickened with rice, barley, farina, tapioca, sage, and the like, over clear soups. They are more easily managed by a novice, and perhaps usually more nourishing, although considered less elegant for dinner-parties and other formal entertainments. Broths are good family fare—provided always that the strength of the materials used in the manufacture of them is thoroughly extracted before the liquor is drawn off. Clear soups are without flavor or nutriment unless this be done. The failure to comply with this essential regulation lies at the bottom of much of the contempt felt and expressed by many who have never seen or tasted good *bouillon*, or so much as heard of clear gravy soup.

If this preamble to our practical talk upon soup-making seems superfluous, and the directions following it ridiculously simple and minute, the reader, in extenuation of what bores her, will please believe my statement of the gross and general ignorance on the subject of this paper, illustrated in thousands of kitchens by such facts as I have just stated.

Before leaving this point of the distinction between broths and soups, let me remark that good clear (and strong) soup cannot be extracted from *cooked* bones and meat. Family broth of fair quality may be made from the carcasses of poultry and game, and from bones and scraps of underdone beef, mutton, and veal.

Let your materials be what they may, they should be put over the fire in cold water, and kept at a low temperature for the first hour, at least. Bones should be cracked in several places, meat cut into dice, vegetables sliced or grated. But the chief secret in the, to many, occult art of soup-brewing is steady, slow cooking for a long time. To be hasty in the process is to mar. Impatience but accelerates ruin. The first fast boil hardens the outer network of fibrous skin and the albumen next to this into a case almost impervious to water; seals the generous juices away from influences that would else draw them to the surface.

It is Grimm, I think, or may be Hans Andersen, who tells the story of the peasant girl whom the king made into a great lady, because when left to watch the soup-pot she never once suffered it to boil. Our energetic Yankee housewife, whose specialty is "driving" herself and subordinates, including fire and water, might go to school to the German girl. For two hours the contents of the pot should simmer drowsily beneath a closely fitting lid. Then the heat may be increased until a gentle bubble agitates the liquid, little more decided than that which shakes the water in a "singing" tea-kettle. From the beginning to the close of the operation nothing is gained and much imperilled by a "good hard boil." But neither should the "bubble, bubble" be allowed to intermit. The practised ear of the cook, busied about other matters, will soon detect irregularity on this head. The best soup-maker I ever had in my kitchen was a young woman who only knew enough when she took the place to obey orders with

Casabianca-ish doggedness. She would leave her meals; drop knife and the potato she was peeling in the sink; interrupt me in the middle of an order—I verily believe would have started up from the soundest slumber of healthy youth—to dash at the range with "*Is that soup a-bilin' hard?*" if the smothered murmur from the covered pot was quickened by but a few beats in a minute.

Next—put no salt nor other seasoning in the soup until meat and vegetables have yielded up their goodness. As a rule, season just before you are ready to remove it from the fire. Condiments have a tendency to harden the fibres and flesh, and thus resist the persuasiveness of heat and water upon the object to be steeped into pulp. Whenever you can, make soup the day before it is to be used on the table. The important process of freeing it from every particle of fat is then made easy by the congelation into a firm cake upon the top of the liquid of the oils that will arise even from lean meat. Circles and eddies of hot grease in one's plate of soup are offensive to sight and taste —demoralizing to the stomach.

The soup made, the stock-jar comes to the front. A wide-mouthed stone pot with straight sides is best for this purpose. It should be well glazed on the inside, that it may not absorb fat or liquid. Pour the soup—unstrained —into it and set by until the morrow, when it must be carefully skimmed. If you have allowed a quart of cold water to each pound of meat—independent of marrow-bones and vegetables—you should now have a rich, gelatinous "stock" above the residuum at the bottom. Strain off from this, day by day, enough to supply soup for your family. If the stock is very strong you can dilute it for daily use. The stock-pot must be kept in the cellar or other cold place. When the jelly runs low, put the entire contents of the jar over the fire, adding enough cold water to cover all well, and cook gently for a couple of hours. Then drain and press in a colander, and run the liquid thus obtained through your soup-strainer. Good broth may be made of this, but do not attempt to get clear soup from it. The mass left in the colander is as unfit for food as would be so much wet, raw cotton.

I state this distinctly, lest economic zeal, but not according to knowledge, should induce our cottage housekeeper to trim it up into ragout or hash. Throw it away—not disdainfully, for it has done its work well if you have yours, and parted with every element of nutrition. I have heard of a rich family, the daughters of which wear velvet and fine laces every day, whose breakfasts, for some weeks, consisted chiefly of hashes variously seasoned and gravied, but all based upon the minced meat from which beef-tea had been made for the invalid mother. This is meanness—not frugality. The two differ as widely as do prodigality and parsimony.

But to our stock-pot—a much more agreeable subject. When it has been thus emptied, and before fresh soup is poured into it, cleanse it thoroughly, washing with hot soap-suds, scalding several times, rinsing out with clear water in which a teaspoonful of soda has been dissolved, and finally setting it in the open air for some hours until it is perfectly odorless. This process should be repeated at least once a week even in winter; in summer twice as often. Bits of underdone meats, scraps of lean *corned* ham, bones from roast, boil, and broil as they accumulate, may go into the stock-jar. Vegetables should not be added after the soup is cooked, as they are apt to sour. But a few spoonfuls of stewed tomato, canned corn, beans or peas, are often a pleasant contribution to stock taken out for to-day's dinner. Nothing of the sort should be thrown away. A half-cupful of cold boiled rice, a cup of milk and an egg, joined judiciously to a pint of stock, can be wrought up into a delicious white soup. No fat or smoked fragments should be consigned to the stock-jar or soup-kettle. Festoons of cobweb in the drawing-room are not more sure indices of slovenly housewifery than are oily soups of unskilful cookery.

If I seem to recur with needless frequency and emphasis to this point, it is because I have come to regard *Fat* as the evil element of American culinary effort. And nowhere else is its rule more rampant in all the phases of boiled fat, stewed fat, fried fat, and foulest reek of all—burnt fat! than in our cottage kitchens.

Fish Soup.

2 cups of soup stock.
1 small cup of fine crumbs.
1 coffee-cup of cold fish, minced very fine and cleared of bones, fat, and skin.
1 cup of boiling milk.
1 egg, beaten light.
1 tablespoonful of butter.
1 tablespoonful of chopped parsley.
Pepper and salt to taste.

Skim the stock carefully, heat it to boiling, and stir in the fish, add pepper and salt, and boil gently forty minutes. Heat the milk in a vessel set within another, the outer containing boiling water. When the milk is hot pour it upon the beaten egg, mix well, put over the fire again and stir in the butter, then the crumbs and parsley. Stir two minutes and turn into a heated tureen. Set a hot colander above it and rub the soup through it. Stir up well and serve.

Oyster Soup.

1 quart of oysters.
2 cups of milk.
1 tablespoonful of butter.
1 cupful of boiling water.

Drain every drop of the liquor from the oysters through a colander, and set them aside in a cold place while you put the liquor and boiling water, with pepper and salt to taste, on the stove over a good fire. Bring the liquid quickly to a boil, add the butter, and when this has melted, the oysters. Let them heat rather slowly, and when they ruffle, which should be about five minutes after they reach the boil, take them from the fire. Have ready the milk, boiling hot, in another vessel. Put oysters and soup into the tureen, stir in the milk, cover the tureen, and let it stand two minutes in hot water before sending to the table.

Send around crackers with oyster soup.

Clam Soup.

Drain the liquor from the clams, set these last aside in a cool place; add to the juice an equal quantity of water, season well with pepper and salt and a little finely-minced onion, and bring to a boil. Strain through a coarse cloth; return to the fire, and chop the clams quite small before stirring them into the hot liquor. Stew all together half an hour, add two tablespoonfuls of cracker-crumbs, a tablespoonful of butter and one of minced celery, or a teaspoonful of essence of celery. Simmer five minutes, while you scald in another vessel, set in boiling water, a cup of milk, slightly salted. Pour this into a hot tureen, then the soup, stirring well, and it is ready for use. In warm weather, add a bit of soda, not larger than a pea, to the milk before scalding it.

Clam soup can be made without milk, water being used instead. When this is done, use more crumbs.

Another way is to chop a whole *parboiled* onion fine and mix with the minced clams, cooking the mixture forty-five minutes instead of thirty. This makes a nourishing and savory soup.

Clam Chowder.

¼ lb. of fat salt pork.
75 clams.
2 small onions or 1 large one, parboiled and chopped small.
1 tablespoonful of parsley.
12 Boston crackers, split and soaked half an hour in 1 cup of milk, slightly warmed.
Cold water, pepper and salt.

Chop the pork fine, and sprinkle a layer in the bottom of a pot. Cover this with the clams, season, scatter on it minced onion, and lay in a coating of the split, soaked crackers. Then more pork, clams, seasoning, onion and cracker, until the materials are used up. Cover an inch deep with cold water and bring to a slow simmer. Cook forty-five minutes after the bubble begins, taking care that the fire does not touch the bottom of the pot, as the crackers will be apt to scorch. Strain the chowder, but do not shake or press it. Put the clams and crackers into a hot tureen, the liquor back in the pot, stir in a generous tablespoonful of fine crumbs, and, if you have it, half a cupful of tomato-juice, drained from the can which is to furnish a dish of stewed tomatoes for dinner. Boil up once and pour over the chowder. If you have not milk to spare, soak the crackers in boiling water.

It is a common mistake to imagine that chowder, like some other dishes reckoned as dainties by "high-livers," must therefore be excluded from the poor man's table. A moment's computation of the cost of the dish described in this receipt will prove that the cause of this exclusion is not necessity.

Such a chowder as the one described below is a dinner of itself and a good one, and can be put before a tired and hungry man at an expense of about thirty cents—at some seasons of the year for less.

Cod Chowder.

2 lbs. fresh cod, cut into bits an inch square.
6 potatoes, peeled, sliced, and parboiled.
1 sliced onion.
$\frac{1}{4}$ lb. fat salt pork, chopped.
6 split crackers, soaked in 1 cup of warm milk or in boiling water.
Pepper, salt, and a handful of minced parsley.

Put first a layer of pork in the pot, then one of potatoes well peppered, next fish, onions, parsley—beginning a second round with pork. Cover with boiling water, and stew gently half an hour. Line the tureen with the soaked crackers, and set in hot water until the chowder is done. Pour it in, cover, and send to the table.

Send around green pickles with it. A little pickled cucumber, chopped, is an improvement to the chowder if added just before taking it up.

In the country, where butter is abundant, the housemother may better the chowder by buttering the hot sodden crackers before pouring the contents of the pot over them.

Catfish Soup.

4 fresh-water catfish, or about 2 lbs. in all.
$\frac{1}{2}$ onion, parboiled and chopped.

1 cup of milk scalded, with bit of soda stirred in, not larger than a pea.
1 teaspoonful essence of celery.
1 beaten egg.
3 pints of cold water.
1 tablespoonful of corn-starch wet up in cold water.
1 tablespoonful of butter, and same of minced parsley.
1 slice fat salt pork, minced.

Skin and clean the fish, remove their heads, and cut up small.

Lay the pork in a pot, the fish on it, then the onion, and cover with the cold water. Stew forty-five minutes, or until the fish falls to pieces. Strain and squeeze through a colander, put over the fire again, stir in the corn-starch, butter, pepper, salt, and celery essence, boil one minute. Meanwhile have ready in a tin pail set in boiling water, the milk scalded and cooked one minute with the beaten egg and parsley, or until it begins to thicken. Pour this into a heated tureen, stir the boiling soup into it, and it is ready for the table.

You may, if you like, line the tureen with split water- or butter-crackers soaked in hot water or milk.

A good soup in country neighborhoods where catfish are plentiful in ponds and creeks. Even in town they are among our cheapest fish. If you cannot get parsley, use celery-tops, omitting the celery essence.

Lobster Bisque.

1 can of lobster, or 2 small fresh lobsters.
2 cups of milk.
3 pints of boiling water.
1 heaping tablespoonful of butter.
½ cup finely-powdered cracker.
Salt to taste.

As much cayenne pepper as will lie on a silver half-dime.

Chop the lobster rather coarse with a keen-bladed chopper, taking pains not to tear it. Put boiling water, salt, pepper, and lobster into a saucepan and cook *gently* forty minutes. At the end of this time have ready in a tin vessel (set in another of hot water) the scalding milk in which the crumbs have soaked for twenty minutes. Stir the butter into the stewed lobster, then the soaked crumbs and milk, turn out into a covered tureen, set in hot water five minutes, and send to table.

Don't be frightened at the French name, or by the notion that lobster is an expensive luxury. On some parts of our coast they retail for fifty cents a half-dozen. Preserved lobster is seldom more than 30 cents a can. The *bisque* is very delightful, costing little except for the fish.

Eel Soup.

2 lbs. of eels, cleaned, cleared of fat, and cut into short pieces.

1 small onion, minced.

1 tablespoonful of butter.

1 slice fat salt pork, chopped.

1 cup of milk, scalding hot.

1 tablespoonful of flour rubbed up with the butter.

2 quarts cold water.

Pepper and salt to taste.

1 tablespoonful of chopped parsley.

Put eels, onion, and pork on in the cold water and stew one hour, or until the fish is in rags. Rub all except the bones through a colander back into the pot, boil up and add the floured butter, parsley, salt, and pepper. Boil one minute. Put the hot milk into a tureen, stir in the soup, and send to the table.

If you choose you may line the tureen with toasted split crackers, very dry and buttered.

A Lenten Soup.

1 large potato.
1 onion.
1 turnip.
1 egg.
1 quart of boiling water.
2 cups of milk.
2 tablespoonfuls of butter rolled in flour.
½ of a small cabbage.
½ cup fine dry bread-crumbs.
Parsley, pepper and salt to taste.
A stalk of celery.

Chop the cabbage, peel and mince the other vegetables, put into a pot with cold water enough to cover them, and let them get scalding hot, but not boil. Drain off the water through a colander and throw it away. Return the vegetables to the pot, add a quart of boiling water, and stew slowly until they are very soft. Rub all through a colander—water as well as vegetables—season, and heat again to boiling before stirring in crumbs and butter. Have the milk hot in another vessel, drop in a bit of soda the size of a pea, and stir into the soup. Draw to the side of the stove, dip out a cupful and mix with this the beaten egg. When this has been done, pour the egg and liquor back into the soup, stir well over the fire for one minute, and turn into a hot tureen.

This pottage is especially commended to those who raise their own vegetables and keep a cow. At a nominal cost an excellent dish can be set on the table, one that will be very popular when once tasted.

Katherine's Soup.

Like the last, this is made without meat.

- 1 onion, sliced.
- 1 carrot, grated.
- 1 turnip, grated.
- 3 tablespoonfuls chopped cabbage.
- ½ can tomatoes.
- 4 tablespoonfuls of raw rice soaked one hour.
- 1 cup of milk.
- 1 lump of white sugar.
- 1 teaspoonful essence of celery, or a teaspoonful of celery-seed tied in a muslin bag, or a stalk of celery chopped.
- 2 tablespoonfuls of butter, cut up and rolled in flour.
- 3 pints of cold water.
- Pepper and salt.

Parboil the onion and cabbage and throw away the water. Put all the vegetables, sliced and grated (except the tomatoes), in a pot with the soaked rice, cover with the cold water, and stew one hour. Then put in the tomatoes, and cook twenty minutes longer. Press and squeeze all that will pass the colander-holes back into the pot, leaving behind only hard lumps and tough fibres. The pulped vegetables should be like a very soft paste in the pot. Heat again and season, stirring often, then put in the floured butter. When the soup bubbles all over, turn into the tureen and stir in the milk, which should have been scalded in another vessel.

A little chopped parsley is an improvement. It should be added when the butter goes in.

Onion Soup (*without meat*).

- 3 onions, parboiled ten minutes, then chopped and the water thrown away.

SOUPS AND THE STOCK-POT.

1 stalk of celery, or a teaspoonful of celery essence.
1 grated turnip.
2 eggs.
2 tablespoonfuls of butter, rolled in a tablespoonful of flour.
1 tablespoonful of chopped parsley.
3 pints of cold water.

Cook the vegetables in the water slowly, until they are very tender. Rub through a colander with the water in which they were boiled, season with pepper, salt, and parsley, and simmer ten minutes before stirring in the floured butter. Dip out a cupful and beat into it the whipped eggs. Stir this well into the soup, cook one minute, keeping the spoon going all the time to prevent the eggs from clotting, and pour at once into a hot tureen.

A relishful and wholesome stormy-day broth.

Quick Potato Purée (*without meat*).

6 large mealy potatoes, boiled and mashed while hot.
3 pints of boiling water.
1 cup of scalding milk.
1 tablespoonful of chopped parsley.
2 tablespoonfuls of butter.
1 heaping tablespoonful of corn-starch, wet up in cold milk.
Salt and pepper to taste.

Put the water over the fire with the mashed potato and simmer twenty minutes. Run through a colander back into the pot to get rid of all lumps, put in parsley, salt and pepper, and cook ten minutes more, stirring up from the bottom now and then to avoid the chance of scorching. Now stir in the butter, then the corn-starch, and, when the mixture thickens well, the hot milk. Let it *just* boil and pour out.

Potato Soup.

The only meat needed for this is a small piece of salt pork—say a quarter of a pound—chopped into bits.

8 mealy potatoes, peeled and sliced.
1 small onion, or half a large one, also sliced.
1 stalk of refuse celery, such as your green-grocer will give you for nothing—minced.
1 heaping tablespoonful of butter, cut up in the same quantity of flour.
1 cup of milk.
Pepper, salt, and chopped parsley.
2 quarts of cold water.

Lay the sliced potatoes in cold water half an hour; then cook five minutes in boiling. Drain and put into the soup-pot with onion, pork, and celery. Add the water, and boil steadily one hour. Strain, rubbing all through the colander. Return to the fire; season, and when it boils anew, stir in the floured butter. Heat the milk in a separate vessel, and add after the soup is put into the tureen, mixing in well.

There should be less than three pints of this vegetable soup, or *purée*, when ready for table, the two quarts of water put in at first having reduced at least a pint in boiling. It is a nutritious and savory soup.

Bean Soup.

1 quart of dried beans.
½ lb. of fat salt pork chopped.
1 small onion.
1 tablespoonful of flour, wet to a paste with cold water.
4 quarts of cold water.
1 stalk of celery (if convenient), minced.
Pepper to taste, and (perhaps) salt.

Soak the beans all night in cold water. Drain them in the morning and cover with lukewarm water. After soaking two hours in this, drain them again, put into a large pot with the pork, onion, celery, and cold water, and set where it will, in an hour's time, come to a slow boil. Keep this up four or five hours, and rub all well through a colander, leaving nothing but dry husks behind. Return to the pot, season to your liking, stir in the flour-paste, boil up well once, and serve.

This soup is better the second day than the first, and good always. You may, if you like, fry some strips of stale bread crisp and put into the tureen before pouring in the soup.

The above receipt will make a large quantity. Set aside a quart, and in a day or two make—

Bean and Tomato Soup.

Open a can of tomatoes, put into a saucepan with a teaspoonful of sugar, and stew gently half an hour. Rub through a colander; return to the fire with the bean soup saved from yesterday, and simmer together after they begin to boil, about twenty minutes, before serving.

Or you may, if you prefer, have—

Bean and Corn Soup.

Chop the contents of a can of corn in your chopping-tray until they are like fine hominy, and cook half an hour in just enough boiling water to cover it. Rub through a colander into the cold bean soup, add a teaspoonful of sugar, and when it comes to a boil, a tablespoonful of butter cut up in one of flour. Simmer five minutes, and it is ready for use.

Purée of Peas.

1 pint of split peas, soaked over night.
3 quarts of liquor in which corned beef has been boiled.
1 onion, sliced (a small one).
1 cup of milk.
2 tablespoonfuls of corn-starch, wet up in cold water.
1 tablespoonful chopped parsley, and, if convenient, a stalk of celery, chopped.
Pepper to taste. No salt.

Skim all the fat from the cold beef-liquor and pour the latter upon the soaked peas, sliced onion, and celery. Cook slowly four hours at least, or until the peas are boiled very soft. Rub them through the colander with the liquor; return to the fire, stir in parsley, pepper, and corn-starch. Simmer five minutes, and pour into the tureen. Heat the milk separately, and add. Small squares, or dice, of stale bread fried in dripping, drained, and put into the tureen before the soup, are a pleasant addition to it. It is very nice made of green peas—fresh or canned. These, of course, need no soaking.

Green Pea and Potato Soup.

8 mealy potatoes, parboiled and sliced.
1 pint of green peas, or same quantity of canned.
1 sliced onion—small.
1 tablespoonful corn-starch wet with cold water.
Pepper and chopped parsley.
2 quarts corned-beef or corned-ham liquor.

Put the skimmed liquor, onion, peas, and parboiled potatoes over the fire, and cook slowly one hour. Rub through the colander with the liquor, pepper, and return, with the parsley, to the kettle. Boil up once, stir in the corn-starch, cook two minutes, and pour out.

In helping bean, pea, and other purées, put the ladle well down to the bottom of the tureen, and stir before pouring out the first plateful.

The French canned peas are too expensive to be used for soup. The American are cheap, and only fit for this purpose.

Pea and Rice Purée.

1 quart of green peas, fresh or canned.
½ cup rice, soaked three hours in a cup of warm water.
2 quarts corned-beef liquor, or other weak stock.
1 tablespoonful of butter cut up in same quantity of flour.
Pepper to taste.
½ small onion, chopped.

Drain the peas, if canned, and put into the stock with the onion and rice. Cook slowly forty-five minutes, strain and press through a colander. Put over the fire, season, stir in the floured butter, boil up once and serve.

Tomato and Rice Broth.

1 can of tomatoes.
½ cup raw rice which has been soaked three hours in a cup of warm water.
1 lump of white sugar.
2 quarts weak broth, in which a leg of mutton was boiled yesterday or the day before.
Pepper and salt to taste.
1 tablespoonful chopped parsley and same of onion, minced.

Put tomatoes, soaked rice, and onion in the cold,

skimmed broth, and stew gently one hour. Season with sugar, salt, and pepper. When you have rubbed through the colander, boil up once and pour out.

Tomato Soup (*without meat*).

1 dozen ripe tomatoes, peeled and sliced, or a can of tomatoes.
1 small onion, sliced and fried to a light brown in some nice dripping.
1 tablespoonful of butter rolled in same quantity of flour.
½ cupful of hot boiled rice, very soft.
1 teaspoonful of sugar.
1 quart boiling water.
Pepper, salt, and chopped parsley or celery tops.

Put three tablespoonfuls of clean dripping into the soup-pot, bring to a boil and fry the sliced onion. Add the tomatoes, and stir together over the fire until smoking hot before the boiling water goes in. Stew steadily forty minutes, and put all through the colander back into the pot; season, bring again to a boil, add the rice; simmer ten minutes, stir in the floured butter, boil one minute, and pour out.

Canned Corn Soup (*without meat*).

- 1 can of corn, drained and chopped fine.
1 pint of milk.
1 quart of boiling water.
2 tablespoonfuls of butter rolled in 1 tablespoonful of flour.
2 eggs.
1 teaspoonful of sugar.
Pepper and salt to taste.

Put the chopped corn over the fire in the boiling water and cook for an hour. Work through a colander; return to the pot with sugar, pepper, and salt. Boil one minute and stir in the floured butter. Have the milk ready scalded, and add it gradually to the beaten eggs. When the butter has entirely melted, stir eggs and milk into the soup for one minute, then pour it out.

Turnip Purée (*without meat*).

12 turnips of medium size, white and firm.
3 cups of milk.
3 pints of boiling water.
2 tablespoonfuls of butter, cut up in 2 tablespoonfuls of flour.
½ small onion, parboiled and sliced.
1 tablespoonful of minced parsley.
Salt to taste, and pepper rather profusely.

Peel and slice the turnips and put on in the hot water with the onion. Cook forty minutes, or until the vegetables boil to pieces. Pulp through a colander into the water in which they were boiled, season with pepper, salt, and parsley, and set over the fire. Stir in the floured butter, simmer five minutes, add the milk, which should have been heated in a separate vessel with a bit of soda not larger than a pea, and take at once from the fire.

Ham Soup.

Skim and clear two quarts of the liquor in which a *corned* (not smoked) ham was boiled. To clear it put it over a quick fire (with half an onion sliced), and when more than blood warm drop in the white and shell of an egg, or the freshly-broken shells of two. Boil fast three minutes, and strain through a thick cloth. This will give you a clear-looking liquid. Return it to the fire, bring it to a boil, wet two tablespoonfuls of corn-starch in half a cup of milk and stir into the soup. Beat two eggs light in a bowl, add to them a cup of the boiling soup, mix well, and return to that in the pot, with a tablespoonful of minced parsley. Chop two hard-boiled eggs fine and put them into a hot tureen, before pouring in the soup.

A Family Soup.

2 lbs. cracked bones, beef, veal, or mutton.
¼ lb. of liver, chopped fine.
¼lb. *corned* ham, also chopped, or a ham bone, broken well, or some salt pork bones.
1 carrot, chopped.
2 tablespoonfuls of minced cabbage, and as much onion.
½ can of tomatoes.
2 tablespoonfuls of raw rice.
Pepper, salt, and sweet herbs minced.
2¼ quarts of cold water.

Put everything except the seasoning and rice over the fire in the cold water, cover, and let all cook slowly four hours. Meanwhile soak the rice in just enough warm water to cover it. Strain the soup, pulping liver and vegetables through the colander, season and return to the fire; add the rice, and simmer half an hour, or until it is soft.

Bone Soup.

Make this, and all soups that have meat in them, the day before they are to be eaten.

4 lbs. of bones (raw), pounded to pieces, saving every bit of the marrow to enrich the soup.
1 small onion.

1 turnip.
1 carrot.
2 or 3 stalks of refuse celery, a cabbage leaf and bunch of "soup herbs," all chopped.
2 tablespoonfuls of tapioca, soaked three hours in enough water to cover it.
3 quarts of cold water.

Put minced vegetables, herbs, and cracked bones on in the cold water, cover, and let them "bubble" gently at the back of the stove for five hours. At the end of this time bring to a quicker boil, and check this suddenly by throwing in a cup of cold water. Skim carefully, season, turn all into the stock-pot, and set in the cellar until morning. Then remove the fat from the top, strain, without pressing, and clear the liquor by warming it to more than blood-heat, dropping in the white and shell of a raw egg, boiling up hard for three minutes, and straining, without squeezing, through a thick cloth. Return the clear liquid to the fire in a clean pot, add the soaked tapioca, and simmer fifteen minutes.

This is a cheap and good "stock," susceptible of many variations in the final preparation.

Chicken and Corn Soup.

Even in the country, where old fowls must be disposed of in some way, it is seldom economical to boil them to pieces just to make soup. But if you will save the liquor in which these have been boiled the day before, for the table, a delightful soup may be supplied good enough for city-boarders and company.

2 quarts of the liquor left from boiling a chicken, cleared of fat after it is cold.
1 can of corn, chopped, or 8 ears of green corn, rather too hard for table-use, grated from the cob.

1 tablespoonful of butter cut up in one of flour.
1 tablespoonful minced parsley and same of green onion-tops.
Pepper and salt.
1 cup of boiling milk.

Boil corn and liquor slowly together one hour after they begin to bubble. Rub thoroughly through a colander, season and add herbs. Heat to boiling, stir in the floured butter, simmer five minutes, pour into the tureen and add the boiling milk.

Clear Sago Soup.

2 lbs. lean beef—the coarsest cuts will do—chopped as for mince-meat.
2 lbs. veal bones, well cracked.
½ onion.
1 carrot, chopped.
3 quarts cold water.
½ cup German sago (or tapioca), soaked three hours in cold water.
Pepper and salt.

Put meat and minced vegetables on in the cold water and boil slowly five hours. Season and turn into the stock-pot until next day. Strain, then, squeezing all the strength out of meat and vegetables, return the liquor to the fire, and clear as directed in "Bone Soup." Strain—this time through a cloth, without pressing—rinse the soup-pot, put in the clear stock, add the soaked sago, and simmer ten minutes.

Giblet Soup.

In roasting a pair of chickens or a turkey, save the necks, the feet, and the giblets. Put them in three pints of cold water, and cook slowly down to one quart. Season, and set aside in the liquor until perfectly cold. Remove the fat, take out the bones, and chop all the meat you can get off these, with the giblets, very fine. Strain and season the stock, and set over the fire to heat. When it boils, add the chopped meat and giblets, some minced soup-herbs, and cook three minutes. Beat two eggs light in a bowl, pour a cup of hot soup on them, stir well together and then into the soup-pot, for one minute, just long enough to cook, without curdling the eggs.

Mutton Broth.

- 2 lbs. lean mutton—a coarse part—say, from the scrag, and if tough, no matter. Chop as for mince-meat.
- $\frac{1}{2}$ onion, sliced.
- 1 cup of milk.
- $\frac{1}{2}$ cup of raw rice.
- 2 quarts of cold water.
- Some chopped parsley.
- Salt and pepper.

Boil meat and onion in the water, slowly, four hours after the bubbling begins. Season, and set by until *perfectly* cold. Take off the fat and strain, pressing out every drop of nourishment from the meat. Return the soup to the pot with the rice, previously soaked three hours in just enough water to cover it. Simmer half an hour, or until the rice is soft and broken to pieces; add the parsley, simmer three minutes, turn in the milk, which should be scalding hot, stir one minute and pour out.

A Scotch Soup.

1 sheep's head, cleaned as butchers do calves' heads, the wool being removed, leaving the skin on.
1 turnip.
1 small onion.
1 carrot.
Bunch of sweet herbs, minced.
4 quarts of cold water.
Pepper and salt.

Be sure the head is clean. Sometimes dirt or grass is left in the mouth. Soak one hour in warm (not hot) water, then put it into the pot, with the cold water, and boil slowly five hours. Season, and let all get cold together. Take off the fat from the top, chop the meat, and put it back with the bones and liquor into the pot, to stew for an hour. Cut the tongue into small dice, and set aside. Cut up the peeled vegetables in like manner, and covering them with salted hot water stew until tender, but not to breaking. Strain the soup through a colander, then through a cloth, return to the fire, drop in the minced tongue and the cooked vegetables, simmer ten minutes and serve.

A cheap and savory dish.

A Scrap Soup.

The carcass of roast turkey, duck, or chicken. A slice of corned ham, or some cold lean boiled ham. Any mutton or beef bones you may have in the pantry.

½ a can of corn.
½ onion, minced.
Bunch of sweet herbs.

3 quarts of cold water.
Stuffing of turkey or chicken.
1 tablespoonful corn-starch, wet up in half a cup of milk.

Set bones, ham, corn, and onion over the fire with the cold water, and cook gently for four hours. Take out the bones, and strain the soup through a colander, pulping the vegetables. Return to the fire, put in the dressing and herbs. Stir until there are no lumps in it, season, and simmer fifteen minutes, taking care it does not burn. Then stir in the corn-starch and milk, boil one minute, and it is fit for use.

MEATS.

FAMILIAR TALK.

Of late years, the "meat question" has been fraught with deepening perplexity to the frugal housewife. That vegetarian theories have not grown in favor with the American public in the same period is presumptive evidence against their reasonableness. Doctors and health-journals, meanwhile, unite in declaring that as flesh-consumers we surpass even our ancestral beef-eaters. If "the scarcity of beasts of meat" is no longer a drawing-room topic, even fashionists do not disdain to declaim against the extortion of butchers, while insisting upon the necessity of having meat in some form as a part of each tri-daily meal.

I remember better than the attack deserves to be recollected, the strictures of a certain journal upon a mild effort on my part to lead popular favor toward simple breakfasts of rolls, boiled eggs, tea or coffee, or if more substantial food were demanded, toward omelette, *fondu*, and porridge.

"Such trash," the writer protested, "might do for lazy men and literary women, but the brawny laborer could not undertake a day's work after breakfasting upon a spongy composition of cream, bread-crumbs, and eggs. He must build up and sustain bone and muscle with strong meat."

In this persuasion is rooted the rustic devotion to salt pork and the rustic indifference to fruits and other vegetables than cabbages, onions, and potatoes. Given the pork, the average cook knows but two ways of preparing it for the craving stomachs of the "men-folks." When she does not boil, she fries it. "A bit of butcher's meat" is a luxury, and as such appears on the farm-house board but seldom unless when served for visitors. It is usually a part of a "critter," slaughtered in the neighborhood and peddled by the slayer from door to door, and here again the methods of cooking it are primitive and few. If "a piece," it is roasted fast and long. If steak or chop, it is fried slowly and until no more fat can be absorbed and no more juice exude. The raw material is expensive; after the second death—by fire—it is unmanageable alike by dental and digestive apparatus.

We eat too much meat, and pay too much for what we buy. What are known to dealer and initiated purchaser as the "best cuts," form so small a proportion of the whole animal that the enterprising meat-vender is thrown upon his imagination to supply enough of these for really good customers. Hence the phenomenal porter-house and tenderloin, the fillets and spring-lamb that disgrace our housewifery as much as they excruciate our pocket-nerves. Our merchant always fails to understand it. He paid at wholesale within a cent and a-half per pound of what he charged us. Mrs. Senator Toploft ordered the other joint, or companion-cut, for a grand dinner-party and sent word to Mr. Cleaver how much delighted she was with it.

We are all cowards in the face of sounding statements of this kind, not one word of which we believe, and we avoid the speaker's eye while we pay "choice-cut" prices for chuck-rib, round-steak and "ram-lamb."

The lesson of this talk, which is in danger of waxing

into a tirade, is—when you cannot afford to pay for the best, ask boldly for the second-best. And out of this honest article, for which you pay something like an honest sum, make nourishing, savory food by cooking it properly and ingeniously. Never buy tainted meat or fowls, but bear in mind that "coarse" and "choice" are comparative terms, and that "roast" is, *per se*, no more elegant a term than "stewed." Make a study of made-dishes and "leftovers," and do not despise scraps—always provided that these preserve their individuality and have not been huddled together into "messes."

MUTTON.

Roast Breast of Mutton.

Lay in a dripping-pan, and half-fill this with warm—not hot—water slightly salted. Turn another pan of the same size as the lower upside down over the meat and cook in a moderate oven, thus covered, about twelve minutes to the pound, or until a fork goes easily into the thickest part and is not followed by red gravy. In this time, baste six times with liquor from the pan. Have ready in a plate a handful of fine dry crumbs, salted and peppered. Ten minutes before taking up the meat, rub a tablespoonful of butter over it, and strew the crumbs thickly and evenly over the top. Or, you can omit the butter and wash well in gravy from the pan. Close the oven to brown the crumbs and remove the meat to a hot dish. Cover, and keep warm over a pot of boiling water while you pour the gravy into a cold bowl or pan and set it out of doors in winter, in very cold water in summer to make the fat rise. Take all of this off, strain the gravy back into the dripping-pan, stir in enough browned flour wet with cold water to thicken it to the consistency of cream, boil up once, and send to table in a gravy-bowl.

Boiled Shoulder of Mutton.

Get the butcher to take out the bones, and use them for soup-stock. Fill the cavity left by their removal with a force-meat made of dry crumbs, peppered and salted, with a slice of fat salt pork chopped fine and a little minced thyme or parsley worked up in it. Sew the meat up neatly in whatever shape you like, in stout mosquito-netting (white) and plunge into a pot of warm water in which has been stirred a tablespoonful of salt. The water should cover the meat well and be just hot enough not to scald your hand. Bring *slowly* to the boil, and after this begins, cook fifteen minutes to the pound, still slowly.

Half an hour before taking it up, dip out a cupful of liquor and cool fast to bring up the fat. Remove this, put the liquid on in a saucepan and stir in a teaspoonful of butter cut up in a tablespoonful of flour. When it thickens, add (if convenient) a tablespoonful of chopped cucumber pickle, or pickled nasturtium-seeds. These last are an excellent imitation of capers. Serve this sauce in a gravy-boat.

Take the meat from the liquor when done, remove the cloth with care, lay the mutton in a hot dish, and dispose some slices of hard-boiled egg upon it.

Very tough mutton can be made eatable by this process.

Stewed Breast or Scrag of Mutton.

Trim neatly and lay, skin-side downward, in a widemouthed pot. On and about the meat strew some slices of onion and a sliced turnip. Pour in two cups of cold water, and if you have it a cup of weak soup or gravy.

Heat gradually, and after the liquor begins to hiss around the edges, stew gently for one hour. Turn the meat and stew an hour longer. Take it up, sprinkle with salt, cover in a hot dish and set over boiling water, while you strain the gravy, season with pepper and salt, thicken slightly with browned flour, and after pouring a cupful over the meat, serve the rest in a gravy-boat.

When green peas and tomatoes are cheap and plentiful, you can slice a couple of the latter and add to the turnip and onion, then boil a pint of peas in a little salted water, drain and put them into the strained gravy when you return it to the pot to heat and thicken. They are a pleasant addition to the dish.

Stewed Mutton with Dumplings.

2 lbs. lean mutton, cut into pieces an inch square.

¼ of an onion, chopped. A slice of fat salt pork, minced. Chopped sweet herbs, pepper and salt to taste.

1 tablespoonful of flour wet up in cold water.

2 cups of cold water.

Put mutton, pork, and onion on in the cold water, and stew very slowly until the meat is tender. Add herbs, seasoning, and stew ten minutes. Take out the meat with a skimmer and put on a hot covered dish over a pot of boiling water to keep warm.

Have ready the dumplings made according to this rule:

1 cup of prepared flour—or flour mixed up well with ¼ teaspoonful of soda and twice as much cream-of-tartar.

1 heaping teaspoonful of lard.

¼ cup of milk, or enough to enable you to roll out the paste.

A little salt.

Chop the lard into the prepared and salted flour until thoroughly incorporated, wet up with the milk, and roll out with as little handling as possible into a sheet about a quarter of an inch thick. Cut into strips, and when you have stirred in the flour for thickening the gravy, and boiled one minute, drop in the strips, a few at a time, and cook from eight to ten minutes. Pile the meat in the centre of the dish, arrange the dumplings like a hedge around it, and pour the gravy over all.

This stew is improved by stirring into the gravy with the flour half a cup of milk in which a bit of soda the size of a pea has been dissolved. But it is a nice family dish without it.

Summer Stew of Mutton.

2 lbs. coarse lean mutton cut into dice an inch square. Have a sharp knife and do this neatly.

3 or 4 spoonfuls of nice dripping.

$\frac{1}{4}$ of an onion, sliced.

Pepper, salt, and summer savory.

Sweet marjoram or parsley, chopped fine—1 tablespoonful (heaping).

Cold water enough to cover the meat.

1 pint of green peas.

Heat the dripping in a frying-pan, put in the meat and onion, and fry to a light brown, first dredging the meat with flour. Drain, and put these in a pot with the herbs, cover with cold water, and stew very slowly until tender and ready to drop to pieces. Take the meat up with a skimmer, lay on a dish, and keep hot over boiling water while you skim and season the gravy, thicken with a little browned flour, and add the pint of peas. Stew gently until these are done, return the meat to the pot, boil up one minute, and turn out into a heated dish.

In winter you may substitute canned peas for fresh.

A Brown Stew of Mutton.

2 lbs. of lean mutton, cut into inch-square pieces.
¼ onion, sliced.
Dripping for frying.
1 slice fat salt pork, minced.
Chopped herbs.
Pepper, salt, and (if you have it) a tablespoonful of tomato catsup.
1 cup of liquor (cold) in which corned beef or mutton has been boiled, or of weak broth, made from scraps and bones, then strained and skimmed.
Pepper and salt for liberal seasoning.
Browned flour.

Fry the mutton and onion in the dripping, drain and put in a saucepan with the pork, herbs, and broth. Simmer gently until the meat is tender and plump; take up, and keep hot while you strain the gravy, heat to boiling, thicken with browned flour, and add the catsup. Bring to a boil, put in the meat again, boil one minute, and pour out.

Mutton Pudding (No. 1).

1 cupful of prepared flour, salted.
1 cup of milk.
1 egg.
1 tablespoonful of melted butter.
Pepper and salt.
Cold roast or boiled mutton, cut into dice.

Lay the meat in the melted butter, and set over hot water to make the one absorb the other, while you prepare the batter. Beat the egg very light, add the milk, then the flour. It should be a *batter*, not paste. Butter a pie-dish, pour in a third of the batter, lay on this the buttered meat, well-seasoned with pepper and salt, fill up with the batter, and bake half an hour in a good oven—that is, hot and steady. Serve at once, for batter soon falls.

Mutton Pudding (No. 2).

4 mealy potatoes, mashed fine while hot, with 1 tablespoonful of butter and 3 tablespoonfuls of milk.

1 egg.

1 tablespoonful of prepared flour.

2 cupfuls of cold mutton, minced, seasoned highly, and wet to a soft paste with weak broth.

Whip the potatoes, butter, and milk to a cream; add the egg, already beaten light, and whip all one minute before working in the flour. Put the moistened mutton in a greased pudding-dish, and spread the potato over it. Bake, covered, for forty minutes, then brown nicely.

Minced beef—corned or fresh—is very good prepared in this way.

Minced Mutton on Toast.

1 cupful cold mutton, chopped.

½ cupful of drawn butter.

1 tablespoonful of chopped onion, and same of minced sweet herbs.

1 egg, well beaten.

Pepper and salt.

Stale bread cut into crustless rounds and toasted.

To draw the butter, put half a cupful of hot water, in which the onion has steeped, then been strained out, in a saucepan. When it boils stir in a generous teaspoonful of butter, and, this melted, an equal quantity of flour, wet up with cold water. Stir until it begins to thicken, put in the meat, and this hot, the egg and herbs. Season, toss, and stir for one minute, and set in boiling water at the side of the stove where it will not cook while you get the toast-rounds ready.

Lay these on a hot platter, and if you have gravy or soup-stock to spare, heat it, and pour a little on each piece. If you have none, wet with boiling, salted water, butter, and heap equal spoonfuls of the mince on it.

Another Mince of Mutton.

Prepare the mince as directed in the last receipt, but moisten it more abundantly, using a cupful of drawn butter. Grease a pudding-dish; strew a good coating of dry crumbs on the bottom, pour the minced meat on this, cover with an inverted plate or tin "lid," and bake until it bubbles all over the top. Draw to the oven-door and break quickly four or five eggs on the surface, drop a few bits of butter, with pepper and salt, on them, and shut up again until the whites are set.

Serve in the dish in which it is cooked.

VEAL.

Stewed Breast of Veal.

Remove the largest bone, and fill the cavity left with a force-meat of crumbs, pepper, salt, and a little fat pork cut up fine. Pin with skewers into a good shape and lay it in a broad pot, on the bottom of which are several thin slices of fat salt pork, well peppered. Put two or three more on the veal, pour in a cup of hot water, and fit a *close* cover on the pot. If you have no lid that exactly fits it, use several thicknesses of stout paper—not printed —to fill out the cracks around the edges. Or cover the pot with a folded cloth and press the lid down on this, setting a flat-iron on it, to exclude the air and keep in the steam. Heat slowly, and do not open the pot for one hour. Then, turn the meat over, cover again, and do not touch it for another hour. All this time it should be gently simmering, never quite still, yet never cooking rapidly. When the two hours are up, remove the veal to a hot dish, pick out the pork and lay around it, and keep all warm over boiling water; while you strain the gravy, heat it, thicken with browned flour, and (if convenient) add some juice from a can of tomatoes. Pour a few spoonfuls over the dished meat. Send the rest to table in a boat. A knuckle of veal may be thus prepared.

Veal cooked in this way is juicy, digestible, and savory.

Veal Scallop.

A good dish to succeed the stewed breast of yesterday.

To 2 cups of minced cold veal allow a cup of dry bread-crumbs. Season the meat spicily, and have ready a cup of gravy or broth with which to wet the crumbs. If you have not enough, make out the quantity with warmed milk. Strew the bottom of a pudding-dish with crumbs, scatter some butter-bits with salt and pepper on it, and a few spoonfuls of liquor—broth or milk. A thicker stratum of minced veal comes next, then, more crumbs, etc. When the veal is used up, cap the top with crumbs, well-moistened, cover as closely as you can and bake half an hour before uncovering, in order to brown the surface. Send to table in the pudding-dish.

Veal Pie.

2 pounds lean veal; a slice of corned (not smoked) ham; 1 hard-boiled egg; flour for thickening; pepper and salt; paste for crust; 1 tablespoonful butter.

Cut the meat into dice, and stew tender in enough cold water to cover it well. Fill a deep bake-dish with this, interspersing the hard-boiled egg, minced small. Cut up a tablespoonful of butter in one of flour, and stir into the liquor in which the meat was cooked. Pour into the dish over the meat, cover with the paste, and bake in a good oven until browned.

Make the crust by rubbing a tablespoonful of lard or nice dripping into a cupful of prepared flour, salting it, and wetting it up with a little milk. Water will do, but is not quite so good. Roll out with a few quick passes of the rolling-pin into a sheet half an inch thick, and lay over the pie, printing or pinching hard at the edges. Make a gash or two in the middle, to allow the escape of the heated air. Use a top-crust only with meat-pies.

Savory Stew of Veal.

3 lbs. knuckle of veal or other "coarse" part.
¼ lb. corned pork, fat.
½ an onion.
Chopped sweet herbs.
Salt and pepper.
½ can tomatoes.
Browned flour.

Cut the meat from the bones in neat strips, and set aside in a cool place while you make the gravy. Do this by putting the bones—well-broken up—with the onion and herbs into a saucepan, covering them with a quart of cold water, and stewing down gently until the liquid is reduced by one-half. This should take several hours. Just before you take it off, fry the veal in nice dripping, put it in a pot and strain the hot gravy over it. Chop pork and tomatoes fine and add with the seasoning. Cover closely, and simmer for two hours. Thicken with browned flour wet up in cold water, boil up once and dish.

If you put on the bones, etc., for the gravy before breakfast, you can easily have the stew for an early dinner. As will be seen by looking over the directions, the preparation requires little labor or expenditure of time. As with most stews, the excellence depends mainly upon slow and steady simmering.

Veal Cutlets.

2 lbs. veal cutlets, trimmed into a neat shape.
1 lb. ham.
1 egg, beaten light.
Crushed cracker—about half a cupful.
Pepper and salt.
Dripping.

Cut the veal and ham into strips two inches wide, three long, and half an inch thick. Roll, first in the egg, then in the crumbs. Have the dripping hissing in the pan, and fry the ham, then the veal, turning as they brown. Take up, pepper the ham, pepper and salt the veal, and lay on a hot dish in alternate and overlapping slices. Eat fresh and hot.

N.B.—Never throw away a drop of "dripping" skimmed from the top of gravies and soups. Melt it down, and strain, while hot, through a coarse cloth; set away in a cold place, and use instead of lard and butter for frying.

Veal Chops

Cost less than cutlets, are less dry, and more wholesome. Trim into shapeliness, and broil on a warm gridiron, turning several times. Lay on a hot dish, pepper, salt, and put a bit of butter on each into which has been worked some *finely* chopped parsley.

Or, dip in egg and cracker-crumbs, and fry as you would cutlets.

When you can do so conveniently, serve tomatoes, stewed or baked, with veal.

Calf's Head.

I have hesitated to give any preparation of calf's head as cheap, in the unpleasing recollection of my surprise, when having once ordered one for soup, I received with it a bill for $1.25!

"We had to order by Express from Boston," was the cool response to my expostulation. "There wasn't a calf's head to be had in our town!"

"Not in *your* establishment!" cried a graceless youth present. "That does surprise me."

I could not reprove the impertinence as severely as it merited, for, up to that hour, I had never paid more than forty cents for a dressed calf's head that furnished soup and meat for a dinner. In the country I have had the head *given*, the butcher charging fifteen cents for cleaning it. This is done by scalding it whole in boiling water, after rubbing pounded rosin well into the hair to make it come off more readily. A handful of potash or of clean wood-ashes stirred and boiled into the water will loosen the hairs. Split the head lengthwise to get at the brains.

Wash the head carefully in cold water, remove the brains, and set them by in a cold place. Soak the head one hour in cold, salted water, then put it over the fire with three quarts of boiling water, and cook gently an hour and a half, *or* until tender. Take it out without breaking or tearing it, and lay in *cold* water five minutes to make it firm. Wipe dry, set in a dripping-pan, brush over with beaten egg, dust thickly with cracker-crumbs, invert a pan over it, and bake half an hour before removing the cover, and browning it for perhaps ten minutes more. As it browns, baste with a cupful of the liquor in which it was boiled. Transfer to a hot dish, strain the gravy left in the pan, thicken with browned flour, boil up, pour a few spoonfuls over the head, the rest into a gravy-boat.

The liquor in which a calf's head is boiled makes delicious soup for the next day's dinner. You can treat the stock as you would that made from bones or chopped meat, but instead of adding tapioca or sago, after clearing it, thicken with two tablespoonfuls of browned flour and a quarter spoonful of allspice rubbed up with a tablespoonful of butter and the juice of a lemon. Drop in force-meat balls made of calf's brains, scalded for ten minutes in boiling water, rubbed smooth in a bowl, seasoned well, and beaten light with a raw egg and a teaspoonful of flour put in to hold the ingredients together. Flour your hands, make the mixture into small balls, and keep cold until the soup boils. Drop in gently, cook five minutes, take up with a split spoon, put into the tureen, and pour the soup over them.

Calf's Liver (*larded*).

Soak a whole calf's liver (that is, not sliced) in cold, salted water for half an hour. Wipe dry; with a narrow-bladed knife make incisions in the liver, holding the knife perpendicularly. The slits should be half an inch apart, and run quite through from top to bottom. Into these thrust strips of fat salt pork, long enough to project above and below. Put the liver into a saucepan that has a tight-fitting lid, sprinkle with two tablespoonfuls of chopped onion, some sweet herbs, salt, and pepper. Pour in two cupfuls of cold water, and set where it will not boil under an hour, keeping the lid on. Open at the end of this time, baste well with the water, put the lid back to keep in steam and flavor, and cook slowly, never boiling hard, for another hour. Then boil up briskly for one minute, and take out the liver. Keep hot on a dish; strain the gravy back into the saucepan, thicken with browned flour, boil up once, and put into a gravy-dish. Carve the liver horizontally, at table. It will be found singularly tender and good, if these directions are exactly obeyed.

Calf's Liver—Smothered.

2 lbs. liver, sliced half an inch thick.
¼ lb. fat salt pork or fat bacon, chopped.
2 tablespoonfuls minced onion.
1 tablespoonful sweet herbs, chopped or powdered.
Pepper. The pork salts it.

Cover the bottom of a tin pail with chopped pork, lay in some of the liver, sprinkle with onion, herbs, and pork, then another stratum of liver, and more pork, until all are used up. Fit a close cover on the pail, and set in a pot of cold water. Bring slowly within a few degrees of a boil—that is, to the scalding, but not bubbling point, and keep it at this for an hour. Then increase the heat until the water in the pot boils steadily, and leave it an hour longer. Now, for the first time, open the inner pail, take out the tender, unctuous liver, and keep it hot in a covered dish over boiling water. Set the pail directly on the stove, thicken the gravy with browned flour wet up in cold water, boil two minutes, pour over the liver, and send to table. Beef's liver, also pig's liver, may be cooked in the same way.

Breakfast Stew of Liver.

1 lb. cold, cooked calf's (or beef's or pig's) liver.
2 slices cold boiled pork or ham.
1 tablespoonful minced onion.

Pepper and sweet herbs to taste.
1 cup of weak broth made from soup or gravy.
Browned flour.

Chop the liver and pork into coarse bits. Heat broth, onion, and herbs in a saucepan, and when these boil, put in the meat. Draw to a place on the stove where it will not quite boil, stir now and then for ten minutes, or until the whole mass is smoking hot; add a tablespoonful of browned flour wet with cold water, boil once, and turn out.

If you have in the pantry half a cupful or so of stewed tomato saved from yesterday, add to the gravy before liver and pork go in.

Spiced Liver.

Treat exactly as you do larded liver (see receipt on page 49) until the larding is done. Then have ready in a frying-pan some hot dripping, with a tablespoonful of minced onion. Lay the liver in this, and fry five minutes, turn over, and cook for the same time, or until it is of a pale brown. Put all into a close saucepan, add two tablespoonfuls of vinegar and a cup of warm (not hot) water. Cover closely, and simmer for an hour and a half without lifting the lid. Take out the liver, and keep hot on a dish over boiling water; strain the gravy, return to the saucepan with a teaspoonful of mixed mace and allspice (ground); thicken with browned flour, boil once, put the liver in again, and set in hot water five minutes, turning the liver over twice before dishing it. Lay the liver on the heated platter; send the gravy in in a boat.

This is very nice cold for tea, almost as good as when hot.

BEEF.

Boiled Beef with Vegetables.

6 lbs. of lean beef, larded with strips of salt pork, and bound into shape by a broad band of muslin sewed about it.

2 carrots.

2 turnips.

2 small onions.

2 cups of string beans cut into inch lengths.

2 potatoes, peeled and parboiled for fifteen minutes.

2 beets, parboiled for one hour.

Pepper and salt.

4 quarts of boiling water.

Put the beef into a broad pot when you have thrust the pork lardoons thickly through it. (The larding should not be done until the strip of cloth is secured around the sides.) Cover with the water, and cook slowly, twelve minutes to the pound. An hour before the time is up, dip out a quart of the liquor, strain, cool until the fat rises, skim, and heat in another pot. Put the prepared vegetables—leaving out the potatoes—into this, and cook tender. Fifteen minutes before taking them out, drop in the potatoes.

Undo the cincture from the beef, trim off ragged and rusty edges, and lay it upon a hot dish. Slice the vegetables—excepting, of course, the beans—and lay all in neat heaps about the meat, each by itself. Pepper, salt, and butter, and keep very hot to the last.

Make a sauce by cooling and skimming a cupful of liquor taken from the pot an hour ago, heating it to a boil, stirring in a tablespoonful of butter cut up in a teaspoonful of flour, boiling up once, and seasoning with salt, pepper, and made mustard. Serve in a gravy-dish.

The pot-liquor must be reserved for to-morrow's soup. This is an elegant variation of the "boiled dinner" much affected by farmers and those who were reared on farms. In the season other vegetables may be added.

Braised Beef.

Take a good, firm piece of beef weighing four or five pounds, and without bone, trim neatly, and put into a wide-mouthed pot. Strew some sliced onion over it, with pepper and salt, add a cup of boiling water, fit on a *tight* top, and cook slowly one hour and a half, turning once during this time. The water should be reduced to half the original quantity. Dredge the meat with flour when you have taken from the pot, lay in a dripping-pan, pour the gravy over the top, and brown for ten minutes, basting five times. There should be a brown glaze on the surface. Transfer to a hot dish, and keep warm. Add a little boiling water to the gravy, strain, and set in cold water to throw up the fat; skim this off, heat in a saucepan, thicken with browned flour, boil up once, and serve.

Tough meat may be made eatable in this way by cooking two hours. The steam from the hot water and seething meat should do most of the work.

Beef à la Mode.

Bind about the upright sides of a round of beef a band of stout, unbleached muslin, stitching the overlapping ends together. Make perpendicular incisions with a sharp knife an inch apart, and plug these alternately with lardoons of salt pork and a spiced force-meat made of chopped pork and onion and bread-crumbs soaked in vinegar, all seasoned highly with allspice and mace. Rub this well into the upper surface of the beef also. Lay in a dripping-pan; pour enough boiling water over it to half-fill the pan; cover closely, and cook very slowly, basting often, for at least three hours.

Leave the meat in the gravy all night with a heavy weight on top. Next day remove the muslin band, trim the beef into neat form, and when you use it cut horizontally.

A tough, leathery round, or a piece of very "chuck-rib," can be bound into comeliness and made really good if treated as above. If you have a broad pot with a close cover, cook it in that, leaving it in four or five hours. The liquor in which it was cooked—when the caked fat has been taken from the top—makes excellent soup-stock.

Beef Steak.

If you cannot afford to buy porter-house steak, get the best you can; have it cut an inch thick, *at least*, and in cold weather keep it several days to "mellow." If you want to use it the day it is bought, hack it closely from end to end, lengthwise, crosswise, and on both sides, with a dull, heavy knife. Having done this, rub the juice of a lemon deeply into it, and set it by for three or four hours. If you have not a lemon, use a tablespoonful or two of sharp vinegar. Broil the steak without washing or wiping off the acid over a clear fire, turning often that it may not drip. In twelve minutes it should be done for those who like it rare. Lay on a hot dish, pepper and salt; put bits of butter all over the surface. Cover with another hot dish, and let it stand five minutes—not longer—before sending to table, to draw out the juices. Steak and chops lose their flavor if not served soon after they are cooked.

Beef Stew.

2 lbs. of lean beef—the "inferior" bits will do, brisket or round.
½ onion, chopped.
¼ teaspoonful of allspice.
1 tablespoonful of sweet herbs minced, thyme, parsley, marjoram.
Pepper and salt.
1 tablespoonful browned flour.
2 cups cold water.

Cut the meat into inch-square dice. Put into a saucepan with the water, fit on a close top, and set where it will heat gradually, but not boil under an hour. Move it then to a spot where it will just bubble, and stew an hour and a half longer, all the while closely covered. Add onion, spice, herbs, and seasoning, and stew, covered, half an hour longer. The meat should be so tender as to fall to pieces when a fork pierces it. Stir in the browned flour and boil one minute. Send to table in a deep dish. It should be deliciously savory, if this receipt be exactly obeyed. Slow boiling in a close vessel, and piquante seasoning, are the essentials to success.

Roast Beef.

Lay the meat in a clean dripping pan; pour a cup of *boiling* water all over it, set in a moderate oven, and do not open under half an hour. After that, baste every ten minutes plentifully with the water in the pan, pouring ladleful after ladleful on the smoking meat. Do this quickly, not to lower the heat of the oven. Allow ten minutes to the pound in roasting. Five or six minutes before taking it up, sift flour pretty thickly over the top of the meat; shut the oven until this begins to brown, stir salt to taste in the gravy, and baste the roast liberally with this. Leave in the oven two minutes, transfer the beef to a hot dish, and keep warm while you pour the gravy into a bowl; wait a few moments to let the fat rise, skim it off, strain the gravy into the dripping-pan, heat to boiling on the top of the stove, and thicken with browned flour wet up in cold water. Boil once and pour into a gravy-boat.

Many people do not like made gravy with roast beef, preferring the red essence that flows from it when carved. But save the contents of the dripping-pan for dripping and the substratum for the "cup of gravy" required for so many made dishes.

Irish Stew.

2 lbs. of lean beef, leaving out bone and gristle, cut into inch-square bits.
½ onion, chopped.
4 large or six small potatoes, parboiled for ten minutes, then sliced.
Pepper and salt.
1 tablespoonful flour.
1 quart of cold water.

Put meat on in the water, cover and stew *gently* one hour and a half, or until tender. Add onion and seasoning; stew half an hour, and drop in the sliced potatoes. They should not be too thin, or they will boil to pieces. Simmer ten minutes longer, or until the potatoes are soft all through, stir in the flour wet up in cold water (or half a cup of milk if you can spare it), and boil one minute. Take up the meat first with a split spoon, heap on a hot flat dish, and arrange the potatoes about it like a hedge. Serve both to each person helped.

Beef Steak and Onions.

Cook the steak as directed on page 54. Have in a frying-pan some dripping heated to hissing. Slice two small onions, or one large one, thin, and fry quickly during three of the five minutes spent by the steak under cover, to draw the juices to the surface. Drain the onions in a colander, and turn and spread smoking hot upon the steak. Cover closely, leave it for two minutes, and send to table.

The flavor imparted to the steak by this style of serving onions with it is incomparably more pleasant than that of the dish generally known under the above title.

Scalloped Beef.

1 cup minced beef, boiled or roast, corned or fresh.
½ cup soup or gravy.
1 cup cold mashed potato.
1 tablespoonful of butter.
½ cup of milk.
1 beaten egg.
½ teaspoonful made mustard.
Pepper and salt.
Handful of fine crumbs.

Put the mashed potato, hot, into a bowl, and whip light and powdery with a fork. Beat in gradually the butter, the milk, finally with your egg-beater (I hope you have a "Dover!") the whipped egg. Salt to taste, and whip to a smooth cream. Season the minced meat highly, moisten with gravy, work in the mustard, and put it into a greased pie-dish when ready. Spread the prepared potato over all smoothly, sift fine crumbs on the surface, and set in a quick oven until nicely browned.

Beef Pie.

Cut 2 lbs. of lean beef into inch-lengths, put into a pot with half of a sliced onion, cover with cold water and stew gently one hour. Parboil in another pot three or four potatoes. Let all get nearly or quite cold while you make a crust like that directed on page 46. Strain the gravy from the meat, skim off the fat and season. Stir into it a tablespoonful of browned flour, but do not heat it. Lay in a pie or pudding-dish some of the meat, well-seasoned, cover with sliced potato, salted and peppered. Proceed in this order until the materials are used up, pour in the gravy, and fit on the crust, not forgetting the slit in the middle.

Potato-crust for Beef Pie.

1 cup cold mashed potato.
1 tablespoonful of melted butter, and the same of *clean* beef-dripping.
Yolk of 1 egg, beaten light.
2 tablespoonfuls of prepared flour.
Salt to taste.
1 cup of milk.

Beat the butter and dripping into the potato, then the egg, salt, and milk; when all are light, the flour. There should be just enough of this last to hold the paste together. Roll out into a pretty thick sheet, handling it carefully, and spread over your pie.

Corned Beef (*hot*).

It is not economical to buy any piece of meat that has much bone in it. Corned beef is no exception to the rule. The brisket, however, is a good and fairly cheap family dish, selling several cents less in the pound than the round. This last, unless too fat—and this must be guarded against—is perhaps the best, even for small purses.

Soak the meat five or six hours in plenty of cold water, when you have washed off the salt and scum. Put then into a pot, cover deep in warm, not boiling water, and bring slowly to the boil. Cook fifteen minutes per pound. It is a good plan to bind it into shape with strong twine before it goes into the pot. Remove the pot from the fire and leave with the meat in it on the table or sink, while you make drawn butter to go with it, using for this purpose a strained cupful of the liquor, adding a tablespoonful of butter as it heats, a heaping tablespoonful of flour wet up in cold water, boiling up once and stirring in some chopped green pickle.

Transfer the beef to a hot dish, and send the sauce in in a boat. Save the pot-liquor for bean, pea, and other vegetable soups. The fat from the top makes tolerable dripping.

Pressed Corned Beef.

When you dish the hot meat, set over the fire a saucepan containing a cupful of the liquor, with a teaspoonful of chopped onion in it. When the meal is over, and while the meat is still warm, tear, rather than cut it apart with knife and fork, separating fat and lean. Shred the latter with the fork and chop the fat fine. Pack a layer of the lean in a small pan or a tin pail, moisten with the hot liquor when you have strained and peppered it. Do not get it wet—only juicy. Now press on the lean a thinner layer of minced fat, then a second of lean moistened, and so on until the meat is used up. Lay on the top a stout plate or saucer that works easily inside of the tin mould, set two heavy smoothing-irons or a stone, or the weights from your scales, on the plate, and put aside in a cold place until next day.

Turn out of the mould and carve in thin slices.

Beef Hash.

To cold corned or roast beef, minced and freed from gristle and strings, add an equal quantity of mashed potato. Mix together well, and season with pepper and salt. Put into a frying-pan a large cupful of boiling water, with half as much gravy from which the fat has been skimmed, and a teaspoonful of made mustard. If you have no gravy, substitute soup-stock, or a cupful of soup left over from yesterday. Boil up briskly before stirring in the chopped meat and potato. Toss and stir until the contents of the pan are a bubbling, smoking heap. Be careful that the hash is not too stiff. Add more boiling water should the meat and potato absorb the liquid too rapidly, and do not let the hash stick to the bottom of the pan. The country housekeeper, who has plenty of butter, can improve this dish by stirring a tablespoonful into the hot water and gravy. If she has neither gravy nor "stock," let her double the quantity of butter, dissolving in the boiling water. Serve in a deep, covered dish.

A friend of mine had a cook, Justina by name, and Italian by nationality, whose modest boast, when kitchen-lore was under discussion, was, "Well, I suttinly" (certainly) "can make a puffeckly good, upright hash."

It is not a common accomplishment. The very name "hash" is a by-word and a hissing, fraught with associations of second-class boarding-houses and boarding-schools, where gristly, fatty, lumpy hashes relieve guard with sour, smoked, and garlicky, and all are miscellaneous in composition, innutritious in effect. It is such culinary failures that bring disgrace and suspicion upon "made" dishes. I know a family where the manufacture of these is a study and a success. The grown members of the household own, without a blush, to a preference for "surprise-scrap-dinners," and the eight-year-old daughter, on being allowed to make out the bill-of-fare for her birthday dinner, produced, after much thought, the following *menu*: "Mock-turtle soup, larded sweetbreads, fried potatoes, bananas, white grapes, ice-cream, and *hash!*"

Do not, then, stir your hash to an indiscriminate, clay-like mortar, or convert it into a lump of pudding-stone by leaving chunks of potato and gristle uncompounded in the whole. Chop meat and mash potato; cook only until it begins to boil all along the line, and season smartly.

Chipped Beef.

Instead of serving dried (chipped) beef in the crude state in which it is sent home from market, cut it up small and boil in clear water fifteen minutes. Drain dry, and put into a frying-pan with a teaspoonful of butter and a little pepper. Stir until "frizzling" hot, when turn out into a hot dish.

Or, when eggs are plenty, break a couple into a bowl, and beat just enough to mix yolk and white. Stir these into the beef, treated as above, just before taking it off, tossing all together for a minute to mingle the ingredients well.

Still another way.—Chop the beef after boiling it. Put a tablespoonful of butter into the frying-pan, and when it hisses add three or four slices of onion. Fry three minutes, take out the onion and turn in the beef. Any and all of these methods of preparing dried beef are preferable to serving it raw.

PORK.

Pork and Beans.

1 quart of dried white beans.
½ lb. of streaked salt pork.
1 tablespoonful of molasses.
1 teaspoonful (small) of made mustard.

Soak the beans overnight in cold water. Throw this away in the morning, and cover well with water a little more than lukewarm. Soak two hours, drain, and put on in a pot well covered with cold water; boil gently until soft, but not broken. Meanwhile, boil for ten minutes a square half pound of pork; take it up, score the top in lines the width of a slice apart; drain the beans, put them into a bake-dish, season with molasses and mustard, and bury the pork up to the rind in the middle. Cover with boiling water, fit on a tin lid, or a stout plate, to keep in the steam. Cook in a moderate oven three hours, then uncover and brown lightly.

Stewed Pork.

2 lbs. lean fresh pork, from the leg, or "trimmings" left from cutting up pigs.
4 large potatoes, parboiled.
Pepper, salt, and dried sweet herbs to taste.
1 teaspoonful of minced onion.

Cut the pork into inch-long strips, put into a pot with two cups of cold water, and stir slowly one hour. Cut the parboiled potatoes into dice an inch square and add to the stew with onion, herbs, and seasoning. A little tomato-catsup will improve the flavor. Cook slowly forty minutes, and serve in a deep dish.

Salt Pork and Potato Stew.

¼ lb. salt pork, chopped small.
12 or 14 small potatoes.
¼ onion, minced.
1 large tablespoonful minced parsley.
Pepper and a little salt.
2 cups of hot water.

This is a good way of using up small bullet-like old potatoes. Parboil them and rub the skins off. Drop into a pot with the minced pork, onion, and hot water, and cook slowly about forty-five minutes. Add parsley and pepper with salt (if needed), simmer five minutes and turn out. You may, if convenient, add at the last half a cup of milk into which you have stirred a small teaspoonful of flour. Boil one minute after these go in.

Pork Chops.

Trim off most of the fat, and put it into a hot frying-pan. Fry quickly until the grease is all extracted, strain the fat, salt slightly, return to the frying-pan, and cook the chops slowly, that they may be done to the bone. Lay them on a hot dish; add half a cup of boiling water to the fat left in the pan, with a teaspoonful of minced onion and half as much minced sage, green or dry, with (if you have it) a tablespoonful of tomato-catsup or twice as much juice from canned tomatoes, pepper and salt. Simmer three minutes, stir in a teaspoonful of browned flour, boil up once and pour over the chops.

Pork Pie.

2 lbs. lean fresh pork.
4 winter apples, tart and juicy.
1 heaping tablespoonful of brown sugar.
1 tablespoonful of butter.
Good plain crust made as for veal pie, page 46.
Pepper, salt, mace, and a pinch of cloves.
Browned flour.

Cut the pork into inch-lengths, cover with a cup of cold water, and stew gently half an hour. Let it get cold, skim the fat from the gravy, take out the pork and arrange a layer in the bottom of a pudding-dish. Season with pepper and salt. On this spread sliced apple, sprinkled with sugar, spice, and butter-bits. Proceed in this order until pork and apples are used up, having apples for the upper layer. Pepper and salt the gravy, stir in the browned flour, pour it into the pie, and cover with the pastry.

Bake forty-five minutes, not too fast.

Eat hot, and only make it in cold weather. It is very nice.

Pork-and-Pea Pudding.

¼ lb. streaked fat pork.
1 quart dried peas—or small white kidney beans.
1 tablespoonful of butter.
2 eggs.
Pepper and salt.

Soak the peas or beans all night in cold water. In the morning exchange this for lukewarm, and soak two hours longer. Then put them over the fire in plenty of cold water, and boil until tender, but not broken. Drain, and rub through a colander until only husks are left, and season the hot pulp with pepper and salt. Beat in the butter, lastly the whipped eggs thoroughly. The mixture should be smooth and thick. Flour a pudding-cloth, pour in the pudding, leaving plenty of room for swelling.

The pork should also have been soaked overnight, but not with the peas. Ten minutes before the pudding is ready for boiling put on the pork in hot water, which must boil hard when the pudding is dropped in. Keep at a steady boil for one hour. Take up the pork, and slice neatly. Dip the pudding-bag for one minute in cold water to loosen the contents from the sides, untie, and turn out the pudding upon a flat dish, arranging the sliced pork about it. Serve at once.

What is left of this dish is good sliced and fried. Some like a little onion and celery boiled with the peas.

Barbecued Ham.

Cut liberal slices of cold ham, and fry in their own fat. When they are done take out of the pan, and arrange on a hot dish. Keep warm while you add to the gravy a teaspoonful of made mustard, a good pinch of pepper, a saltspoonful of white sugar, and three tablespoonfuls of vinegar. Mix these well together before stirring into the gravy; heat all to a sharp boil, pour over the ham, and let it stand, covered, for a minute before sending to the table.

There is nothing more appetizing than this dish. The very odor is provocative of hunger and suggestive of good cheer.

Bacon and Apples.

Cut thin slices of breakfast bacon, and fry quickly, taking them up the instant they are done, and laying on a hot dish. In the fat left in the pan fry round slices of firm apples—not too tart—which have been cored but not pared. Turn as they brown, and as fast as they are cooked take out of the fat, that they may not soak up grease. When all are ready, arrange in the middle of a flat dish and lay the fried bacon around them.

A homely dish, but if cooked as above directed, so good that you will be solicited to repeat the experiment once and again.

Bacon and apples consort agreeably and wholesomely with Graham biscuit.

Sausages.

Buy, when you can, the sausage-meat "in bulk," in preference to that put up in skins. It is cheaper, goes further, and is more easily cooked. Make into round cakes, flouring your hands that the meat may not stick to them. Have ready a warm frying-pan, put in the sausages, and cook over a clear fire, in their own grease. Instead of sending to table swimming in fat, take each out on a split spoon or broad fork, and lay on a hot dish. The gravy (lard) strained from the frying-pan, being highly seasoned, will do to use for frying eggs or potato croquettes. The sausages look nicer and are less unwholesome without it.

FAMILIAR TALK.

COUNTRY BOARDING.

THE following paragraph, clipped from a newspaper lying on my table, is the text for our talk upon a matter which is getting to be almost as truly "the vexed question" as domestic service in America.

A gentleman and lady in the month of August boarded in an interior town with a widow and her two daughters. Soda-bread, hot at every meal, and pork were the diet; never a bit of meat nor a chicken killed; not an egg cooked, and never a vegetable plucked from the garden, nor milk offered in quantities to be drunk. Other parties boarded two weeks on the sea-coast in the month of August, and ate hot soda-bread and fish, not once seeing a bit of fresh meat of any kind. The cooking was excellent of its kind, and the table and house were as neat as wax-work.—*Brunswick (Me.) Telegraph.*

Almost a score of years ago I wrote for a popular monthly a series of saucy sketches entitled, "Taking Boarders for Company." These professed to depict the miseries of a city family, seduced by an advertising letter from home and comfort to tempt the uncertainties of summer board in a farm-house. When I read the articles in print they seemed to me rollicking caricatures, the best point of which was that, taking probabilities with improbabilities, the story hung well together. To my surprise, and at first amusement, at last to my chagrin, I was pelted with letters from all parts of the country—from farm-house boarders and from farm-house keepers—grateful, deprecatory, defensive, and menacing. A few were coarsely abusive, and, to cap the climax, I finally received formal intimation that unless I promptly and publicly retracted certain statements contained in the offensive papers, a libel suit would be instituted by an aggrieved spinster, who had for many years "solaced the solitude of rural seclusion by opening her hospitable doors during the summer season to guests from the city."

I took no notice of letter or threat, and heard nothing more of the libel suit. But the inference of the experience was not to be mistaken. Instead of a burlesque, I had achieved a pre-Raphaelite cartoon that commended itself alike to oppressor and oppressed. I have seen much since to confirm the opinion then formed that summer boarding, while it is becoming more and more general every year, is, as a rule, conducted upon principles that would insure the ruin of any other business.

I would make it plain at the outset that I do not deny the exactions, the rudeness, and general unreasonableness of many of the mighty army of vagrants from city streets that overrun sea-shore and farm with each recurring heated term. They mean as resolutely to save money as their hosts intend to make it. They are captious as to featherbeds, intolerant of husk mattresses; sarcastic upon salt pork, consumptive pillows, and dingy coverlets; and in the trifles of clean towels, poultry, cream, and fresh vegetables, "pennickety"—as the New England Mrs. Billickin would put it, beyond rhyme or reason known in Berkshire, or dreamed of in the Mohawk Valley or Jersey Mountains. I confess freely and promptly that they hire board and lodgings of Mrs. Billickin with the foul design of getting for every dollar paid down the value of one hundred cents in health and comfort. But I find no specification in common sense or in business precedent to the effect that the boarders are, over and above the money's worth, under personal and usually painful obligations to the Billickins—one and all—for the privilege accorded them of spending so many weeks or months under their roof.

If the curious student of this social and domestic problem were to offer a reward for a truthful statement from a veteran farm-house boarder that he ever concluded an engagement for the season without being assured with that engaging candor without which Mrs. Billickin were not herself—"Of course, I don't expect to make anything by taking boarders. All I hope for is barely to meet expenses"—I doubt if the prize would be claimed soon, if ever. There would seem to be no propriety in my wasting time and paper in declaring this to be an absurdity. Even the rural Billickin is not so unsophisticated as to invite toil and annoyances all summer long through sheer benevolence, nor so consumed by generous compassion for the denizens of the man-made city as to invite them by paid advertisements and private letters to descend wolf-wise upon her peaceful fold, there to raven until frosty nights compel their departure. And after all this to be quite satisfied if she has "just covered expenses!"

Let us be reasonable. You—my dear hard-working, honest, and kindly farm-house matron—have an undoubted right to eke out your income or solace your solitude by taking summer "guests." It is a legitimate business transaction on both sides, the character of which is not affected by the low terms upon which you plume yourself in the negotiations with Mr. Urbanus. You ask, as much as you think he will pay, and, all things considered, as much as the accommodations are worth, or you are unfit to manage this or any other moneyed transaction. Nor are you prone to the conviction stated by your English namesake, that—"Though not Professed but Plain, still your wages" (or board-money) "*should* be a sufficient object to you to stimilate to soar above mere roast and b'iled." That you, with your narrow experience of polite society and its usages, should be content with your cookery, does not imply, necessarily, the satisfaction of your guests, however modest their requirements. Soda-biscuits and pork are seldom the diet of people of the class who engage your rooms by the season. The very children would not eat it were it not for the keen hunger created by the out-door living, to gain the advantages of which the parents are willing to forego the ease and refinement of home.

The beginning of a much-needed reformation is in a right comprehension on the part of the rural hostess of the tastes and habits of her boarders. The effort to break them in, during their brief sojourn with her, to country living and country thinking as regards pork, codfish, and saleratus-bread, will result in mutual disgust. Nor, on the other hand, is it to be expected that course-dinners and elegant lunches, expensive *entrées* and accomplished waiters will be imported for the summer months by farmers and their hard-working wives. The wise medium is so judicious and simple that our wonder grows at thought of the small number who adopt it.

Give to your city boarders country dainties. This is what they come to you for, not for salted meats and sal soda. The oleaginous chunk of pickled pork is the more difficult to swallow and to digest when through the open windows they hear the cheerful clamor of the fowls you are fattening for the Thanksgiving market. They would complain less of the tough rump steaks, the mottled, clammy biscuits, the insipid coffee and bitter tea, if you would give them plenty of milk and cream. When the pastures and woods are full of fresh, fragrant berries, do not insult human stomachs by dried-apple pies, rhubarb stewed in molasses, or that abomination of desolation, "huckleberry-slump." Cultivate other vegetables as well as cabbage and potatoes. Fatten the girls and boys on green corn and peas; delight their elders with egg-plant; sweeten the blood and strengthen the brains of all with abundance of tomatoes and young onions. Learn how to cook eggs in a tempting variety of styles, and let there be no stint of these while it costs you no more to rear one hundred than fifty fowls.

Finally—study how to prepare in the best manner the materials at your command. The wealthiest and most fastidious of your lady-boarders cannot, when at home, purchase vegetables that bring to table with them the sweetness of morning dews and juices drawn that day from the generous earth, nor such cream and eggs as you can put before her. Nor yet such plump and clean fowls as you might—but seldom do—carve in her sight. Abjure pastry unless it is imperatively demanded. Pies are the rock on which the Yankee Billickin is apt to wreck her boarders' patience and digestion—and her own reputation as a cook. Plunge freely into the realm of blanc manges, custards, "whips," and the innumerable puddings of which eggs and milk are the wholesome base.

Many of the "Cottage Kitchen" receipts have been prepared with especial reference to this class of busy and tried housekeepers. For them the summer vacation is crowded with labors many and cruel, and those for whom they cater are too apt to regard the race as the natural enemies of their—*i.e.*, the city—kind. Do not be afraid of progressive cookery in the form of directions that would have seemed odd to your grandmother.

While paying due regard to reasonable suggestions, however uncivil their wording, cultivate a spirit of modest independence toward supercilious cockneys. Well-bred people are superior to the affectation of fine-lady and lordly airs in their intercourse with those who live and dress more plainly than themselves. The less your boarders discourse of the luxurious appointments of their homes, the more likely it is that these are faultless, and the owners accustomed to the use of wealth. You are every whit as respectable as they so long as you fill your appointed station with modest dignity. You may not be able to vie with the Purseprouds in the non-essentials of clothes and furniture, may be totally ignorant of olives, *patés*, champagne, and truffles, yet be entirely competent to give them lessons in good manners based on the golden rule of equity and courteous forbearance.

Be consistent in the conduct of your suddenly-enlarged household—swollen into an "establishment." She who does not pretend to skill or knowledge she does not possess, can never in any circumstances be ridiculous. Stay your dismayed soul on this axiom when likely to be borne down by the disdainful looks or coarse criticism of those who are to be pitied for knowing no better than to betray the base metal under the plating of gentility.

Let your homespun be honest. Patches of cheap silk and cotton velvet make a pitiable contrast that provokes —and deserves—contempt.

One direct and practical hint: Buy—and use—*a gridiron.*

CHICKEN.

Boiled Chicken and Rice.

Clean, wash, and stuff a full-grown fowl as for roasting, and sew it up snugly in a piece of clean, white mosquito-netting. Have ready a pot of scalding—not quite boiling—water, put in the fowl and bring to a steady, but not violent boil. Allow in cooking twelve minutes to the boil. Half an hour before it is done, take out a cup of the liquor, skim, and strain it into a tin pail, and season well. Have ready a cup of rice which has been soaked two hours and boiled ten minutes, then drained. Put it into the broth in the pail, set in a saucepan of boiling water, and simmer slowly until the rice is soft, shaking from time to time but never stirring. It should soak up all the broth. When done, stir in *with a fork* a teaspoonful of butter and the same of minced parsley. Beat one egg light and stir in in the same way, cook one minute and take from the fire.

When the chicken is done, undo the netting, make a flattened mound of the rice, and lay the fowl on top. Serve hot. Send around a boat of drawn butter with it, using for it another cupful of liquor, strained, a teaspoonful of butter, a tablespoonful of flour, salt, pepper, and if you can spare it, a beaten egg. Boil two minutes.

An old fowl can be made tender by putting it on in cold water, and cooking *very* slowly fifteen minutes to the pound. Of course you will set aside the broth for next day's soup.

Chicken Stewed Whole.

Prepare as for roasting, but without stuffing. Do this soon after breakfast, and set away in a cold corner. Cut giblets, neck and feet to pieces, cover with a pint of cold water, add a little chopped onion, and stew gently two hours, closely covered, then boil fast half an hour with the lid of the saucepan off. This should give you a large cup of broth after the giblets and bones are strained out of it.

Have in the bottom of a broad pot, four tablespoonfuls of minced fat pork, lay the chicken on this, pour the cooled gravy over it, cover tightly, and set where it will heat to a gentle simmer in about an hour. Open the pot, turn the chicken, fit on the top, boil slowly half an hour longer, and turn again. Cover tightly, and it should be done at the end of another half-hour's gentle stewing. Transfer to a hot flat dish; strain the gravy, season well, add parsley, thicken with browned flour, boil up, and pour over the chicken.

A delicious dish.

Brown Fricassée of Chicken.

Clean, wash, and cut the chicken into joints, making two pieces each of breast and back. Large pieces are unsightly in a stew of any kind. Chop a quarter-pound of fat salt pork and half of a small onion, put the chicken with these into a pot with a pint of cold water, and stew *slowly* until the meat is tender. Take out the chicken, put into a colander, and keep hot over a pot of boiling water, throwing a thick cloth over the colander. Strain the gravy back into the pot, season with parsley, pepper, and, if needed, salt. Thicken with a great tablespoonful of browned flour, boil up once, return the chicken to the gravy, simmer ten minutes and dish.

Smothered Chicken.

Split down the back as for broiling, when you have cleaned and washed the chicken. Lay it, breast upward, in a dripping-pan ; pour a cupful of boiling water over it, cover with another pan that fits it exactly, turned upside-down ; set in a good oven, and cook half an hour without looking at it. Then baste abundantly with the hot water. In half an hour more rub a tablespoonful of butter over the fowl, re-cover, and in ten minutes more baste again, very profusely, and pepper and salt the chicken. Cook in this manner, basting every ten minutes and keeping covered between-times, until a fork enters the breast easily. The color should be a soft, yellow-brown all over. Lay the chicken on a dish, cover and keep hot while you add a little boiling water to the gravy, with chopped parsley and browned flour, and stir to a boil on the top of the stove. Boil up well, pour a little on the chicken, the rest into a boat.

A Virginia receipt and a nonpareil.

Old-fashioned Chicken Pot-pie.

Cut the chicken as for a fricassée. Chop a quarter-pound of fat salt pork, and with it cover the bottom of a wide-mouthed, rather shallow pot. Next lay in the pieces of chicken ; sprinkle with minced onion, and just cover with cold water. Over this lay a thick biscuit crust, pretty short. Stew one hour and a half, then brown by holding a red-hot shovel close to the crust, or if you have a stove-cover that fits the pot, heat this very hot and fit it on, leaving it five minutes or so, the pot being drawn to the side of the stove, where it will be hot without boiling.

Now, lift the crust out with a fork and cake-turner, and cover to keep warm. Take out the chicken and set over boiling water. Add a little boiling water to the gravy, thicken with a tablespoonful of browned flour, season with pepper, salt, and parsley, and boil one minute. Then, put in squares or strips of pie-crust, cook gently ten minutes ;

arrange the chicken on a flat dish, lay the dumplings on it, pour the gravy over them, and cover with the crust.

Chicken Scallop.

This is an excellent way of disposing satisfactorily of an old, very tough fowl.

The day before it is to be eaten, cut up as for fricassée, put into a pot with a gallon of cold water, and set where it will heat slowly to a boil in perhaps an hour. Just simmer for four hours—and if not tender then, for six. Never boil fast in all this time. A minute's rapid bubble will toughen tendons and flesh irretrievably. Let it get cold in the broth, and save the latter for soup.

Next day, cut the chicken from the bones, tossing back these into the broth. With a sharp knife cut the meat into inch-lengths about half an inch wide. Take out a cupful of broth, strain, and put into a saucepan over the fire. When hot, season well with pepper, salt, and chopped parsley; stir in a tablespoonful of butter, rolled in one of flour. Boil up well and pour upon a beaten egg in a bowl. Mix the chicken into this, cover the bottom of a pudding-dish with fine crumbs, put in gravy and meat, cover from sight under a thick layer of crumbs; divide a tablespoonful of butter into bits and drop on the top; bake, covered, half an hour, then brown nicely. Serve in the pudding-dish.

Chicken and Egg Scallop.

Make as above; cover and bake until the gravy bubbles up at the sides. Then take off the plate or pan that covers it, draw to the oven-door and break four or five eggs upon the seething surface, enough to cover it well. Pepper and salt these, shut up the oven, and bake until the eggs are set.

In the country, where eggs are abundant and tough hens *ought* to be unmarketable, this is a cheap dish, and would be a favorite even with summer boarders.

A Virginia Stew of Chicken.

1 large fowl.
1 pint of tomatoes, fresh or canned.
3 potatoes, large ones, parboiled and sliced.
4 ears of green corn cut from the cob.
¼ lb. fat salt pork, chopped.
1 cup shelled Lima beans.
2 tablespoonfuls of butter rolled in as much flour.
½ teaspoonful black pepper and half as much cayenne.
1 tablespoonful—even—of salt.
1 teaspoonful sugar.
1 small onion, minced.
1 large tablespoonful of chopped parsley.
3 quarts of cold water.

Joint the chicken, put on in the water with the onion, and stew gently until tender. Add, then, the pork and all the vegetables except the tomatoes; cover closely and stew one hour, still slowly, stirring up from the bottom now and then. Now, put in the tomatoes and sugar with the seasoning, stew forty minutes, and add the butter cut up in the flour. Boil one minute, and turn out into a deep dish or a tureen. Eat from soup-plates as you would chowder. Before taking it up, taste to make sure it is seasoned right.

This was a famous dish at the "barbecues" of Old Virginia. In the season squirrels were substituted for chickens.

EGGS.

Boiled.

Lay clean, fresh eggs two minutes in warm—not hot—water; transfer them to a saucepan of boiling water; take it directly from the fire, fit on a close top, and let it stand for six minutes. By this time the eggs should be like a soft custard throughout. Send to table wrapped in a warmed napkin.

Eggs cooked thus are far more digestible, and to most people more palatable than when the white is boiled into solid albumen that resists the action of the gastric juices.

Baked Eggs.

Put two tablespoonfuls of nice gravy in a pie-plate; set in the oven until the gravy begins to hiss, break into it enough eggs to cover the bottom of the dish, pepper and salt, and bake until the whites are set. Serve in the pie-plate.

Scalloped Eggs.

Lay a layer of bread-crumbs, soaked to a soft paste in milk, then peppered and salted, into a pie-dish, set in the oven until hot through. Beat up five eggs to a stiff froth, add a tablespoonful of melted butter and the same of cream, salt and pepper, and pour over the bed of crumbs. Bake five minutes in a quick oven.

Or,

Instead of the crumbs, you can put a bed of minced ham or veal or chicken in the dish, moistened with gravy or soup.

Eggs on Toast.

6 eggs.
1 cupful drawn butter—drawn in milk.
Slices of stale bread, toasted and buttered.
Chopped parsley.
Pepper and salt.

Heat a cupful of milk to scalding; mix in a large teaspoonful of butter, a teaspoonful of flour wet with cold water and rubbed smooth, and stir until it is as thick as custard. Add chopped parsley, pepper and salt to taste. All this should be done in a tin vessel set in boiling water, and over the fire.

Have ready the toast (not forgetting to pare the crust from each slice before it is toasted), buttered, and laid in close rows on a hot dish. Pour a tablespoonful of hot water on each piece. Beat the eggs very light, and stir fast into the drawn butter until they are a rich yellow sauce, almost stiff enough to stand alone. Heap upon the toast and send *hot* to table.

Stewed Eggs.

Boil five or six eggs ten minutes, and throw them into cold water until they are perfectly cold. Then peel and cut crosswise in slices with a sharp knife. Have on the fire in a frying-pan a cupful of soup-stock or gravy, in which half an onion has been stewed five minutes, then taken out. The gravy should have been strained, and seasoned with pepper and salt. When it comes to a boil, heat in a tin plate a tablespoonful of butter, roll each slice of egg in it, coat it with flour and lay gently in the frying-pan. Set the pan at one side of the stove to do this, then remove to a warmer spot, but do not allow the gravy to boil again—merely to simmer around the edges. Leave the eggs thus five minutes.

Line a flat dish with very crisply-toasted bread, dipped in salted boiling water and buttered. Lay the sliced eggs on this, and pour on the gravy.

A savory breakfast-dish. Chopped parsley improves it.

Breaded Eggs.

Boil and slice the eggs as directed in the last receipt. Beat up one raw egg light in a bowl, and have a handful of fine crumbs ready, peppered and salted, in a plate. Dip the egg-slices first in the egg, then in the crumbs, coating them well. Heat some nice dripping in a pan, and fry them to a yellow brown. Take up the instant each is done, and lay in a hot colander.

Heat a cup of gravy or soup in a saucepan, well-seasoned and thickened with browned flour. Transfer the eggs to a hot platter, and pour the hot gravy over them.

Egg-cups.

6 hard-boiled eggs.
1 cupful of minced cold meat—ham, veal, or poultry
    —well seasoned.
1 cupful of drawn butter, or strained gravy.
A little chopped parsley.

Cut the eggs smoothly around, dividing each into two cups, extracting the yolk. Cut a small piece from the bottom of each cup, so that it will stand upright. Mash the yolks to powder with a potato-beetle or bowl of a spoon, mix with them the chopped meat, and mould into pellets about the size and shape of the displaced yolk. Put one of these in each "cup," arrange them in a dish, and pour over them the gravy or drawn butter, made very hot and seasoned with the chopped parsley. Set in the oven for five minutes to heat the eggs, and serve.

This is a pretty dish, and may be made prettier by sticking a tiny spray of parsley in the top of each of the yellow pellets. Should you wish to add further to it, cut stale bread into rounds with a cake-cutter; scoop out a hollow in each to fit the bottom of the egg; toast and butter them, and put one under each egg-cup before you pour the gravy over all. You then have cups and saucers. In this case there should, of course, be more of the liquid, as the toast would absorb much of it.

Eggs in the Nest.

Prepare the yolks as above directed, but shred the whites into thin strips; put a tablespoonful of butter on a hot tin plate and lay these in it, turning now and then, and keeping warm over boiling water, until the yolks are ready. Heap the yolks on a hot dish, arrange the whites around them like hay or straw, pour over all a cupful of drawn butter in which some chopped parsley has been stirred, set in an open oven three minutes, and send to table.

Devilled Eggs.

Boil eggs very hard, throw into cold water, and when perfectly cold remove the shells and cut in two in the middle. Take out the yolks and rub smooth with a little melted butter or cream. Salt, cayenne pepper, and dry mustard to taste. Fill each hollowed white with this mixture, place the halves neatly together, and wrap in tissue-paper.

Some prefer two or three drops of onion juice added to the seasoning.

A very nice *entrée* for picnic parties. The ends of the

4*

tissue-paper should be cut into fringe and twisted lightly about the eggs. Arranged on a bed of lettuce in an open round basket or dish, they are a pretty addition to the meal spread under the greenwood tree, or the lunch-table at home. You can make a salad of them by serving a lettuce-leaf and egg, stripped of the paper-covering, upon each plate, and pouring over them mayonnaise dressing.

Dropped Eggs.

Pour two cupfuls of boiling water into a clean frying-pan, stir in a teaspoonful of salt, and when it dissolves, break your eggs, one at a time, into a cup, slipping each upon the water, carefully, holding the lip of the cup close to the surface to keep the egg from scattering. Do not put more than three into the pan at a time. As the white forms and a film gathers over the yolk, slip a perforated skimmer or split spoon under the egg and lay it on a slice of toast which has been dipped in *boiling* salted water, then laid on a hot dish. There should be as many rounds of toast (always crustless) as there are eggs.

Scrambled Eggs.

Melt a tablespoonful of butter with a saltspoonful of salt in a frying-pan, but do not let it brown. Have ready six or eight eggs, broken into a bowl, and as the butter warms pour them into the pan. Stir them from this minute until they are a *soft* mass. As soon as they can be heaped together, they are done, and should be dished. Scrape from the bottom with every stir, and toss the mass upward as you work it. Most people cook scrambled eggs too long. When they cease to run on the pan, turn them out upon a hot dish, heap neatly but not smoothly, pepper, and serve.

Scrambled Eggs with Shad Roes.

When you have shad for dinner, scald the roes ten minutes in boiling water (salted), drain, throw into cold water, leave them there three minutes, wipe dry, and set in a cold place until next day, or whenever you wish to use them. Cut them across into pieces an inch or more wide, roll them in flour and fry to a fine brown. Scramble a dish of eggs, pile the roes in the centre of a heated platter, and dispose the eggs in a sort of hedge all around them.

A very nice breakfast or lunch-dish.

A Plain Omelette.

7 eggs.
½ cup of milk.
Salt and pepper.
Butter or clean fresh dripping for frying.

Beat yolks and eggs together for two minutes. Put in milk and seasoning, and give a few strokes more. Have ready in a frying-pan two great spoonfuls of butter or dripping. The fat from the top of the liquor in which corned ham has been boiled is the next best thing to *good* butter, and much better than bad. When this is hissing hot, pour in the beaten eggs. Keep the omelette clear of the pan while it is cooking, by working a broad-bladed knife carefully under it now and then. In eight minutes it should be "set." With a cake-turner double it down upon itself; invert a hot flat dish over the pan, and turn it out. Serve before it falls. This will make a breakfast for five people.

Baked Omelette.

Prepare as above-directed; but instead of frying the beaten eggs turn them into a pudding-dish, well-buttered, and bake ten minutes in a quick oven, or until the centre is set and the whole a puffy mass, delicately touched with tan-color.

Dyspeptics who dare not eat fried omelettes can partake of baked without injury.

Tomato Omelette.

When the omelette is ready to be taken from the pan, have at hand a cup of tomato, stewed with half a teaspoonful of sugar, a little pepper and salt, and a teaspoonful of butter cut up in fine crumbs, then rubbed through a colander and left in the saucepan while the omelette is in cooking. It should be a smooth purée. Dish the omelette, lift the upper flap, put in the tomato, and fold down upon it again. Serve hot.

Ham Omelette.

Make in the usual way, and when dished, put a layer of chopped ham between the folded halves.

Chicken or veal, well seasoned, may be substituted for the ham, also cheese, grated, salted, and lightly sprinkled with cayenne pepper.

Omelette aux fines herbes

Is made by mincing green parsley and thyme very fine, and sprinkling over the whole surface of the omelette just after it is put into the pan, and before it sets.

SALADS.

Cabbage Salad.

1 small head of white cabbage, shred fine with a keen knife. Chopping bruises salads of the green kinds.

½ cup of vinegar and the same of boiling milk.
1 tablespoonful of butter.
1 beaten egg.
1 tablespoonful of white sugar.
Pepper and salt to taste.

Scald the milk in one saucepan, the vinegar in another. Put into the latter, when hot, the butter, sugar, pepper, and salt, boil up once, and stir in the shred cabbage. Cover closely, and draw to the side of the stove where it will scald but not boil. Pour the hot milk on the beaten egg, return to the fire, and stir until it begins to thicken. Turn the cabbage into a bowl, pour the hot milk-and-egg upon it, and mix thoroughly with a silver fork. Cover the bowl while the contents are hot, and set away where it will cool suddenly. Eat cold. It will be found very delightful.

Lettuce Salad.

Dress your salads on the table, and eat at once, when lettuce, celery, cresses, and other succulent and green things are the material. Wash the lettuce and pick apart before it is sent in, leaving out stalks and coarser leaves. Set on the table in a broad plate, lined with a napkin to absorb the ice-cold water from which it has just been drawn dripping. Take, leaf by leaf, gingerly, with the tips of your fingers, tear apart and pile in your salad-bowl. Sprinkle with salt, pepper, and white sugar, turning the lettuce over and over with a fork as you season. Then, measure and pour over it two tablespoonfuls of salad oil to four of vinegar, adding the vinegar last. Toss lightly but thoroughly until each bit has its coating of dressing, and pass to the rest, that each person may help himself. *The fork only should be used in eating salad.* It toughens and wilts lettuce to lie long in dressing.

Water-Cress Salad.

Wash the cresses well in cold water and shake off the wet. Cut the sprigs apart with a sharp knife, not to bruise them too much. Heap in a bowl or deep dish, and season in the following proportions: 1 teaspoonful white sugar, and the same *scant* of salt and of pepper. 2 tablespoonfuls of salad oil and twice as much vinegar. Put the vinegar in last of all, and toss up well. Eat soon after dressing the salad.

Potato Salad.

2 cups of mashed potato, rubbed through a colander.
¾ cup of firm white cabbage, chopped fine.
2 tablespoonfuls of cucumber or gherkin pickle, also chopped.
Yolk of a hard boiled egg, pounded to powder.
Mix all well together.
Dressing: 1 raw egg, beaten light.
1 saltspoonful of celery-seed.
1 teaspoonful of sugar.
1 tablespoonful of melted butter.
1 teaspoonful of flour.
½ cupful of vinegar.
Salt and pepper to taste.

Heat the vinegar to boiling, and stir into it the beaten egg, sugar, butter, and seasoning. Wet the flour with cold vinegar and add to these. Cook the mixture, stirring constantly, until it thickens, when pour scalding hot upon the salad. Toss up with a silver fork, and let it get perfectly cold before eating.

Tomato Salad.

Pare and slice the tomatoes, and put into a salad-bowl. Make a dressing of one saltspoonful each of salt, pepper, sugar, and made mustard, worked to a paste, with two tablespoonfuls of oil; then beat into it gradually four tablespoonfuls of vinegar. Add the beaten yolks of one raw egg, and pour over the tomatoes. Set on ice until wanted.

Beet Salad.

Boil half a dozen sweet beets until tender; scrape off the skins, and slice round. While still warm, pour over them a dressing made of one tablespoonful of oil, two of vinegar, a teaspoonful of sugar, half a teaspoonful each of mustard, pepper, and salt. Work the oil well into these, beat light, and add the vinegar gradually. Cover the beets, and set away where the salad will get cold quickly. You can keep it two or three days.

Celery Salad.

Pick out the crisp stalks, wash and scrape, lay in very cold water until you are ready to send it to the table, then cut into short pieces, arrange in a bowl, and pour over it a seasoning made in the same proportions as that for beet-salad.

Mayonnaise Dressing.

The yolks of 6 eggs, carefully freed from the whites.
4 tablespoonfuls of salad oil.
2 tablespoonfuls of vinegar.
1 saltspoonful of salt, and half as much cayenne pepper.

Put the eggs, vinegar, and oil on ice for several hours before you begin to make the dressing. When quite ready, break the yolks into a *cold* bowl, set amid cracked ice, or in ice water. Keep the vinegar and oil in another vessel of ice, close at hand. Be careful that your egg-beater is cold, clean, and dry. "The Dover" is incomparable for this purpose. Begin to beat the yolks with even, not hurried, strokes, husbanding your strength for a possibly long siege. As soon as they are fairly broken up, let fall upon them *one drop* of oil. Beat one minute, and add another, and do this at like intervals for ten minutes. Then, put in three drops every minute, keeping the egg-beater going all the time. By this the mayonnaise should be as thick and smooth as cake-batter. Add a teaspoonful of vinegar when it reaches this point, beat two minutes, and drop in the oil every few seconds until it is all used up, still whipping the mixture steadily, "without haste, without rest." Alternate the last forty or fifty drops with tiny "spills" of vinegar, whip all smooth, put in salt and pepper, beat vigorously to mix these in, and set on ice until wanted. As you will see, the preparation of a dressing so famous and elegant is neither expensive nor difficult. Keep all the ingredients at the lowest temperature compatible with liquefaction, have fresh eggs and oil, beat steadily, and do not hurry the dropping of oil and vinegar, and failure is an impossibility.

This dressing is suitable for *every kind of salad*, and I know of no other that is.

Salmon Salad.

1 can of salmon, drained, and broken into rather large flakes with a silver fork.
2 heads of nice lettuce, picked apart, washed carefully, and laid in ice-cold water until the salad is served.
1 cup of mayonnaise dressing. (See receipt.)

Put the salmon into a glass bowl, and salt slightly.

Serve the lettuce in another dish, the dressing in a gravy-boat or small pitcher. Put on a plate, in helping each person, a leaf of crisp "heart" lettuce; on this, as in a cup, a great spoonful of salmon, and pour a spoonful of dressing on it.

Lobster, Crab, and Halibut Salad

Are made in the same way.

Tomato and Lettuce Salad.

Peel ripe tomatoes with a sharp knife, cut each crosswise through the middle, and lay within a curling leaf of crisp, cool lettuce, on a small, deep plate. Pour mayonnaise dressing on the tomato.

A simple and elegant salad for summer weather.

FISH.

Boiled Codfish (*fresh*).

Leave the fish in cold, salted water half an hour. Take it out, wipe dry, and sew it up in white, strong mosquito-netting, keeping the shape of the piece of fish. Plunge deep in boiling water, salted, and cook in this twenty minutes to each pound.

Clip the stitches, remove the cloth, and pour half a cupful of drawn butter over it while very hot. Send to table with the rest of the drawn butter in a boat.

Make this sauce in the usual way, with the addition of chopped parsley, and a hard-boiled egg, chopped *very fine*.

How to Use up Cold Fresh Cod, Halibut, etc.

Pick the cold fish carefully from the bones, and to every cupful allow half as much well-mashed potato. Have ready in a sauce- or frying-pan a cupful of boiling water, salted and peppered, with a large spoonful of butter, and (if you have it) the remains of the drawn butter that did duty as sauce to the fish when hot. When the butter is melted, stir in the codfish and potato, mixed well together. Stir and toss with a fork until the whole is a smoking-hot mass. If stiff, add more boiling water. It should be just consistent enough to heap on a hot dish, not so soft as to run.

Boiled Codfish (*salt*).

Divide a piece of the thick part of a salt cod into strips an inch wide, cutting crosswise. (A pound will make a good meal for two people.) Soak all night in lukewarm water. In the morning soak two hours in cold water. Then wash and scrape all the salt from the skin and flakes, and set it over the fire in warm water in which you can easily bear your hand. Heat *almost* to a boil, and keep it at that gentle simmer two hours. Half an hour before it is needed, drain off the water, lay the fish on a dish, pick out skin and bones, breaking the fish as little as possible. Have ready in a frying-pan a cupful of scalding water—or enough to cover the fish well. Lay it in, and again simmer—never boil—while you prepare the sauce.

Draw a tablespoonful of butter in a cup of milk (with a bit of soda the size of a pea dropped in), thicken with a teaspoonful of flour, pepper well, and when it boils stir in well a beaten egg with a little chopped parsley. Again drain the fish, arrange in the centre of a hot dish, and pour half the sauce upon it, the rest into a gravy-dish.

Cover, and set over boiling water three minutes, and send *hot* to the table.

There is no better method of cooking salt cod than this.

Fried Fish.

Clean carefully, washing out the inside of perch, smelt, or other pan-fish, and wiping perfectly dry. Have ready a little dry, salted flour, and coat each fish (or piece of fish) well with this. Heat lard, or clarified dripping very hot in a frying-pan, and lay in the fish carefully, not so many at once that you cannot turn them with ease. This you should do so soon as the underside is nicely browned, and when both are of a yellow-brown take the fish out of the grease. If small, transfer them to a hot colander, to rid them of every drop of fat. Send to table in a hot dish.

When eggs are plenty you can make a really elegant dish of our small pan-fish by dipping them, after wiping, into beaten egg, then rolling in pounded cracker, or bread-crumbs, before frying.

In any case, serve your fish dry—not crisp—neither soaked in grease, nor slowly converted into cindery chips.

Creamed Mackerel.

Wash a salt mackerel, and soak it all night in cold water. To prepare it for breakfast, wipe it well to get off the salt crystals that may be lodged in the creases, put into a broad pan of boiling water, and cook steadily half an hour. Drain when done, and transfer to a hot dish. Pour over it a sauce made by stirring into a cupful of boiling water a heaping teaspoonful of corn-starch, two teaspoonfuls of butter, one of vinegar, and a little pepper. Instead of the vinegar you can put in a teaspoonful of green pickle minced fine. Stir over the fire until smooth and as thick as custard, when add minced parsley, if convenient. Pour upon the fish; cover, and let it stand five minutes in a warm place before it goes to table.

Scotch Herrings.

Instead of eating them raw, put them in a tin plate, turn another over it to keep in the heat, and set in a good oven until they are very hot. A few drops of lemon-juice or vinegar are an improvement in the estimation of some. Indeed, nearly all salt relishes, especially fish, are more wholesome and pleasant when qualified by some agreeable acid. Pepper the herrings in the dish, and serve very hot.

Clam Fritters.

12 clams, chopped fine.
1 cup of milk.
2 eggs.
¼ teaspoonful of soda.
1 cup of flour.
Liquor from clams.
Pepper and salt.

Sift soda and salt through and with the flour. Put clam-liquor and milk together. Beat up the eggs, add milk, then flour, lastly, chopped clams and pepper. Fry as you would cakes on a griddle, rubbed well with a bit of salt pork, and eat hot.

In making batter for these as for other fritters and cakes, you must exercise your own judgment in the matter of flour. Some brands "thicken up" more than others. Prepared flour, for example, must be used more sparingly than barrel-flour. But it is excellent for muffins, cake, batter, and, indeed, all purposes where yeast and sour milk are not used. If you substitute it for plain flour in this receipt, omit the soda.

Salmon Strips.

Soak half a pound of salt, smoked salmon one hour in cold water, then boil gently twenty minutes. Drain, lay in very cold water for ten minutes, wipe dry, and with a sharp knife cut into strips about as long as your middle finger and half an inch wide. Have some butter or nice beef-dripping hot in a frying-pan; roll each strip of fish in flour and fry to a fine brown. Serve hot and dry, piled like sticks in a heated plate.

Salmon Pudding.

1 can salmon.
2 eggs.
1 tablespoonful melted butter.
½ cup bread-crumbs.
Pepper, salt, minced green pickle.

Pick the fish to pieces, when you have drained off every drop of the liquor for sauce. Work in melted butter, seasoning, eggs, and crumbs. Put into a buttered bowl or tin cake-mould, cover tightly with a tin pail-lid or plate, and set in a dripping-pan of boiling water. Cook in a hot oven—filling up the water in the pan as it boils away with more from the tea-kettle—for one hour. Set in cold water one minute to loosen the pudding from the sides, and turn out upon a hot platter.

Make the sauce by adding to a cupful of drawn butter the liquor from the can, a raw beaten egg, a teaspoonful of chopped pickle, pepper, salt, and minced parsley. Boil up and pour over the pudding.

Fricassée of Salmon.

1 can preserved salmon.
1 raw egg and 1 hard-boiled.
1 cup of drawn butter.
Pepper, salt, and minced parsley.

Drain the liquor from the salmon, and heat in a saucepan with half a cupful of boiling water. When it simmers put in the salmon, from which all the bones have been picked, breaking the fish as little as possible. Salt and pepper, and bring slowly to a boil. Turn into a colander; drain the liquor off, and heap the fish on a very hot dish. Have ready and boiling the drawn butter, add the beaten raw egg, cook, stirring all the time, one minute; put in the hard-boiled egg, minced very fine, and the chopped parsley. Boil up once, and pour over the salmon.

Salmon Croquettes.

1 can preserved salmon.
1 raw egg, well-beaten.
½ cup fine bread-crumbs.
1 tablespoonful of butter.
Salt, cayenne pepper, a pinch of nutmeg.
Juice of half a lemon, or a teaspoonful of vinegar.

Drain off the liquor and mince the fish. Melt and work in the butter, season to taste, and moisten with the liquor and vinegar before the crumbs go in. Beat up a raw egg, and mix well with the fish, etc. Flour your hands, and make the paste into rolls as long as your middle finger and more than an inch in diameter. Roll over and over on a well-floured dish to shape them, flatten the ends by standing them on the same, and when thickly crusted with flour, set aside in a cold place for an hour or more. They should be firm before they are cooked. Heat nice, cleared dripping or sweet lard hot in a frying-pan—enough to "swim" the croquettes. Put in a few at a time, turning over gradually as they brown. When done, put them in a hot colander to rid them of grease, then pile neatly on a warm dish.

N.B.—Strain lard or dripping left in the pan through thick cloth, and set away for frying fish, unless it is burnt black.

Lunch or Supper-dish of Salt Cod.

Boil a pound of soaked codfish as directed in receipt for "boiled codfish—salt." When cold mince it *fine*. Heat a cup of drawn butter, stir in the fish, pepper to taste, mix in well two tablespoonfuls of grated cheese; butter a baking-dish; pour in the fish, strew fine dry crumbs on top, and set in the oven until delicately browned.

Cold fresh cod, halibut, or other firm white fish is very good prepared in this manner.

Baked Halibut.

When halibut is cheap (as does happen sometimes) buy a cut weighing three pounds or so. Lay in strong salt and water one hour, to draw out the fishy taste. Wash with pure water, wipe dry, make through the tough skin on top incisions a quarter-inch apart, and lay in a dripping-pan. Dash a cup of boiling water, slightly salted, over it, invert another pan above it and cook one hour, basting three times with the salt water. Remove the upper pan, rub the top of the salmon well with a tablespoonful of butter, and brown delicately. Baste again with the hot water and transfer the fish to a hot dish, keeping warm while you get the sauce ready.

Strain the water from the dripping-pan into a saucepan, stir into it two tablespoonfuls of liquor from canned tomatoes, or some tomato-sauce strained, *or* a liberal spoonful of tomato-catsup, pepper to taste; add lemon-juice or a little vinegar, thicken with an even tablespoonful of browned flour, boil up and turn into a gravy-dish.

The remains of this dish can be used for halibut-salad, or in some other of the various methods given for preparing cold fish. Never throw away a bit of salt or fresh cooked fish.

FAMILIAR TALK.

TABLE MANNERS.

"It is not a sin, *per se*, for a man to put his knife into his mouth," remarked I, to a friend.

"No?" half-interrogative and reluctant. "But I wish it were! Then Christians would not do it."

In no other country upon earth is the cultivation of the minute courtesies of daily life—domestic and social—so nearly a Christian duty as with us. The answer most frequently made to kindly strictures upon our notorious carelessness in this regard, is that we do not compare unfavorably, rank for rank, with foreigners, that our yeomanry and mechanics are far better behaved than those of England, Germany, and Russia. The reply to this is plain and pertinent. The German or Irishman who tears bones apart with his fingers, thrusts peas by the knifeful down his throat, and helps himself to butter with the same reeking blade, eats as did his grandfather—as his great-grandson will—unless he should emigrate to America. Here there is no more a fixed rank for any family or individual than an Established Church. Mill-boys, rail-hewers, tanners, and canal-boatmen may in the course of time control senates and sit in the Presidential chair.

I write it down, then, as good common sense—if not, as

my friend would imply, Christianity—that the head of every household should insist upon and conscientiously maintain a certain degree of cleanliness, order, and what, for the want of an English word, we name "etiquette," in each department of the home. And since, in the fulfilment of this and other duties involving the adornment and general pleasantness of the dwelling, the mother is minister of the interior, my talk will be mainly with her.

We will begin, if you please, with the morning meal in the farm-house kitchen. If, of the three hungering boys who troop in from the barn-yard and milking-pen at "father's" heels, Eben should one day go to Congress, Oliver become a potentate in the money market, and Ethan governor of a powerful Western State, it would be only what has happened over and again, until we have learned to look to the farmer's boy for brain as well as brawn. Sarah, who has cooked the breakfast and strained and skimmed the milk, may be an ambassador's wife in time; and Hannah, who has already "done up" the bedrooms, set the New York fashions before she is forty-five. Excluding these startling possibilities, it is almost certain that each will, by the Lord's good and gracious appointment, govern a household of his or her own, and pass down to another generation the stamp received from the pressure of the mother's hand. Bearing this in mind when these hands hang down through continual housework, making and mending, and the knees are feeble with much "stepping around," the refining no less than the feeding one's offspring will rise into the dignity of a solemn duty, a privilege to be accepted thankfully.

Your table-cloth may be coarse. It must be clean. *My John maintains gravely that there is something demoralizing in a dirty table-cloth, degradation more serious than the damage sustained by appetite and stomach.* Put under the linen cloth (don't use cotton!) a sub-cover of thick Canton-flannel, if you cannot afford the heavier "table-felt" sold for this purpose. Or an old blanket, darned, washed, and kept for this use only, will do, if you can spare it. The upper cover will lie more smoothly, look like a much better quality of napery, and keep clean a third longer than if spread upon the bare boards. Have mats of some kind—crochet- or basket-work—under the dishes, and a napkin at each place. Beside these, have knife and fork laid straight, and side by side, at the right hand, a clean tumber or goblet, and an "individual" butter-plate. The fashion of using these last is not only cleanly, but economical, since the bits of butter left can be collected after the meal and used for cooking without clinging associations of gravy, crumbs, or sweets.

Do not let the boys wash in the eating-room, nor comb their hair with a family comb hung over the sink; nor yet produce each his pocket-comb and make straight and sleek his locks in sight of the assembled family. It is almost as objectionable, make him understand, to clean or pare his nails at table, or in the parlor. If obtuse on this particular point, impress upon him, at the risk of seeming coarse, that the cuttings and scrapings of the human body are interesting only to the possessor thereof. The shock of the idea may prevent him from falling into the habit of cleansing and trimming his finger-nails during divine service, after he becomes a city millionnaire, in the persuasion that it is a seemly and not ungraceful diversion for the time and place.

When seated at table, let the helping be done in decorous turn as the parents shall decree. An overloaded plate is, in this day, considered unsightly. Nor should the few articles taken at the same time upon it be stirred together and compounded as a druggist makes up a prescription, the knife taking the place of the spatula. Especially, inculcate the principle that the specific and only use of the knife is for cutting the food and dividing the joints. Putting the knife into the mouth is always, everywhere and essentially, a *vulgarity*.

Yes, Mrs. Homespun, I know "some very nice people do it." Dickens tells us that the Cheeryble Brothers "ate with their knives." But their mother, we also learn, died early. And "nice" (otherwise) people would never have fallen into a habit so incorrigible that example, ridicule, and self-watchfulness often fail to cure it, had not "mother" tolerated the abomination as of "no consequence" when they were ravenous children. When the food is properly cut, let the knife be laid on one side or at the back of the plate, and the fork be taken in the right hand. Teach the children, next, to chew well and slowly, with the lips closed to avoid the sound of crunching and smacking. Fast eating has more to do with our national dyspepsia than have pies and fresh bread. Never allow the sopping or wiping up of gravy or molasses with bits of bread when the solid contents of the plates are consumed. If the young people use water as a table beverage, see that they acquire the habit of wiping their lips before drinking, thus leaving the glass unsoiled.

Tea and coffee must be drunk noiselessly, not sucked, from the side of the cup, leaving the spoon in the saucer, and the cup be held by the handle. I have sat at table with a ponderous D.D., LL.D., and F.F.A., who made me tremble for the dainty china by grasping the cup with his whole hand, the thumb overlapping the brim, while he imbibed the contents as one might quaff a bumper, succeeded by a loud "Ha!"

Dr. Samuel Johnson made inarticulate noises over his food resembling the grunting of a pig. But he was English, and plebeian in every molecule and muscle—one whom not even early emigration could have transformed into a gentleman.

Demand that requests for food, acceptance and declinature of the same, be conveyed in set and courteous phrase; that all the members of the family seat themselves at the same time, and without bustle. Exact from the chance laggard a sentence of apology, addressed to yourself. To you, also, as hostess, should be directed the "Please excuse me," or "May I be excused?" without which no one, old or young, should be permitted to quit the table until all have finished, put spoons in emptied cups, laid knife and fork in close parallels across the plate, the handles to the right, folded napkins, and left them on the same side between plate and cup or goblet. When all rise, the chairs should be lifted, not pushed, back, and set quite out of the way of the turning figures.

"When you leave the table, leave the room," is an excellent rule in most households. If servants are to clear away dishes and plates, the presence of mere lookers-on will be unwelcome. If the mother and daughters perform the work, "Father" and the boys are apt to be in the way, loath as the kindly women are to hint this.

I seem to hear the pettish or disdainful comment that will follow the reading of the above practical hints in some —perhaps many—home circles. The foundation of much that offends people of good taste and breeding is in the dread of routine and fretting restrictions where one would be most comfortable: in his own home—the poorest man's liberty hall. The truth is, that due and early attention to such simple rules as I have mentioned should be as general and as lightly felt as are the customs of sleeping in beds instead of on the floor, and sitting down to tables rather than on the ground around the fire and eating from one big pot with unwashed fingers.

It is well to have the "instincts of a gentleman," but I speak that which I do know in asserting that the expression is oftener used in connection with apologies for boorish habits, than in commendation of the person thus endowed. Such "instincts" are the more graceful for pruning and direction.

I have not written out all this for those who will wonder that I have thought it worth my while to take pains to say what everybody—that is, their everybody—knows already. Said a lady of this class to me the other day, illustrative of the platitudinal utterances of one who thought he was bestowing useful information:

"Such tiresome triteness! I should as soon have thought of enunciating portentously: 'I eat with my fork!'"

"But," I could not help retorting, "you see there are those who do *not!*"

I receive scores of letters that tell me, if my own observation had not already convinced me of it, that there are many who would like to know how better-bred people behave at table, and to conform their usages to a higher standard than that which prevails in their own homes. Some have come into sudden possession of riches, or into communication with neighbors and entertainers whose ways and means subject the plainer personages to distressing embarrassments. "I don't feel at ease!" is the cry often uttered, a thousand times oftener smothered in very shame. I should lay aside my pen and fold my hands with a devout "*nunc dimittis!*" could I be enabled to convince my countrywomen that *refinement in action and speech should not wait upon wealth;* that elegance and what we are apt to call lowly life are not incompatible. If the mothers of our land would come up to the full measure of their duty in this regard, there is no reason why the plough-boy of to-day, who is to stand before princes in eighteen-hundred-and-ninety-something, should not carry with him to that exalted station habits and language befitting it and his patrician associates; deportment that has become second nature through the only means that will qualify one to carry a mantle of any fashion easily—accustomedness.

VEGETABLES.

Old Potatoes (*boiled*).

Wash, but do not peel, put on in cold water, and cook until a fork passes easily through the heart of the largest. Peel quickly, laying each in a hot colander as it is skinned, sprinkle salt over them, then twist them, one at a time, in a soft, warm, dry cloth, until they crack. Have ready a deep dish, made hot and lined with a napkin. Lay in the potatoes, cover with the napkin-corners, and serve.

Old Potatoes (*stewed*).

Pare very thin and lay in *cold* water for three hours. Put over the fire in cold, salted water, and cook until tender. Drain off the water, sprinkle with salt, and set the pot, uncovered, at the back of the stove until the potatoes are perfectly dry. Have ready in a saucepan a cup of scalding milk, stir into it a tablespoonful of butter, cut up in a teaspoonful of flour; boil up, add salt, pepper, and parsley to taste. Turn out the potatoes on a wooden tray, press each with the back of a wooden spoon until it breaks through the middle, and drop it into the hot milk. When all are in, simmer three minutes and serve.

Whipped Potatoes.

Peel thin, cut in halves or quarters, lay in cold water one hour—longer if the potatoes are old ; put over the fire in boiling water, salted, and cook until tender. Drain off every drop of water, strew salt on the potatoes, and set them in the uncovered pot at the back of the range to dry. Turn out into a hot bowl, and whip with a four-tined fork until light and mealy. Beat in then a tablespoonful of warmed butter, and for every dozen large potatoes, nearly a cup of hot (*not* boiled) milk, with salt to taste. The product should be as smooth as cream, but thicker. Heap in a deep dish.

Browned Potato.

Mash Irish potatoes very light, or, what is better, whip them with two stout forks to a powdery heap ; beat in enough milk with a little butter to make them soft and creamy ; salt to taste, and mound upon a greased pie-plate. Set this in the oven until nicely browned on top, and slip, by the help of your cake-turner, to a hot dish.

You can vary this dish by strewing the top of the mound with fine dry crumbs, then browning as directed. This is "potato *au gratin.*" It is well for every woman to become familiar with the French names of the dishes known to us by common titles. They taste no better for the foreign garnish, but it is a convenience to be able to interpret the barbarous affectations of hotel *menus.*

Scalloped Potatoes (No. 1).

Mash or whip as above directed, beating in at the last a raw egg, whipped light. Butter a pudding or pie-dish ; spread a thick stratum of mashed potato in the bottom ; cover this with slices of cold hard-boiled egg, pepper and salt these, and put in another layer of potato. Cover all with fine dry crumbs, strew a few bits of butter over them; cover closely, and bake until very hot throughout, then brown on the upper grating of the oven.

Scalloped Potatoes (No. 2).

Treat as you would whipped potatoes, but add pepper and a *very* little nutmeg. Fill some buttered patty-pans with this, cover with fine crumbs, salt and pepper, put a bit of butter on each, finally, strew finely-grated cheese over the top. Bake quickly to a light brown, and serve in the patty-pans.

The sooner you make experiments upon the appetite of your family with such unfamiliar and un-American dishes as the above the more rapidly and satisfactorily will your bill of fare be varied and improved. Come out of the deepening rut of commonplace cookery, and develop just and delicate tastes in those for whom you cater. There is no reason why you should live more meanly than the rich, although you may live more frugally.

Fried Potatoes.

Peel the potatoes and cut very thin. Lay in ice-cold water half an hour to make them crisp. Dry by spreading on a clean towel and covering with another, patting down the upper closely to absorb the moisture. Do not take from the water for drying until you are quite ready to fry them, as they become tough and limp as they get warm. Many fail utterly in cooking potatoes in this way through neglect of the simple rule just mentioned. Have ready plenty of salted lard or dripping in a pan, made very hot. Fry the sliced potatoes, a few at a time, to a yellow brown; take out with a perforated skimmer and throw into a hot colander. When all are done, shake briskly to clear them of grease, and put into a dish lined with a hot napkin.

The potatoes ought to crackle crisply between the teeth, and be so dry as hardly to soil the napkin.

Potato Puff.

2 cupfuls of cold mashed potato.
2 eggs, beaten light.
1 cupful of milk.
⅓ tablespoonful melted butter.
Salt and pepper.

Beat the butter into the potato until the latter is like whipped cream. Add seasoning, eggs, and milk, and bake in a greased pudding-dish rather quickly to a fine brown. Serve in the bake-dish, and soon—as it becomes heavy if left to stand long after leaving the oven.

This is a very nice preparation of potato, and easily made.

Potato Croquettes.

Into two cups of cold, mashed potato beat a half-teaspoonful of butter, a little salt, and a raw egg. Make into rolls about four inches long and an inch in diameter; coat these liberally with flour, and set by to get cold and stiff. Heat plenty of clean dripping in a frying-pan, and fry the croquettes, a few at a time, rolling them over carefully in the fat as they brown, to keep them in good color and form. Take up with equal care, leave in a hot colander for a moment to drain off the grease, and send to table in a heated platter. These croquettes are a nice garnish for roast beef. They should be laid neatly about the meat.

Stewed Potatoes.

Peel and cut the potatoes into dice. Lay in cold water half an hour; then put over the fire in enough hot salted water to cover them very well. Stew until tender; turn off nearly all the water, and add a cup of hot milk in which have been melted a teaspoonful of butter and a teaspoonful of flour previously wet up with cold water. Cook five minutes, and stir in a teaspoonful of finely-minced parsley. In one minute more serve in a deep dish.

Stuffed Potatoes.

Bake large, fair potatoes, until they yield readily to the pressure of thumb and finger. Cut a "cap" from the end of each, and with a small teaspoon, or the handle of a spoon, scrape out the contents, taking care not to tear the skin. Add to the scraped potato, when all the cases have been emptied, a dessert-spoonful of butter for each cupful of potato, a teaspoonful of milk, the same quantity of grated cheese, with salt and pepper to liking. Work all into a creamy mixture, beating up with a fork or split spoon, and fill the skins with this. Fit each "cap" in its place and set the potatoes back in the oven, cut ends uppermost, for eight or nine minutes, until they are hot again. Send to table in the skins, and eat from these. The result will well repay you for the little trouble required to prepare the potatoes.

Potatoes Stewed in Gravy.

Peel and cut into inch-lengths. Lay in cold water for an hour—longer if they are old—and cook in slightly-salted boiling water until tender, but not to breaking. Drain, and add a cup of weak broth made by adding to half a cup of gravy as much hot water, straining and seasoning well with pepper, salt, parsley, and a little finely-minced onion. Heat to boiling after the potatoes go in, stir in a teaspoonful of butter cut up in the same quantity of flour, simmer five minutes, and turn into a deep covered dish.

How to Stew Cold Boiled Potatoes.

Cut them into half-inch dice with a sharp knife. Have ready in a saucepan a cup of hot milk in which a bit of soda no larger than a pea has been dropped. Set this pan in an outer vessel of boiling water. Stir into the milk a tablespoonful of butter cut up in flour, pepper and salt to taste; add the potatoes, fit on a close top, and simmer ten minutes. The potatoes should just come to the boil. If you can spare the white of an egg, beat it to a stiff froth and stir into the saucepan one minute before it is taken from the fire.

Serve hot in a deep dish.

Potato Soufflé.

Thin a cupful of mashed (cold) potato with half a cupful of milk, and rub through a fine colander. Beat three eggs *very* light, yolks and whites together, and whip in the potato. Season with pepper and salt. Have ready some cleared dripping in a frying-pan—about two great spoonfuls—and when hissing hot pour in the potato-mixture. Cook as you would an omelette, loosening from the bottom with a knife, and, when quite firm in the middle, invert a hot dish over the pan and turn it out.

It should be eaten directly, as it gets very heavy if allowed to stand. The dish on which it is served must be *very* hot.

Lyonnaise Potatoes.

Cut cold boiled potatoes into dice, salt and pepper to taste. Heat a great spoonful of cleared dripping in a frying-pan and fry slowly an onion cut up. Strain the onion out, return the fat to the pan and put in the potatoes. Stir from time to time, but without breaking them, until they are very hot all through. A minute before taking them up, stir in a tablespoonful of finely-cut parsley. Drain in a hot colander, and serve in a deep dish.

Some people prefer to leave the minced onion with the potatoes. You can try both ways.

ASPARAGUS.

Asparagus on Toast.

Cut away the wood before cooking. These portions may give a pleasant flavor to your soup, but are unfit to be served as a vegetable. Have the stalks of uniform length; tie up in small bunches with soft packthread, cover well with boiling water, salted, and cook half an hour, or until tender. They should not break.

Pare the crust from half a dozen small slices of stale bread, toast nicely, and as each piece comes from the fire dip quickly in the water in which the asparagus is boiling, and lay on a hot dish. Pepper, salt, and butter while smoking hot; drain the asparagus, take off the strings, and lay neatly on the toast, salting, peppering, and buttering to taste.

Or,

You can pour a cupful of drawn butter, well-seasoned, upon the asparagus after arranging it on the soaked toast.

Asparagus Pudding.

1 cup of cold boiled asparagus—the green part only—chopped very fine.
1 tablespoonful of butter.
2 eggs.
1 cup of milk (a bit of soda the size of a pea stirred in).
½ cup fine crumbs.
Pepper and salt to taste.

Whip the eggs very light; warm the butter and add next, then the crumbs, which should have been soaked in the milk, the asparagus, pepper, and salt, and beat all together very hard. Turn into a greased tin pail with a close cover, if you have no pudding-mould; set in a pot of boiling water, and cook one hour and a half. Dip the pail in cold water to loosen the pudding, turn out and pour half a cupful of drawn butter over it.

A good way of using up cold asparagus. The pudding is very delightful.

Asparagus and Eggs.

1 cup of cold boiled asparagus—the green part—chopped very fine.
4 eggs, beaten light.
½ cup of drawn butter.
Pepper and salt.
2 tablespoonfuls of milk.

Make the drawn butter by putting half a cupful of boiling water in a saucepan, and stirring into it a tablespoonful of butter cut up and worked well into a heaping teaspoonful of flour. Cook until smooth and thick, and beat in a bowl with the asparagus until you have a soft paste.

Season well. Put this into a buttered bake-dish, set in a quick oven, covered. When the mixture is bubbling hot, remove the cover and pour on the surface the eggs, whipped light and stirred into the milk, then peppered and salted. Set back in the oven—indeed, you should not take it out, only draw it to the door—and so soon as the eggs are set, send to table in the dish in which it was baked. Eat before it falls into clamminess.

Asparagus Biscuit.

Scrape the crumb from the inside of stale biscuits, leaving a thin wall on all sides, except the tops. These should be carefully cut off and set aside. Rub the inside of each biscuit with butter, also the under part of the crust-cover, and set them, open, the crusts beside them, in a moderate oven. Heat in a saucepan a cupful of boiled asparagus, chopped and prepared with drawn butter, as in the last receipt. Do this when the biscuits are crisp and hot, and so soon as the asparagus-mixture is heated throughout, smoking as you stir it, fill the prepared cavities with it, fit on the tops, and send *hot* to the table.

BEANS.

Stewed Beans (*dried*).

Soak a quart of beans overnight in lukewarm water. Next morning, change this for hotter—not scalding, however—and leave the beans to get cold. Two hours before dinner, put them on in cold water slightly salted, and cook soft. They should not break. When done, turn off all the water except about half a cupful, and stir in four or five great spoonfuls of diluted gravy or weak soup-stock in which a small onion has simmered for half an hour. This gravy should then be strained, and a little chopped parsley added before it goes into the beans. Stew gently ten minutes, and dish, without draining.

Cold beans may be made savory by warming them up slowly in weak gravy seasoned with onion and parsley. Pepper and salt to taste.

Boiled Beans (*dried*).

Soak all night in water that was lukewarm when poured over them. In the morning exchange this for warmer, and leave two hours. Put the drained beans over the fire with plenty of cold water and a bit of salt pork—just a slice to flavor them. Cook very slowly until soft, but not broken to pieces. Drain off the water, dish the beans, pepper to taste, and, chopping the pork very fine, mix well through them.

Buttered Beans.

These make a pleasant variety in the winter bill of fare. Treat as directed in the foregoing receipt, omitting the pork in boiling, and salting the water slightly. Cook two hours slowly, and when the beans are soft and mealy, and the skins show signs of breaking, drain off all the water, leaving the beans in a hot colander. Set this over an empty saucepan; lay a cloth lightly folded on the beans, put the saucepan where it will keep hot for half an hour, or until the beans are dry, very mealy, and slightly cracked throughout. Salt, pepper, and stir, with a fork, a tablespoonful of butter through them, turn into a hot dish, and eat hot.

They are very nice.

Beans with White Sauce.

Soak a quart of white dried beans all night in lukewarm water. Drain this off in the morning, and cover with more as hot as you can bear your hand in. Soak in this two hours, throw this away, and put the beans over the fire in plenty of cold water slightly salted. When they have cooked slowly until soft, heat in a saucepan a cup of milk (adding a bit of soda not larger than a pea) and half an onion, cut small. Simmer ten minutes, and strain, squeezing hard to get the onion-flavor; return to the saucepan, stir in a tablespoonful of butter rolled in a teaspoonful of flour, pepper, salt, and a little minced parsley. Drain the beans dry, and turn into a hot, deep dish, pour the sauce over them, set the dish, covered, in hot water ten minutes, and send to the table. Try it!

Beans à Lyonnaise.

Soak and boil as directed in the foregoing receipt, drain perfectly dry, throw in a little salt, and leave over an empty pot in the colander at the side of the range as you would potatoes, to "dry off." Have ready in a frying-pan a great spoonful of clarified dripping (that from roast beef is best), with half a small onion minced *very* fine, and a little chopped parsley. Salt and pepper to taste, and when hissing hot put in the beans. Shake over the fire about two minutes, until the contents of the pan are well-mixed, and as hot as may be without scorching, then serve.

Beans left from yesterday may be cooked over in this manner, and are very savory. Fresh Lima and other shell-beans are nice when thus served on the second day.

Fried Beans.

Soak and boil in the usual way, and let them get perfectly cold, after draining them. *Or*, take shelled beans of any kind—Lima, kidney, fresh or dried—that were boiled for dinner yesterday, and mash them partially in a bowl with the back of a wooden spoon. Cook in a frying-pan three or four slices—narrow ones—of salt pork until crisp, take them out and keep warm. Pepper the fat left in the pan, and put in the beans. Stir with a fork until very hot, dish, and lay the strips of crisp pork about the heap.

Lima and Other Shelled Beans.

Shell into cold water, and leave there half an hour. Put over the fire in plenty of boiling water, slightly salted, and boil one hour, or until tender. Drain off all the water through a colander, shake lightly, and turn into a deep dish. Pepper and salt to taste, stir in a spoonful of butter, and eat hot.

String-Beans (*fresh*).

Top and tail, and unless they are very young, pare both sides with a sharp penknife. The superiority of the dish when thus prepared will repay you for the trouble. Cut into inch-lengths, boil one hour in plenty of boiling water, a little salt. When tender, drain in a warm colander, turn into a hot deep dish, and pepper and salt. Stir in a tablespoonful of butter, and send to table. Pass vinegar for those who like it with beans.

String-beans, cooked as above, and served as soon as done, are a very different vegetable from the woody, rank, or insipid dull-green lengths floating in a pond of dingy milk or greasy water and served in saucers—the form and condition by which they are known to so many.

String-Beans (*canned*).

Drain off all the liquor and leave the beans in an open bowl in a cool place for some hours, to rid them of the close airless taste inseparable from what are sold as "canned goods." Then, cook gently half an hour in enough salted boiling water to cover them, drain well, season with pepper, salt, and butter.

Before cooking, look them over and pick out bits of fibre, also, cut into lengths as nearly uniform as you can make them.

TOMATOES.

Stewed Tomatoes (*canned*).

Open and empty the can some hours before you mean to cook the contents. The flavor will be much improved by this precaution. Drain off half the liquor, and set away for future use. It will add piquancy to soup, gravy, and meat-sauces, and will be especially valuable for macaroni. If you do not foresee an early occasion for it, pour it into a saucepan, pepper and salt it, and boil fifteen minutes. It will keep several days when this is done.

Season the tomatoes for to-day with a saltspoonful of salt, half as much pepper, and an even teaspoonful of sugar. Some like the addition of a little minced onion. Stew *fast* half an hour in a tin pail or saucepan, set in a vessel of water kept at a hard boil from the moment the tomatoes go in. Then, stir in a heaping teaspoonful of butter, simmer ten minutes, covered, in the hot water, and they are ready for the table.

This receipt is less troublesome than the usual method

of stewing tomatoes, and the result far more satisfactory. If there are hard, green·bits and cores in the can, remove before stewing, and break up whole tomatoes.

Stewed Tomatoes (*fresh*).

Throw boiling water. over them to loosen the skins, peel and cut into small pieces. When all are sliced, drain off two-thirds of the juice, put the tomatoes over the fire in a saucepan, and stew gently twenty minutes after they begin to boil. Season then with salt, pepper, and a little white sugar, and five minutes later with a *good* teaspoonful of butter. Simmer five minutes longer, and serve.

Baked Tomatoes (*canned*).

Drain off at least two-thirds of the liquor and reserve for purposes designated in receipt for stewed canned tomatoes. Strew fine, dry crumbs in the bottom of a buttered pie or pudding-dish, lay the tomatoes on this, seasoned with a little salt, pepper, and sugar. Scatter some bits of minced onion and a tablespoonful of butter, cut small, on the surface, and cover with a layer of crumbs. Cover the dish and bake half an hour; then remove the lid, and set on the upper grating of the oven until lightly browned.

Baked Tomatoes (*fresh*—No. 1).

Choose fair tomatoes, ripe and of good size. Cut a piece from the top of each, scoop out the pulp and chop it in a tray with a handful of bread-crumbs, pepper, a little sugar, some minced onion (not too much), and a slice of cold boiled salt pork—fat. Mince fine, mix well, and fill the tomato-shells with this force-meat. Replace the pieces cut from the tops, arrange closely together in a buttered pudding-dish, and bake, covered, half an hour. Take off the cover and brown, before sending to table.

They are delicious.

Baked Tomatoes (*fresh*—No. 2).

Peel with a sharp knife, and slice. Chop very small two good slices of fat salt pork. Put a layer of tomatoes in a buttered pudding-dish, pepper and salt lightly, sugar as lightly, and strew with pork. Many like a little chopped onion as well. Cover with fine dry crumbs. Fill the dish in this order, having crumbs at top. Bake, covered, thirty minutes, then brown, and serve in the pudding-dish.

Scalloped Tomatoes and Corn (*fresh*).

Pare and slice the tomatoes, and cut—or if full-grown, grate—the corn from the cob. Cover the bottom of a pudding-dish with dry fine crumbs, and these with slices of tomato. Sprinkle with salt, pepper, sugar, and butter-bits, and strew thickly with corn, also salted and peppered. Fill the dish with alternate strata of tomatoes and corn, seasoned; coat thickly at top with crumbs, cover and bake thirty minutes, then brown.

A fair substitute for this dish may be made by using canned tomatoes, carefully drained, and canned corn, also drained and chopped fine. The half-can of each ingredient left from soup or stew may be utilized thus, or the remains of stewed tomatoes and corn cooked yesterday.

Stewed Tomatoes and Corn.

Pare and cut up the tomatoes, and pack them in a saucepan with grated corn, as directed above, omitting the crumbs and butter, and adding a little minced onion. Cover closely, and stew gently half an hour. Stir in a heaping tablespoonful of butter, cover, and simmer ten minutes before turning into a deep dish.

Spinach

Is very cheap at some seasons of the year, and always wholesome. Watch the markets, and when you can afford it, by all means set this excellent vegetable, *properly cooked*, on your table. It is too often ruined by bad handling, and is, in consequence, less popular than it deserves to be.

Boiled Spinach.

Wash, and pick over carefully, leaf by leaf. Boil twenty minutes in plenty of boiling water, a little salt. Drain in a colander, pressing gently to get out the water; turn into a tray and chop *very* fine, until you could rub it through a colander and leave nothing behind. It should be a smooth purée. Transfer from the chopping-tray to a saucepan, and stir in a tablespoonful of butter, a teaspoonful of sugar, two tablespoonfuls of milk, salt and pepper to taste, and a mere dust of nutmeg. As it begins to smoke, draw to the side of the stove, and beat hard with a fork or split spoon to a batter. Set over the fire, still stirring, until it bubbles all over, and serve in a deep dish.

Pass vinegar with spinach for those who like it. The excellence of this dish depends upon seasoning and beating, but it is easily made by one who will obey directions exactly.

SQUASH.

Boiled Squash.

Peel, quarter, remove the seeds, and lay in cold water for half an hour. Drain, and drop in enough salted boiling water to cover it well. Boil half an hour in summer, twice as long in winter. Press out the water through a colander, put the squash into a tray, and chop and mash until there are no lumps left in it. Then turn into a saucepan or tin pail, and stir in a tablespoonful of butter, with two of milk, salt and pepper to taste. Set the saucepan in a vessel of boiling water over the fire, and stir and beat the squash to a smooth, smoking mass. It should be very hot when it goes to table, as it soon cools into insipidity.

Scalloped Squash.

If for any reason cooked squash is left over from the family dinner, a nice dish can be made of it the next day in the following manner:

To a cupful of cold squash allow a beaten egg and three tablespoonfuls of milk, warmed until a tablespoonful of butter rolled in flour melts on the top, but not until the milk scalds. Mix up well, pepper and salt to taste, and put the mixture into a buttered pie-plate, sift fine crumbs thickly over it, and brown delicately in a brisk oven. Send to table before it falls. It is very nice.

CORN.

Boiled Corn.

Use well-filled, but tender ears for this purpose. The best method of cooking them is to strip off the coarser outer husks, leaving the thin, silky envelope next the ear on the stalk. Pull this down and pick off all the silk from between the grains, adjust the inner husks in their place, tie together at the top, and drop the corn in plenty of boiling salted water. Boil half an hour, and leave in *hot* water until you are ready to send it in. Cut the stalks off with the husks close to the bottom of the ears, and send to table, wrapped about with a napkin, on a flat dish.

Green Corn Fritters.

Grate, or *shave* off with a keen blade, the grains from six ears of green corn. Have ready in a bowl two eggs beaten light, a cup of milk added to these with a tablespoonful of sugar, and the same quantity of butter warmed and rubbed into a heaping tablespoonful of prepared flour. Season with pepper and salt, beat hard, and fry as you would griddle-cakes.

Canned Corn Fritters.

Canned corn, when simply stewed, is a wretched substitute for that most delicious and succulent of American esculents—green maize on the ear. Chopped fine it may take the place of the summer delicacy in the above receipt with more credit to itself than would be believed by those who have never seen it thus manipulated. Open and empty the can some hours before the corn is to be used, drain dry and mince faithfully, then proceed as with the fresh.

Green Corn Pudding.

6 ears of green corn, full-grown but tender.
2 cups of milk.
2 eggs.
1 tablespoonful butter.
1 tablespoonful of sugar.
Salt and pepper to taste.

Cream, butter, and sugar as for a cake. Beat into the eggs when you have whipped these light, add milk and the corn grated, or shaved thin from the cob with a sharp knife. Season, beat up thoroughly, and bake, covered, in a buttered pudding-dish, forty minutes, then uncover and brown. Serve at once in the dish in which it was cooked.

Canned Corn Pudding.

Empty the can several hours before you need to use the corn, and drain off all the liquid through a colander. Chop the corn very fine, and mix the pudding according to the receipt given for Green Corn Pudding.

Succotash.

6 ears of corn.
1 cup of shelled Lima or of string-beans, carefully trimmed and cut into inch lengths.
½ cup of milk.
2 teaspoonfuls of butter cut up in 1 teaspoonful of flour.
Salt and pepper.

Cut the corn from the cob and add to the beans when they have cooked half an hour in boiling water, slightly salted. Boil thirty minutes longer, turn off the water and pour in the milk. (It is safer in warm weather to add a *tiny* pinch of soda.) As the milk heats, stir in the floured butter, season, and simmer ten minutes.

If canned corn and beans are used, add half a teaspoonful of white sugar.

Chopped Potatoes and Corn.

When cold boiled potatoes and several ears of boiled green corn are found in the refrigerator or store-room, chop the one into rather coarse dice and cut the other from the cob. Heat in a frying-pan a good spoonful of clarified dripping, sweet and good, and stir into this the potatoes and corn, seasoning with pepper and salt; toss and turn until thoroughly heated, and serve.

A good breakfast relish.

Or,

You can, if you have it to spare, heat a cup of milk, stir in a good spoonful of butter, then mix in potatoes and corn, season, simmer five minutes, and dish.

HOMINY.

Boiled Hominy.

Soak the small-grained hominy all night in just enough water to cover it. In the morning put into a pail or saucepan with cold water sufficient to leave three or four inches of clear liquid above the hominy; salt slightly, and set in a pot or pan of boiling water. As the contents of the inner vessel heat, stir up well from the bottom, and repeat this frequently while it boils. It will take an hour to cook it properly. It should be as thick as mush, and a clear white in color.

Eat with milk and sugar, or with milk only.

Fried Hominy.

Cut the remnant of your boiled hominy—now cold and firm—into slices or squares. Dip each in flour and fry to a fine brown. As each piece takes on the right shade, remove from the hissing fat to a hot colander, and when all are ready, lay on a heated dish. There should not be a drop of superfluous grease. Cover with a napkin, and eat hot with sugar or molasses, or, as a vegetable, with meat.

Cold mush is cooked in the same way, and both this and hominy are better, say some, for being coated with meal, instead of flour.

Hominy Croquettes.

To a cupful of cold boiled hominy add a tablespoonful of melted butter; stir well, then add gradually a cupful of milk, stirring and mashing the hominy until it becomes a soft, smooth paste. Then add a teaspoonful of white sugar and a well-beaten egg. Roll into oval balls with floured hands, coat thickly with flour, and fry in plenty of boiling lard or nice clarified beef or pork dripping.

Baked Hominy.

1 cupful of "small" hominy—boiled and entirely cold.
2 cups of milk.
2 eggs, beaten light.
1 tablespoonful of butter.
1 tablespoonful of sugar.
Salt to taste.

Pound and rub the hominy in a bowl with a potato-beetle until it is a mass of fine, dry grains. Carefully remove all bits of skin and rub out lumps. Now melt the butter, and work it in well; next the eggs, beaten up to a cream with the sugar, the salt, and lastly, and by degrees, the milk. Beat well and hard, turn into a buttered pudding-dish, bake covered thirty minutes, then brown. Serve in the dish as a vegetable.

An excellent substitute for green corn pudding.

MACARONI.

Stewed Macaroni, with Cheese.

Boil half a pound of stick-macaroni, broken into inch bits, in hot water, salted, until very tender. Drain well and heap in a deep dish. Have ready a cupful of drawn butter, in which stir three tablespoonfuls of grated cheese. Pour this over the macaroni, lifting the mass here and there to let the sauce penetrate to every part. Cover and leave in a warm corner five minutes before it goes to the table.

Baked Macaroni.

½ lb. pipe, or stick-macaroni.
½ cupful grated cheese.
1 tablespoonful of butter.
½ cupful of milk.
Salt to taste.

Break the macaroni in pieces an inch long, and boil gently in hot water, slightly salted, until tender all through, but not to breaking. Twenty minutes will suffice. Drain in a colander, and put a layer of macaroni in a greased pudding-dish. Over this scatter cheese and tiny bits of butter, with a little salt. More macaroni, until the dish is filled in this order. A thicker layer of cheese should cover the top. Pour in the milk with a little of the water in which the macaroni was boiled. Invert a pan or tin plate over the dish while it bakes, until it has been half an hour in a steady oven. Remove the cover then and brown the top quickly. Send to table in the bake-dish.

Macaroni in Italian Style.

Boil as directed in receipt for Stewed Macaroni with Cheese, but instead of the drawn butter, use for sauce half a cupful of hot weak broth or soup-stock mixed with nearly a cupful of stewed tomatoes, strained, or of tomato-juice drained from a can, the contents of which were used for other purposes. Add a heaping teaspoonful of butter rolled in flour, pepper and salt well. Drain the boiled macaroni, put a layer in a deep dish, sprinkle with grated cheese, and put over it a spoonful of the hot sauce, then more macaroni, cheese, and sauce, until the macaroni is used up. Pour the rest of the sauce over the top, cover the dish, and set in hot water five minutes before sending to table.

This is a delightful side-dish.

Macaroni with Onion Sauce.

½ lb. macaroni.
1 small onion, chopped.
1 cup of milk.
1 scant tablespoonful of butter.
3 tablespoonfuls grated cheese.
Pepper and salt.

Bit of soda no larger than a pea stirred in the milk.

Break the macaroni into inch lengths. Boil twenty minutes in hot salted water. Simmer the milk in a saucepan with the onion ten minutes, then strain through a coarse cloth, pressing hard to get the full flavor of the onion. Return to the saucepan, stir in the butter rolled in a teaspoonful of flour, two tablespoonfuls of cheese, pepper and salt, lastly, the macaroni.

Heat for two minutes; turn into a vegetable-dish, and sprinkle the rest of the cheese on top.

It is very savory.

Bettina's Macaroni.

Boil as above directed, and prepare the sauce without the onion. When the cheese, butter, and seasoning have gone in, stir in two beaten eggs—one if you cannot spare two. Stir and simmer until these thicken up well. Put a layer of the hot macaroni in a deep dish, then a little of the sauce, more macaroni and more sauce until your materials are used up, having a thick coating of sauce on top. Sprinkle dry cheese all over the surface, hold a red-hot shovel close enough to brown this, blowing out the fire should it blaze. This is a good country dish when eggs are abundant, and will be liked anywhere.

Moulded Macaroni.

Boil half a pound of macaroni in salted hot water twenty minutes, drain, and let it get cold. Put it, when quite stiff, in a tray and chop fine, add a half-cupful of any cold meat you may chance to have in the house, minced very fine. Have ready a cupful of milk in which half a minced onion has been simmered ten minutes, then strained out. Add a beaten egg, pepper and salt to taste, a teaspoonful of butter rolled in a like quantity of flour, cook one minute and stir gradually into the minced meat and macaroni. Lastly, put in a tablespoonful of grated cheese, pour the mixture into a well-greased tin mould with a top (use a tin pail if you have nothing better), set in a pot of boiling water, taking care not to submerge it entirely, and boil one hour and a half.

Dip in cold water one minute, to loosen the pudding, and turn out.

Cold boiled macaroni—or baked—left from yesterday, will serve as the base of this pudding. If you have any cold drawn butter or sauce in the pantry, heat with an equal quantity of strained tomato-sauce, and send in in a gravy-boat, to be poured over the pudding when cut at table.

Study such contrivances as are hinted at in this and many other receipts to bring savoriness and cheer out of chill flatness; to make the second appearance of a dish more welcome than the first. It is well worth your while.

RICE.

Rice Boiled Plain.

If we may judge from the infrequency of the appearance of this valuable cereal, *properly* boiled, upon our tables, the preparation of it in this form must be a delicate and arduous business. Every half-trained cook fancies that she can boil rice. Like dish-washing, it has been taken for granted until the simple right way of doing it is likely to fall entirely into desuetude. If the rules given with this receipt are exactly obeyed, we shall see rice boiled as the South Carolina cooks set if before those for whom they cater. It is not surprising that there it should be popular, or that those who have eaten it cooked thus should turn disgustfully from the watery or pasty mass of gray tastelessness which is all thousands know as "boiled rice."

Wash in cold water, picking out discolored grains and bits of chaff. Soak two hours in cold water, drain in a fine sieve or through a cloth, and shake well in this until perfectly dry. Then put over the fire in *plenty* of boiling water, slightly salted. If you have half a cup of raw rice, put at least three pints of water. Cook twenty minutes, shaking the saucepan upward briskly several times to prevent clogging or scorching. Do not touch it with a spoon. Try a few grains to make sure they are tender, and drain off all the water. (You can add it to your soup-stock if you like.) If your colander is too coarse for straining the rice, and you have no fine sieve, lay a bit of coarse net or tarletan in the former. Set it, with the rice in it, back on the stove over an empty pot, and let the rice "dry off" as you would potatoes. Every grain should stand apart from the rest, yet be perfectly done. A little thoughtfulness is all that is required to secure this result.

Boiled Rice and Cheese.

Boil exactly as directed in last receipt, drain off the water, and put the rice back into the saucepan over the fire. With a fork, mix into it a teaspoonful of butter and two tablespoonfuls of dry grated cheese, with a *little* cayenne pepper and salt to taste. Toss and stir two minutes, and dish hot. It is very good, although you may not believe it until you try it.

Rice with Tomato Sauce.

Remember this dish when you find some day in your pantry half a cup of stewed tomatoes left from yesterday, or as much tomato-juice drained from the can you opened for another dish. Skim the gravy, and put with the tomato over the fire to heat at the same time you set the soaked rice to boil. *Or*, if you have also on the cupboard shelf a cupful of cold boiled rice, add a very little boiling water, put into a tin pail, cover, and set in scalding water until very hot. Drain, set back on the stove to dry off; strain your gravy, season well, return to the fire and stir in a teaspoonful of butter rolled in the same quantity of browned flour, a little chopped parsley, if you have it; boil up once, dish the rice and pour the gravy over it.

Savory Rice.

Treat as above, only adding to the rice a half-cupful or more minced meat, well-seasoned, when you put it back on the stove to dry off, and, if you like, a beaten egg. Hard-boiled egg, minced *very* fine, is also a pleasant addition, as it is to many made dishes. Heap the mixture, made very hot, on a dish, and pour the sauce, prepared as directed in last receipt, over it.

Savory Rice Pudding.

½ cup raw rice, boiled as directed for Boiled Rice.
¼ cup of milk.
½ cup soup-stock or gravy, strained.
5 or 6 tablespoonfuls of cold meat, minced fine.
1 tablespoonful chopped onion.
1 raw egg, beaten light.
1 teaspoonful of flour wet in cold water.
Bit of soda no larger than a pea stirred in the milk.

Boil the rice and set to dry off—if you have no cold boiled rice. Heat the gravy with the onion ten minutes; strain and press out the latter. Scald the milk, stir in the flour, cook until it thickens, and add the gravy. Take from the fire and turn into a bowl upon the beaten egg, add the meat, lastly the rice, mix up well, and pour into a greased pudding-mould or tin pail. Fit on the top, set in boiling water, and cook one hour. Dip in cold water and turn out.

A cheap and excellent family dish.

Giblet Rice Pudding.

This is made as the pudding last described, only that, instead of the chopped meat, the giblets of two chickens or one turkey are set on to cook in a cupful of cold water, a tablespoonful of chopped salt pork and a very little onion being added. When the giblets are tender, take them out and chop them small. Strain the gravy, rubbing the pork through the colander into it, thicken with a teaspoonful of flour, turn out upon the beaten egg, and stir in the giblets, then the boiled rice. Cook as directed. When you have poultry, forecast this for the next day's dinner, and keep back the giblets. They go further, and are more popular in this form than when roasted or boiled as mere adjuncts to fowls.

Rice Croquettes.

1 cupful raw rice.
1 raw egg, well beaten.
1 teaspoonful of sugar, and the same of melted butter.
A very little nutmeg.
Salt.

Boil the rice, and let it get *perfectly* cold—not only cool, but stiff. Beat up with the egg the sugar, butter, salt, and nutmeg. Work this mixture into the rice, stirring and beating until all the ingredients are incorporated in the paste, and the lumps rubbed out. Make, with floured hands, into oblong rolls, about three inches in length and half an inch in diameter. Coat these thickly with flour, and set them in a cold place until needed. Fry—a few at a time—in hot lard or dripping, rolling them over as they begin to brown to preserve their shape. As each is taken from the fat, put into a hot colander to drain and dry.

Eat as a vegetable. But they make a good after-meat course, eaten with powdered sugar or sweet sauce.

CABBAGE.

Boiled Plain.

Quarter and wash well, looking sharply for slugs that sometimes nestle in the very heart. Put over the fire in enough hot salted water to cover it well. Boil fifteen minutes, drain off all the water and cover with more, salted and boiling. Cook in this until very tender; take up, drain well in a colander, turn into a tray and chop pretty fine—*fast*—put into a very hot dish and season with pepper, salt, and a little butter. Set in hot water five minutes and send to table. Pass vinegar with it.

Or,

After the first boil of fifteen minutes, turn off the water and put into the second a two-inch square bit of streaked pork. Take this out and keep hot while you chop the cabbage, and when it is dished cut the pork into neat slices and lay about it. Omit the butter in seasoning, and add a little hot vinegar to pepper and salt.

Always boil cabbage in two waters.

Scalloped Cabbage.

1 cup of cold boiled cabbage, chopped.
1 raw egg.
2 teaspoonfuls of butter.
2 tablespoonfuls of milk.
Pepper and salt.
Dry bread-crumbs.

Beat the egg, melt the butter, and add a bit of soda hardly bigger than a large pin's head to the milk; stir into the egg, season, beat in the cabbage, which should be finely minced, and bake, covered, thirty minutes, in a greased pie-plate. Uncover then, sift fine crumbs over it, and brown quickly on the upper grating of the oven.

ONIONS.

Boiled Onions.

Peel, keeping hands, knife, and onions *under water* while the process is going on, and little or no odor will cling to your fingers, none arise to make your eyes smart and water. By such trifling precautions avoid annoyance when you can, and lighten disagreeable tasks.

Put the onions on to boil in *fresh* scalding water. Cook in this fifteen minutes if they are young, twenty if full-grown. Throw away every drop of water and pour in more boiling, add a small teaspoonful of salt, and cook rather gently until they are very tender. Drain in a hot colander, serve in a deep, heated dish, pepper and salt to taste, and put a good lump of butter in with the onions.

Onions, like cabbages, should invariably be boiled in two waters, and thoroughly cooked. Then they take a place among our most nutritious vegetables.

Fricasséed Onions.

Boil fifteen or twenty minutes in fresh water, drain, and cover them with a cupful of weak gravy or soup-stock skimmed, heated to a boil, seasoned well, and strained. Simmer the onions tender in this, add a little minced parsley, and a teaspoonful of butter rubbed in a like quantity of flour, boil up once, and send to table in a hot, deep dish.

Onions should be cooked in a tin or porcelain saucepan, as iron darkens them.

BEETS.

Boiled Beets.

Wash well, taking care not to scratch or break the skin. Boil three-quarters of an hour if young, two hours or more if old, putting them on in boiling water. Scrape off the skins, slice with a clean sharp knife into a warmed deep dish, and pour over them, at once, a sauce made of three tablespoonfuls of vinegar heated with one of butter, a saltspoonful of salt, and half as much pepper. Cover and serve *hot*. Beets cool more quickly than most other vegetables.

When really cold they make a nice salad with the addition of more vinegar, and, if you choose, a little oil.

Lyonnaise Beets.

Boil young beets in the usual manner, scrape and cut them into dice. Have ready in a frying-pan a tablespoonful of butter, two of vinegar, a tablespoonful of very finely minced onion, a saltspoonful of salt, and half as much pepper. When these are very hot, add the beets and simmer ten minutes, tossing often with a fork to prevent scorching. Serve hot.

GREEN PEAS.

Boiled Green Peas.

Shell into very cold water, and leave them in this half an hour. Cook in boiling water, slightly salted, twenty-five minutes. If you buy them in a city market, add a lump of white sugar. Drain *thoroughly*, turn from the colander into a heated dish and stir in a tablespoonful of butter, pepper and salt to taste.

Never throw away so little as a teaspoonful of green peas. They "work in" well in stews, soups, and, as we shall see, in pancakes.

Canned Green Peas.

The canned French peas*(*pois verts*) are a tolerable substitute for fresh, but very expensive. The American are, when simply boiled—*in*tolerable, and cost less than half as much as the imported. They may, however, be made palatable in the winter dearth of green food by two or three processes. First and best, I write down

Green Pea Pancakes.

Mash the peas while hot, and work in butter, pepper, and salt. (If the peas are cold, heat the butter and pound the peas smooth with a potato-beetle.) Beat in two eggs, a cupful of milk, half a teaspoonful of soda, and twice as much cream of tartar sifted *three times* through half a cupful of flour. Beat up well, and bake as you would griddle-cakes.

If you use prepared flour, omit soda and cream of tartar. Never forget to open the can several hours before cooking the peas. Throw away the liquor, and leave the peas in very cold clean water until you are ready for them. This freshens them to taste as well as sight.

Pea Purée on Toast.

Open the can early in the day, throw off the liquor and leave the peas in cold water until you wish to cook them. Boil twenty-five minutes in hot, salted water, mash with a potato-beetle and rub through a colander. Have ready in a saucepan, half a cupful of strained gravy or soup-stock, highly seasoned, a small lump of sugar, a teaspoonful of butter rubbed in the same quantity of flour. When hot stir in the peas, and toss about until they bubble and smoke—say, for three minutes. Toast rounds or triangles of stale bread and lay on a flat dish. Pour a tablespoonful of boiling salted water on each, spread lightly with butter, and heap the purée on them.

TURNIPS.

Boiled Turnips

Are generally the accompaniment of corned beef. If they are young, peel and cut in half, lay one hour in cold water, then dip from the pot in which the beef is cooking a quart of the liquor—*strain through a cloth*, bring to a boil in a saucepan, put in the turnips and cook forty-five minutes. Treat winter turnips in the same way, but cut into quarters and boil twice as long. Drain, and lay about the beef when dished.

Mashed Turnips.

Peel and slice into very cold water. When all are ready, drop into a pot of boiling water a little salted. Cook steadily until tender, when turn into a colander. Mash and press to get out the water; put back into the pot with a spoonful of butter, salt and pepper, and beat smooth while they heat. Serve up hot. Lukewarm, watery, and lumpy turnips are abominable.

Stewed Turnips.

Young turnips should be used for this dish. Peel and lay in cold water, cutting them in halves if of fair size.

Boil twenty minutes in hot, salted water, drain this off and put in half a cup of milk (with a *tiny* pinch of soda) and half a cup of boiling water. Bring to a bubbling simmer and stir in two teaspoonfuls of butter rolled in half as much flour, pepper and salt to taste. Stew gently until very tender, and serve in a deep dish.

PARSNIPS.

Boiled Parsnips.

Boil in hot water until tender. Scrape off the skins and slice lengthwise. As each slice is laid in the dish, butter it well, salt and pepper lightly. Send in covered, and hot.

Parsnips with White Sauce.

Boil, scrape and slice. (Cook winter parsnips nearly two hours, summer parsnips half as long.) Butter well and put into a deep dish. Heat in a saucepan half a cupful of milk, stir in a teaspoonful of butter rolled in one of flour, pepper and salt to taste. Stir until well thickened and pour over the parsnips.

Parsnips are not a cheap dish unless when raised in a country where butter is not dear. They are not eatable without an abundant addition of this.

Fried Parsnips.

This is the most economical way of cooking them. Boil, and let them get cold before you scrape or slice. Roll each piece in flour and fry to a light brown in hot, clarified dripping, turning as they brown. Drain off the fat, pepper, salt, and serve.

Radishes

Are—to alter Mr. Lincoln's famous saying—very much liked by those who are fond of them.

They should be lightly scraped for the table, and the tops removed to within an inch of the pink root. Wash well, set in a glass of very cold water to keep them bright and crisp, and eat with salt, passing bread-and-butter with them.

PORRIDGE OF VARIOUS KINDS.

Oatmeal Porridge.

Soak a breakfast-cupful of oatmeal all night in enough water to cover it well. In the morning drain it and put into a tin pail set in a pot or pan of hot water. If you have no farina-kettle, you can contrive a very tolerable substitute in this way. Add warm water to the soaked oatmeal, and as it heats stir it deeply and frequently, putting in boiling water from the teakettle should it thicken too much. When it has cooked one hour, salt to your taste, taking care not to put in too much, and keep the water in the outer vessel at a hard boil—the inner covered until breakfast-time, except when stirring it. This must be done often.

You cannot cook it too much. It should be like thick batter when poured out, not the lumpy dough one is used to seeing under the name of oatmeal porridge. Should there be any left from breakfast, save it and warm it up the second day by stirring or beating in a little boiling water, and then cooking it as upon the first morning in your improvised farina-kettle. Eat with milk and with or without sugar, as you may prefer.

Indian Meal Porridge.

2 cups of boiling water.
½ teaspoonful of salt.
4 heaping tablespoonfuls of Indian meal, wet up with 2 tablespoonfuls of milk.

Stir the wet meal into the salted boiling water, and cook one hour, stirring often. By putting in half the quantity of meal you have gruel, an admirable laxative for invalids. Leave out the milk in making gruel, when the effect desired is that I have indicated. Eat the porridge with milk, the gruel with salt.

Milk Porridge.

1 quart of milk.
2 tablespoonfuls flour.
A little salt.

Boil the milk and stir in the flour, wet up with cold milk. Salt and stir steadily until the mixture is well thickened. Cook this, as you should all preparations of boiled milk, custard, etc., in a tin vessel set in boiling water. Keep the water in the outer vessel at a hard boil for half an hour, stirring deeply and thoroughly from time to time that the milk may not lump. Turn, when you are ready for it, into a deep dish, and eat with butter and sugar, or with sugar alone.

Mush-and-Milk.

1 quart of boiling water.
2 tablespoonfuls of flour.
2 cups Indian meal.
1 teaspoonful of salt—heaping.

Wet up meal and flour in cold water enough to make a thick paste, salting them while dry. Be sure the water on the fire is boiling when you put in the paste. Boil one hour—not less, and more will not hurt—stirring often down to the bottom, and beating with a wooden spoon to get out lumps. Empty into a deep, uncovered dish, and eat in saucers with milk poured over it. Some sprinkle each saucerful with sugar.

Crumb Porridge.

Imprimis—never throw away bits of stale bread, crumb or crust. Keep them in a dry place until you have quite a dripping-panful, then set them in the oven all night to dry. In the morning, crush them fine on the pastry-board with a rolling-pin, and put them away in a glass or stone jar with a close top. They are invaluable for thickening some kinds of gravy, for scallops, breaded chops, puddings, etc., the many purposes for which crushed crackers are bought —among others for a wholesome porridge which the children will like.

> 2 cups of milk, scalded in an inner kettle or pail set in boiling water.
> 1 cup of hot water in which is soaked a scant cupful of crumbs.
> A scant teaspoonful of salt.
> A good tablespoonful of butter.

Salt the milk, and when it boils remove the skin from the surface before stirring in the soaked bread. Simmer five minutes and put in the butter. Cook gently, stirring often and well, ten minutes, beat hard, and turn into a deep, covered dish.

Eat with sugar and milk. If you can afford it, make it altogether with milk, leaving out the water.

Little Boy's Porridge.

2 heaping tablespoonfuls of Indian meal and a like quantity of flour.
1 cup of boiling water.
2 cups of hot milk.
1 teaspoonful of salt.

Wet up flour and meal with a little cold water and stir into the boiling water. Salt to taste, and cook steadily half an hour in a tin vessel set in a pot of hot water, stirring often. Then beat in the milk gradually, working out all the clots of paste, and cook ten minutes longer. Eat with milk and sugar.

FAMILIAR TALK.

THE MAID-OF-ALL-WORK.

Henry James, Jr., in "Daisy Miller," plays with a national and feminine weakness in depicting Mrs. Miller's amiable familiarity with the courier, who accepts it as his due, while sneering in his sleeve at "these Americans." We are irate with our very international countryman, but thankful, withal, that he is too Anglican in experience to guess how far short of the truth his satire falls. It is a matter of fact that a rich family who had made the European tour under the direction of a clever courier, formerly an Englishman's valet, invited him to visit them in America, and when the fellow actually came, entertained him in their noble mansion as an honored guest, and invited their friends to meet him at a dinner party!

We do get the relations of tourist and courier oddly mixed up. We should be as much at a loss to know what to do with another personage known to us only through books—the English "slavey." In Boston, New York, or Philadelphia, The Marchioness would have run away from Miss Sally Brass by the time she could walk, or been rescued by indignant neighbors. The girl with a smudge on her cheek and a continual cold in her head, slipshod, scantily clad, wretchedly paid and overworked, conscious of misery, yet powerless to resist it—who figures in a hundred British novels, might be sought for in vain in our kitchens and garret bedrooms. We dare not defraud or maltreat our "girls," whom few dare call "servants." I *hope* that we would be kind and just to them if we were not compelled by policy and public sentiment to include them in our catalogue of fellow-beings.

Our maid-of-all-work, if a native, calls herself "the young lady who engages to make herself generally useful." If Celtic, "a gurrel as hires for gineral housewurrek." The good-humored "colored person" is "willin' to do mos' anything 'bout de house, honey." One of these, perhaps each in succession, enters the cottage kitchen and fixes the inexperienced nominal mistress with the eye of a ruler. Kindness goes far with all of them, gentle dignity and impartial justice, combined with a fair knowledge of housewifery, much further. It may seem unfeeling and irrelevant, in this connection, to add that the known possession of wealth and social distinction goes furthest of all. Yet this peculiarity of the ignoble mind must be taken into consideration in our treatment of the subject. "Higher than himself can no man think," is a motto we do well to keep before us if we would be charitable or even fair in our dealings with underlings in breeding and education.

The invariable boast, "I've lived in none but the best of families," with which the applicant (by courtesy) applies for "the place," should move you to pity, not to displeasure. The patronizing stare that comprehends in one slighting sweep the modest dimensions and appointments of her future realm, the resigned shrug with which she unties the red strings of the purple bonnet with blue feathers, and "guesses she may as well stay now she is here," are but the protests the pride which is acquired makes against an ingrain sense of inferiority. If she really knew herself to be your equal, she would not assert it so offensively. There is always something that needs to be concealed when so much dust is raised. Here lies her mistake. Yours, and a more serious one by so much as you surpass her in good sense and knowledge of the world, would be to sink to her level by assuming imperiousness you do not feel, in the hope of keeping her in her place, or to court her favor by servile praise and deference. You will probably never speak of her as a servant, she will certainly never address you as "mistress," should you live together forty years. From the first, then, let the relation of employer and employed be distinctly understood, and act, henceforward, upon this basis. You hire her to do such and such work for a given sum. In engaging to do this, she lays you under no obligation. When you pay her wages punctually, you confer no favor. The moment this principle is lost sight of, confusion begins. As employer you have a right to demand—always quietly and pleasantly—that the tasks committed to her shall be done well and as *you* direct. "My way may not be so good as yours, but it is *mine*, and I prefer it in the circumstances," is a dictum which, if uttered firmly and temperately, will bear down the stubborn and officious when argument would degenerate into altercation. Avoid this latter error as the most dangerous reef that underlies the domestic sea. Instead of proving your authority, you attest her equality when you take up the gauntlet she tosses at your feet—in saucy look, peevish cavil, or bolder questioning. If she has difficulties of her own, if the work puzzles her, or your orders have not been explicit, be tolerant and gentle.

But—*keep your methods of work and management above her criticism.*

Few young housekeepers—I might add, not many of age and experience—appreciate the wisdom of this rule.

Correct your mistakes without spoken comment, or ignore them in your subordinate's presence. A certain degree of breeding and mental discipline is required to enable one to view the blunders of another—especially when that other is a superior in rank—without ungenerous exultation. Of course, your Gibraltar is to be always right; but since this does not consist with youth and human fallibility, be reserved as to your occasional lapses from absolute success.

It is not possible for two mortal and sentient creatures to live in daily companionship without incurring mutual obligations. When your general housework maid does that which is not nominated in the bond, recognize the act of civility as good will, and thank her for it. The courtesy may not be due to her, but it is to yourself. If she is rough in speech and manner, try the refining process of politeness upon her before correcting solecisms by direct admonition. I have seen marvellous results in the way of toning down boisterousness and sweetening asperities achieved by the force of example. It is proverbial how aptly the attendant "catches," as we say, the style of the mistress—her tricks of speech and action, often her very intonations. If you are stronger, better bred, and more steady of purpose than your "girl," this must follow, should the association extend over months or years.

Finally, if you have an honest, faithful domestic who tries to do her duty, think long and seriously before deciding that because she fails in one thing, and habitually, you must "have a change." You will never find one that suits you entirely. The probability is that you try the patience and temper of the present incumbent quite as grievously as she does yours. Remembering this—when Katy, brisk, good-tempered, and cleanly, does not get up John's linen to the pitch of smooth polish it had in his bachelor days, be forbearing while you try to urge her to improvement in this line, instead of tormenting yourself with visions of coming ills you know not of. If Maggie cooks to perfection, irons nicely, and will run her feet off to oblige you, put strong force upon your tongue, and do not provoke her to wrath by caustic note of the dirty apron she forgot to lay aside when she answered the doorbell and admitted a fashionable visitor; or when she leaves her bed unmade and her room "in a state" until late in the afternoon. Overlook Ellen's sullen face when you know, if you will curb natural impatience long enough to reflect that her disposition is warped by dyspepsia, that she is a good conscientious woman, who is sincerely attached to you, and means nothing by her black silence, except that she is suffering.

Give "our girl" a fair trial in everything, with an inclination to the side of humanity and mercy. Should you be disappointed in the effect (apparent) of your wise doing upon her, the discipline will not be thrown away. In watering another, you will have mellowed and enriched your own moral and spiritual being, will have learned to manage yourself, if not her. It is something, in this world of wasted powers and thwarted purposes, for one to be the firm and able mistress of *herself*.

CHEESE-DISHES.

Pot-Cheese.

"Cottage cheese" is the prettier name. Heat the milk which has soured on your pantry shelves until it breaks, and the curd, falling into a cake at the bottom of the vessel, lets the whey rise to the top. Turn all into a coarse muslin bag, and let it hang and drip without squeezing until perfectly dry. Chop the curd in a wooden bowl, salt to your liking, and work up with milk and a little butter into a smooth mass. Mould into balls or cakes, and keep in a cool place. When ready to use it, work yet softer with milk, beating this in, and mould in a cold plate. This pot-cheese is so much nicer than the hard, sour balls sold in the markets and offered to summer boarders under the same name, that the wonder is that the one is so little known and the other tolerated.

Cheese Pudding.

1 cup of dry bread-crumbs, very fine.
⅔ cup of grated cheese, also dry.
2 eggs, beaten light.
2 cups of sweet milk.
2 teaspoonfuls of melted butter.
Salt to taste, and a little cayenne pepper.
A bit of soda not larger than a kidney-bean.

Soak the crumbs and soda in the milk. Beat in another bowl the eggs, adding to them when light the butter, the crumbs, seasoning, and, when these are thoroughly mixed, the cheese. Beat very hard, pour into a buttered pudding-dish, and bake in a quick oven. It should be done in half an hour. Send in in the pudding-dish the moment it is ready. It will then be puffy, light, and delicious— but five minutes' delay will ruin it.

Cheese Cups.

6 rounds of stale bread.
½ cup of milk.
¾ of a cup of dry grated cheese.
1 beaten egg.
2 tablespoonfuls of dry, fine crumbs.
1 teaspoonful of butter.
Cayenne pepper and salt to taste.

Cut from six inch-thick slices of stale bread, with a cake-cutter or tumbler, as many crustless rounds, like large cookies. Press a smaller cutter more than half through each round, marking out an inner cup or circle. Pick out the crumb carefully from these, leaving in a thin bottom, and set in a moderate oven to crisp to a light brown. Butter hot, and set where they will keep warm. Meanwhile, heat the milk (not forgetting a bit of soda the size of a pea) in a saucepan. When it is scalding, stir in butter, seasoning, the crumbs, the cheese, and cook one minute before the egg goes in. Stir and beat hard a minute more, and take from the fire. Arrange the bread-cups on a warmed dish, put an equal spoonful of the mixture in each, and send *hot* to table.

Cheese Sandwiches.

Cut thin slices of bread, buttered on the loaf before each is cut, and spread with grated cheese, in which has been worked a little melted butter, a very little made mustard, cayenne pepper and salt to liking. Put two together, buttered sides inward, for each sandwich, if the slices are small. If large, cut in half and fold over upon the mixture. They are very nice.

Welsh Rarebit.

Pare the crust from slices of stale bread, toast lightly, and spread with this mixture:

  1 cup grated cheese.
  1 tablespoonful of butter.
  ½ teaspoonful of made mustard.
  A good pinch of pepper.
  1 egg, beaten light.
  1 heaping tablespoonful bread-crumbs.
  Salt to taste.

Lay the toast thus covered (thickly) upon upper grating of a hot oven until nicely browned. Eat very hot.

BREAD.

Yeast.

6 large potatoes (new potatoes will not do).
1 cup of loose, or one-third the quantity of pressed hops.
4 tablespoonfuls of flour.
2 tablespoonfuls of white sugar.
2 quarts of cold water.

Put the potatoes, peeled and whole, into a pot containing the water. Tie the hops in a coarse muslin bag, or a bit of mosquito-netting, and boil all together until the potatoes drop to pieces, keeping the pot covered to prevent too much evaporation. Lift these out with a skimmer, leaving the water on the fire, and mash them in a bowl with a wooden spoon or potato-pestle, working in flour and sugar as you go on. When you have a fine meal, begin to put in the water (still boiling) by the great spoonful, mixing well as you go on, until the hop decoction is used up. At the last, squeeze out all the liquid you can from the bag, so as to get the full strength. Let the mixture stand until lukewarm, when put in four or five tablespoonfuls of fermented yeast, reserved from your last making, and set aside in a large bowl to work.

When the whole mass is like syllabub, and the surface is quite still, it is ready to bottle. The process will require five or six hours in summer, twice as long in winter. Fill glass or earthen jars with close tops, or bottles with clean tightly fitting corks, and keep in the coldest place you can find—on ice, if you can. It will keep good a long time.

This yeast *cannot* fail, if the ingredients are good and the directions are obeyed; is more wholesome, surer, and cheaper than the dark soapsudsy stuff bought from baker and brewer, under that name.

Bread Sponge.

2 cups of warm water.
1 tablespoonful of lard, and the same of sugar.
4 tablespoonfuls good lively yeast.
¼ teaspoonful of soda.
2 cups of flour—full ones.

Mix together water, soda, lard, and sugar. The water should be just warm enough to melt the lard. If hot, it will spoil the yeast. Pour, little by little, on the flour, stirring to a smooth batter. At last, put in the yeast, and beat all hard two minutes. Set to rise in a bowl covered with a clean cloth. It should stand in a warm place in winter, and in summer out of the draught, but not in a hot room. When light, it will be many times larger than the original bulk and cracked all over the top. For a forenoon baking it should be set overnight.

Bread raised with Sponge.

If you have set the quantity of sponge given above, sift, when ready to bake, three pints of flour into a bowl or tray, strew with a tablespoonful of salt, make a hollow, like a crater, in the middle, pour in the risen sponge, and work down the flour from the sides into this, until you have a soft mass, *just stiff enough to handle.* Rinse out the sponge-bowl with a little lukewarm water and add, working in more flour if this thins it too much.

Flour your hands and the kneading-board abundantly;

make the dough into a ball and lay it on the board; begin to knead steadily, but not so fast as to tire yourself. Work from you all the time, turning the dough around and over every few moments, until it is dry and elastic, but still soft. Keep this up for fifteen minutes, wash and wipe dry the bowl or tray in which the sponge was set, flour the inside and lay in the dough made into a shapely ball. Sprinkle flour over the top, throw a thick cloth over all, and set out of the wind to rise. This will be accomplished in a few hours in warm weather, in winter it will take eight, perhaps—certainly six.

When it is very light and seamy on the surface, lay it again on the board, floured, and knead ten minutes—*well.* Divide into as many parts as you wish to have loaves, make these out, round or oblong, according to the shape of your pans, grease the pans well with lard, put in the dough, cover and set in a moderately warm place to rise for the last time, a cloth excluding air and dust. In an hour they should be ready for baking. The oven should be moderate, with a steady fire. Do not put fresh coal on while the bread is in baking. Leave the oven-door closed fifteen minutes before glancing in to see how "it is getting on." This gives a chance for rising fairly. Half an hour should bake a small loaf; allow a proportionate time for larger. Test with a clean straw to judge when the bread is done. If it comes out dry and smooth, take out the loaves, and tilt on one end against a clean upright surface, to let the air pass freely beneath them. Cover with a light cloth until cold, then wrap up securely in bread-towels and put into a tin bread-box.

If the weather is very cold, wrap an old blanket about the bread-tray when you have covered it with a towel. Avoid the heat in summer and the risk of "taking cold" in winter. Study the best places for bread-rising at all seasons. A light closet adjoining the kitchen is usually a safe corner for this process. Should the loaves rise unevenly in baking, turn them quickly and gently.

Bread without Sponge.

1 quart of sifted dry flour.
2 cups of lukewarm water.
5 tablespoonfuls of lively yeast.
1 teaspoonful of salt—heaping.

Sift the salted flour into a bowl, pour in yeast, then the warm water, work the flour by degrees into the liquid, and proceed as directed in receipt for Bread raised with Sponge.

It is often convenient to make bread in this manner when there is not time to set a sponge. Mix overnight if you are to bake in the morning—about ten o'clock in the forenoon for tea-rolls and biscuits. Knead the dough twenty minutes after the first and second risings. When it rebounds from a blow, or your fingers come up clean after a thrust into the heart of the kneaded ball, you may leave off working it.

Graham Bread.

2 *full* cups of Graham flour—unsifted.
1 cup of white, sifted flour.
5 tablespoonfuls of yeast.
1 heaping teaspoonful of salt.
1 cup of warm water.
½ cup of molasses.
½ teaspoonful of soda, dissolved in the water.

Put both kinds of flour, salted, into a bowl. Stir up very well while dry. Mix molasses, soda, and warm water together (the water *almost hot*), make a hole in the middle of the flour, and pour first the yeast, then this mixture in. Work down the flour with a wooden spoon, beating hard as you go on. Add just enough Graham flour, if necessary, to enable you to knead the batch. Flour your hands and work it hard twenty minutes in the tray. Set to rise for eight hours; knead then ten minutes, and make into loaves; set near the fire for an hour, and bake. It will require a little longer time than white bread. Cover with white or brown *unprinted* paper, should it seem likely to brown too fast.

Light Rolls.

1 quart of flour—sifted.
½ cupful of yeast.
2 cups of lukewarm water.
1 teaspoonful of white sugar and same of lard.
1 heaping teaspoonful of salt.

Sift the flour into a tray or wooden bowl, and chop the shortening well into it. Make a hole in the middle and pour in the yeast and sugar, working it in with your chopper, adding the warm water gradually as it stiffens. When thoroughly mixed, lay by the knife, flour your kneading-board, and throw the dough upon it. Dust your hands with flour and knead steadily, turning the lump frequently, for twenty minutes, or until the dough is elastic, springing back instantly from a smart blow of the fist, and your finger, if thrust into it, comes out clean.

Put into a floured tray or pan; cover with a clean cloth and set in a moderately warm place until next morning, the mixing having been done at bedtime. An hour and a half before breakfast-time, turn out the dough upon the board and work in the salt. Knead steadily, in doing this, for ten or twelve minutes. Be careful not to make the dough too stiff at night, or by adding flour in the morning's kneading. Cut it into four pieces, and knead each in turn a minute, before you break from it bits for the rolls or biscuits. Mould these with your hands, turning the rough edges underneath. Set closely together in a floured pan and set by to rise, under a cloth and in a warm place. They should be light enough in from thirty to forty minutes. Bake in a moderate oven for fifteen minutes, then lay a clean paper over the top to prevent hardening, and quicken the heat. They should be done in about twenty-five minutes from the time of going in. Break apart before sending to table.

Boston Brown Bread.

1 cup of Indian meal.
1 cup of rye flour.
½ cup of white flour.
½ cup of molasses.
1 cup of milk.
½ teaspoonful of salt.
1 teaspoonful of soda—an even one.

Sift soda and salt three times with flour and meal. Make a hole in the middle, and pour in molasses and milk, mixed together. Work up long and well; put into a buttered mould with a close top, set in a pot of boiling water and cook for two hours. Eat warm.

Quick Biscuit.

1 quart of prepared flour (Hecker's is the best).
2 heaping tablespoonfuls of lard, or very nice beef or fresh pork dripping.
1 cup of lukewarm water.
1 cup of milk.
1 teaspoonful of salt.

Rub the shortening well into the flour; add the salt, milk, and water. Work up rapidly, handling as little as possible. Roll out lightly. Much kneading injures the dough. Cut into cakes half an inch thick, arrange in a floured pan, and bake in a quick oven.

Bonny Clabber Biscuit.

1 quart of sifted flour.
2 cups—scant—of loppered milk.
1 tablespoonful of lard or butter.
1 teaspoonful of soda, and the same of salt.
You may substitute buttermilk for "clabber" if you prefer.

Sift soda and salt into the flour, passing all twice through the sieve to mix them thoroughly Into a hole in the middle of the flour put the lard, and chop up until no bits of it remain. Then pour in the milk, still using the chopper, until the whole mass is a tender, clean dough, that leaves the blade clear. Sprinkle your kneading-board and rub your rolling-pin with dry flour. Turn out the dough upon the former, and roll quickly and lightly into a sheet half an inch thick. Cut into round cakes, dust a baking-tin lightly with flour, and lay these within it. Bake quickly to a nice brown. Eat hot.

Graham Biscuit.

3 cups of Graham flour.
1 cup of white flour.
1 cup of milk.
1 cup of lukewarm water.
1 tablespoonful of lard.
1 heaping tablespoonful of brown sugar or molasses.
1 teaspoonful of salt.
1 teaspoonful of soda.
2 teaspoonfuls of cream of tartar.

Sift soda, salt, and cream of tartar into the flour, rubbing twice through the sieve, to mix all together. Chop the lard into this very thoroughly. Lastly, wet up with milk, molasses, and water, handling as little as possible. Roll out into a sheet with few, but rapid passes of the rolling-pin. Cut into round biscuits, and bake in a steady, quick oven.

Eat hot, but they are also good cold.

Toasted Crackers.

Split Boston crackers and toast on the inside, taking care not to burn them. Butter each lightly as soon as it is done, and pile in a heated plate. They are very nice with picked fish.

SOME WAYS OF USING STALE BREAD.

Water Toast.

Cut stale bread into slices half an inch thick and pare off all the crust. Nobody likes toast-crusts. Even Mr. F.'s aunt (see "Little Dorrit") put them off upon others. Have a clear, smokeless fire, and close by on the range a pan of boiling water, in which put a tablespoonful of butter to a pint of the liquid and half a teaspoonful of salt. As each slice is toasted, scrape off every symptom of a scorch or burn and dip quickly in the boiling water and butter. Pile neatly in a hot, deep dish; pour the little water that remains when all is done on the top, and cover closely to keep hot.

Buttered Toast.

Cut all the crust from slices of stale bread half an inch thick. Toast quickly over a clear fire. If a bit is slightly burnt, scrape the black off at once. Burning is not toasting. Neither is toasting the slow drying and darkening of the slices over a dull fire. To smoke toast is to ruin it utterly. When done it should be a delicate brown all over. Butter each piece lightly as it is taken from the fire, and keep hot until all are toasted. Throw a napkin over the plate in sending to table.

Cream Toast.

Stale bread.
1 cup of boiling milk.
1 tablespoonful of butter.
White of 1 egg.
Salt.
Boiling water.

Pare the crust from the bread and toast quickly. As each slice is taken from the fire dip in a pan of water, salted, standing on the stove and kept at a hard boil all the time. Pile in a deep covered dish, and when all the toast is ready pour over it a sauce made of the milk and butter, the white of egg beaten stiff and whipped in at the last, just before the milk is drawn from the fire. Cover and let stand five minutes before it goes to table.

This preparation of toast is very delightful.

Tomato Toast.

Run a pint of stewed ripe or canned tomatoes through a colander, place in a porcelain stew-pan, season with butter, pepper, and salt, and sugar to taste; cut slices of bread thin, brown on both sides, butter and lay on a platter, and just before serving add a cup of hot milk with a *tiny* bit of soda stirred in to the stewed tomatoes, and pour them over the toast.

MUFFINS, CORN BREAD, AND GRIDDLE-CAKES.

Minute Muffins.

1 cup of milk.
1 tablespoonful of melted butter or lard.
1 tablespoonful of white sugar (powdered is best).
1 even teaspoonful of salt.
2 eggs.
2 cups of (sifted) prepared flour.

Beat the eggs very light; into these the sugar, then the lard or butter, the milk, lastly, the salted flour. Stir until the rather stiff batter is porous and rough all through. Bake in greased muffin-tins. They should puff up to treble the height of the raw material.

Simple as these muffins are, they deserve a high rank among the varieties of breakfast cakes, and are especially valuable because so easily and quickly made.

Risen Muffins (*English*).

1 quart of flour.
1 teaspoonful of salt.
2 cups of warm water.
4 tablespoonfuls of yeast.
1 tablespoonful of white sugar.

Make a hole in the middle of the salted and sugared flour. Mix yeast and lukewarm water together; pour in and work the flour down by degrees with a spoon, beating very hard when all is in. Set to rise in a covered bowl five or six hours, or until very light; beat hard five minutes, and let it rise again for half an hour; stir up smartly, and bake in well-greased patty-pans in the oven, or in greased rings on a griddle, turning once when the ring is full and the batter firm. The rings and pans should be but half filled with raw batter. In the oven they should be done in twenty minutes—or less; on the griddle, which should be hot, in less than ten. Turn out upon a hot plate, split, butter, and eat hot. They are nice split and toasted when cold.

Hominy Muffins.

1 cup of boiled " small " hominy—perfectly cold.
2 eggs.
1 large cup sour or buttermilk.
1 tablespoonful melted lard.
1 teaspoonful of salt.
1 tablespoonful of white sugar.
¾ of a cup of flour.
½ teaspoonful of soda.

Rub the hominy until you have a granulated mass, add the salt, sugar, and lard; beat to a cream, then the eggs whipped very light, the milk, in which the soda should be dissolved *just* before it goes in, at last the flour. There should be just enough to hold the other ingredients together. Beat *hard*, and bake quickly in warmed and greased pans. Eat before they fall. They are wholesome and delicious.

Sally-Lunn.

3 even cups of flour.
1 tablespoonful of butter.
1 tablespoonful of white sugar.
1 cup of milk.
2 eggs, beaten thoroughly.
1 saltspoonful of salt.
1 teaspoonful of soda and 2 of cream of tartar.

MUFFINS, CORN BREAD, AND GRIDDLE-CAKES. 159

Sift cream of tartar, soda, salt, and sugar *three* times with the flour. Rub butter and sugar to a cream. Beat the eggs in a cake-bowl, add the creamed butter and sugar, whip hard, put in the milk, then the flour. Beat one minute up from the bottom, and bake in greased patty-pans, or in a buttered cake-mould—one with a cylinder in the centre, if you have it. It should be done in half an hour. Turn the loaf out on a plate, cover with a napkin, and cut in slices at the table, holding the knife almost perpendicularly, not to crush the hot bread.

Graham Gems.

2 cups of warm water.
1 *full* cup of Graham flour.
3 tablespoonfuls of yeast.
$\frac{1}{2}$ cup of molasses.
$\frac{1}{2}$ teaspoonful of salt.
Soda.

Make a hole in the salted flour, stir in water mixed with molasses, add the yeast, beat five minutes, and set to rise for six hours. Then stir in a half-teaspoonful of soda, dissolved in a very little boiling water, beat one minute, and bake in the quickest oven you can heat, in gem-pans greased and made hot before the batter goes in.

Tear open and eat before they cool.

Risen Corn Bread.

2 cups of Indian meal.
3 tablespoonfuls of sugar or molasses.
2 cups of boiling water.
4 tablespoonfuls of good yeast.
1 tablespoonful of melted lard.
1 scant cup of flour.
$\frac{1}{2}$ teaspoonful of soda.
1 teaspoonful of salt.

Sift salt, soda, meal, and flour three times through the sieve. Mix molasses (or sugar), hot water, and lard together, and beat in the meal and flour until thoroughly mixed, and little more than blood-warm. Then put in the yeast, stir vigorously for two minutes, and set to rise until light. Bake in small greased pans, or in one large shallow one, or in a cake-mould. If baked in a large loaf it will not be done under forty-five minutes.

Boiled Corn Bread.

1 pint Indian meal and half as much flour.
1 tablespoonful of sugar or molasses.
2 cups of buttermilk or "clabber."
1 cup of hot water.
1 teaspoonful of soda.
1 tablespoonful of melted lard.

Sift meal, flour, soda, and salt together three times. Stir sugar or molasses, lard, milk, and hot water together, and pour into the flour by degrees. Beat five minutes, and pour into a tight, greased mould with a top, or into a tin pail with a close cover, and set in a pot of hot water, not so full as to boil up to the top. Put an iron on the lid to keep it from turning over, and boil for an hour and a half. Dip in cold water to loosen the bread from the sides, turn out and eat hot.

Cheap, good, and nutritious.

Indian Meal Sally-Lunn.

2 cups loppered milk or buttermilk.
2 eggs, whipped light.
2 tablespoonfuls melted lard.
1 tablespoonful white sugar.
1 teaspoonful soda.

1 teaspoonful salt.
2½ cups corn meal.
½ cup of flour.

Sift the soda and salt three times through flour and meal. Beat the sugar into the lard, and when this is a cream, whip up with the beaten eggs. Next comes the milk, finally flour and meal, sifted in together. Beat hard two minutes, and bake in a shallow pan or in small tins in a steady oven. Eat hot.

Wafers.

2 cups of flour.
1 tablespoonful of butter.
1 cup of milk, or enough to make stiff dough.
1 teaspoonful of salt sifted with flour.

Rub the butter into the salted flour and work up with the milk. Roll out *very* thin, cut into rounds with a small tumbler, and roll these again into larger rounds as thin as writing-paper. Lift carefully, and lay in a pan lightly dusted with flour. Bake to a faint brown.

These wafers are tedious in the making, by reason of the care required to get them thin enough and symmetrical in shape. But they are delicately delicious when done, and always a treat to invalids.

Buckwheat Cakes.

1 quart of buckwheat flour, mixed well with ½ cup of Indian and a like quantity of oatmeal.
1 heaping teaspoonful of salt.
2 tablespoonfuls of molasses.
1 quart of warm water, or enough for good batter.
4 tablespoonfuls of yeast.

Sift meal and flour together, salt, and pour into the "crater" in the middle the warm water and molasses, then the yeast. Beat long and well, and set in a warm corner to rise overnight. Beat up well in the morning, and bake on a hot griddle rubbed faithfully with a bit of fat salt pork stuck on a fork. Turn as they brown. Should the batter sour in rising, stir in a bit of soda no larger than a grain of corn, dissolved in a little boiling water.

Indian Meal Cakes.

3 cups of corn meal.
1 cup of flour.
3 cups of buttermilk or loppered milk.
1 tablespoonful of lard.
1 cup of boiling water.
2 tablespoonfuls of molasses.
1 egg.
1 teaspoonful of soda, and the same of salt.

Pour the hot water on the salted meal, mix in the lard and stir hard until the paste is smooth. Put the molasses into the milk and add gradually to the wet meal, beating faithfully. Then the beaten egg should go in, lastly the flour, through which the soda has been sifted three times. Beat up for two whole minutes and bake on a well-greased griddle. They are good, even without the egg.

Hominy "Griddles."

1 large cup of small hominy, boiled and perfectly cold.
2 cups of sweet milk.
1 egg, whipped light.
½ cup of prepared flour.
½ teaspoonful of salt.
1 teaspoonful of molasses.
1 teaspoonful of melted lard or other shortening.

Rub hominy, salt, and lard smooth in a bowl. Put molasses and milk together and stir in gradually, then the beaten egg, finally the flour. Whip one minute and bake.

Graham Griddles.

2 cups of Graham flour and 1 of white.
4 cups of clabber or buttermilk.
2 tablespoonfuls of Indian meal.
1 teaspoonful of lard melted in ½ cup of warm water.
1 tablespoonful of molasses.
You can put in a beaten egg, if you like.

Mix as directed in Indian Meal Cakes.

Flannel Cakes (*without eggs*).

2 cups of flour.
1 cup of corn meal.
2½ cups of sweet milk.
1 cup of boiling water, poured on the meal.
1 tablespoonful of lard, melted.
1 tablespoonful of molasses.
1 teaspoonful of salt.
4 tablespoonfuls of yeast.

Mix overnight, beating very hard, and set to rise for breakfast-cakes. Should it thicken up too much in the mixing, add more warm water.

Bread-crumb Cakes.

2 cups of fine, dry crumbs soaked in 2 cups of scalding milk.
2 cups of lukewarm water.
⅔ of a cup of prepared flour.
1 tablespoonful of molasses.
1 tablespoonful of melted lard.
2 eggs, whipped light.
1 teaspoonful of salt.

Beat the soaked crumbs two minutes to a lumpless pulp; stir in lard, molasses, and salt, add the beaten eggs, at last the flour. Grease the griddle particularly well, that they may not stick. They are very fair cakes with only one egg—excellent with two.

Buttermilk Cakes.

4 cups of sifted flour.
4 tablespoonfuls of Indian meal, scalded with ½ cup of boiling water.
1 quart of sour buttermilk.
1 heaping teaspoonful of soda sifted with 1 teaspoonful of salt three times through the flour.
2 tablespoonfuls of molasses.

Put molasses and milk together and pour into the flour, by degrees, stirring patiently and long. Beat in the scalded meal, whip hard three minutes, and your cakes, without shortening or eggs, are ready for baking. They will be found very good.

Mush Cakes.

1 egg.
1 heaping cup cold of boiled mush.
2 cups of milk.
1 scant cup of prepared flour.
1 tablespoonful of melted lard.
1 tablespoonful of molasses.
1 teaspoonful (scant) of salt.
Bit of soda no larger than a grain of corn dissolved in the milk.

Beat the egg very light, and into this the sugar, then the lard, salt, and, gradually, the mush. Take off the outer skin, and mix so well that the result shall be a compound like a thick, smooth custard, even before the milk goes in. Add this, likewise by degrees, and at last the flour. Beat hard, and bake on a griddle. If you like to make the batter a little thicker and bake in rings, as muffins, you will find them very nice. The cakes are light, spongy, excellent.

Waffles.

4 heaping cups of flour.
3 cups of milk and 1 of warm water.
5 tablespoonfuls of yeast.
1 tablespoonful of melted lard, and same of sugar.
1 teaspoonful of salt.
1 egg. (You can omit this, if you choose.)

Set the batter, leaving out one cup of flour, the egg, salt, and lard, overnight as a sponge. Early in the morning add these ingredients, beat well, and let the batter stand one hour before baking in waffle-irons.

A Useful Rule.

While it is impossible to set down absolute laws for mixing "a soft dough" or "a good batter," you will find a valuable suggestion in the rule to mix dough in the proportion of *twice as much flour as you have liquid*, and in batter-making *allow a like quantity of each*. If there is a leaning toward prodigality in the measure of flour and economy in liquid, so much the better. But mix measure for measure, then modify slightly should the flour thicken too much. Different brands vary widely in this respect.

PUDDINGS.

Apple Puddings.

There is a large and most respectable family of these —cheap, wholesome, and generally popular. Practically there is no recognized limit to the variations of which this ancient and honorable fruit is susceptible in the hands of a skilful cook. I have collected a few of the more economical and simple of these preparations in this work, and can safely recommend each of them.

Maude's Pudding.

2 cups of bread-crumbs—very dry and fine.
2 cups chopped apple.
A handful of raisins, seeded and chopped.
1 tablespoonful of butter.
¾ cupful of brown sugar.
Cinnamon and nutmeg to your liking.

Butter a pudding-dish; strew the bottom thickly with crumbs. On this spread a layer of chopped apple, sprinkle with raisins and tiny bits of butter, spice, and cover with sugar. More crumbs follow, then apple, and so on, until the dish is full. The top layer should be crumbs, and well buttered. Cover tightly, and bake until the apple juice bubbles through the crust and up at the sides, when brown on the grating of the oven.

Send to table in the dish, and eat with butter and sugar, or pudding-sauce.

This pudding costs less than an apple pie; consumes one-quarter of the time in making; goes twice as far in feeding a family; is more digestible—and *tastes better*.

Apple Méringue.

2 cups hot apple sauce, very smooth and good.
3 eggs.
½ cup of sugar.
1 teaspoonful of butter.
1 teaspoonful of corn-starch.
1 teaspoonful of nutmeg and cinnamon mixed.
Bitter almond flavoring.
2 tablespoonfuls of powdered sugar.

Stew the apples unsweetened and beat out all the lumps. Return to the saucepan, sweeten and season, stir in the corn-starch rubbed into the butter, boil one minute, take from the fire and pour gradually upon the yolks of the eggs, whipped thick and smooth. Beat two minutes and turn into a buttered pudding-dish. Bake fifteen minutes in a quick oven; draw to the oven-door and spread rapidly over the surface a méringue of the whites whipped stiff and the powdered sugar, flavored with bitter almond. Shut up again and brown *delicately*. Eat cold, with or without cream.

Tapioca Apple Pudding.

6 apples—ripe and fair—pared and cored.
1 cupful of tapioca.
3 cups of cold water.
1 teaspoonful of salt.
½ cupful of sugar.
A dozen whole cloves.

Soak the tapioca all night in the water. In the morning, or about two hours before you wish to cook it, arrange the apples in a pudding-dish, add a very little water, cover closely, and set in the oven until they are tender throughout. Fill the hole in the middle of each with sugar, put in a clove or two where the core was, and pour the tapioca over all. Cover again, and bake somewhat slowly one hour.

Eat with milk or with sweet sauce.

Toad-in-a-hole Pudding (*English dish*).

6 large juicy apples, cored and pared.
½ cup of sugar.
2 cups of milk.
2 cups of flour (prepared).
2 eggs, beaten very light.
1 teaspoonful of salt.
1 tablespoonful of lard, chopped into invisibility in the flour.

Peel and core the apples, pack in a pudding-dish and fill the centres with sugar. Salt the flour, chop in the lard, wet up gradually with the milk. Finally, whip in the beaten eggs, and stir *hard* one minute before pouring over the apples. Bake one hour in a steady oven. Eat hot with butter and sugar, or with sweet sauce.

Apple Bread Pudding.

6 fine juicy ripe apples.
6 slices stale bread, an inch thick.
Grated peel of a lemon.
1 scant teaspoonful of cinnamon.
Butter enough to spread the bread.
¾ of a cup of brown sugar.
A little hot milk.

Pare each slice, butter on both sides, and arrange a layer in the bottom of a buttered pudding-dish. Peel and slice the apples and cover the bread thickly with them, sprinkle well with sugar, sparingly with spice and lemon-peel, and put in a second stratum of buttered bread. More apple, sugar, and spice, and so on, until the materials are used up. The top layer should be of bread, buttered on the lower side, pressed into place, then soaked in hot milk poured over it, before butter is spread on the upper. Cover closely, and bake an hour and a quarter; uncover and brown lightly.

Eat hot with sauce.

Or,

You can bake it in a dish set in a dripping-pan of boiling water, replenishing with more from the teakettle as this boils away. When the pudding is done, turn out on a hot dish, and cut in slices at table.

Apple Scallop.

3 cups of good apple-sauce.
Nearly a cupful of sugar.
1 tablespoonful of butter.
Nutmeg to taste.
1 beaten egg.
½ cupful of fine crumbs.
1 heaping teaspoonful of corn-starch rubbed into the butter.

Stir into the apple-sauce while hot the sugar, butter, corn-starch, and spice. Beat hard, boil up once, and let it get cold. If the apples are very juicy, drain off half the liquor before the sugar, etc., are added. Heap, when cold and firm, upon a buttered pie-plate, wash all over with beaten egg, coat with crumbs, and bake half an hour. Slip to a heated dish, or serve in the pie-plate, as most convenient.

Eat hot with sauce, or milk and sugar.

Apple Snow.

6 apples.
Whites of 2 eggs.
3 tablespoonfuls of powdered sugar.

Peel and grate the apples into the whites, which must have been whipped to a stiff froth. Beat in the sugar with a few light sweeps of the egg; whip and set in a cold place until wanted.

Eat with crackers or cake.

Baked Apple Dumplings.

2 heaping cups of prepared flour.
2 tablespoonfuls of sweet, clean lard (if you can afford it, put 1 tablespoonful of lard and 1 of butter).
1½ cup of milk (or 1 of milk, ½ of ice-cold water).
1 saltspoonful of salt.

Chop the shortening into the salted flour, until they are thoroughly incorporated. Wet up with milk; roll into a paste less than half an inch thick, handling as little as possible; cut into squares about five inches across every way, lay in the middle of each a juicy ripe apple, peeled and cored, fold the corners of the paste neatly together and pinch hard. Put in a floured baking-pan, the seamy sides down, and bake to a nice brown.

Eat hot with sauce.

Boiled Apple Dumplings.

Make as above, and boil in square, stout cloths, each dumpling being tied up in one of these, with room to swell. Wring out the cloths dry in boiling water, and flour on the inside before the apples go in. Plunge into boiling water and cook one hour.

Bread Puddings.

For these you will find your jar of fine crumbs accumulated from day to day excellent, and a genuine time-saver. It is a good plan to crumb stale bread for puddings overnight, or at least some hours before they are to be used. Have no bits of crusts or hard lumps in the mixture, and compound as carefully as you would pound-cake.

Sugarless Bread Pudding.

2 even cups of crumbs.
3 cups of milk.
2 eggs, beaten very light.
1 tablespoonful of melted butter.
Cinnamon and nutmeg to taste.
Bit of soda the size of a kidney-bean dissolved in a tablespoonful of hot water.

Beat the eggs long and light while the crumbs are soaking in the milk. Add the butter and spice to the crumbs, the soda, and whip to a smooth pulp, lastly, stir in the eggs. Beat all one minute, pour into a buttered pudding-dish, bake until lightly browned and well "set" in the middle.

Eat warm with sauce. It is very nice.

Bread-and-Raisin Pudding.

2 even cups of crumbs.
3 cups of hot milk—full ones.
3 eggs.
½ cup of raisins, seeded and chopped.
1 tablespoonful of butter.
½ cupful of sugar.
½ teaspoonful mixed nutmeg and cinnamon.

Rub butter and sugar to a cream and set aside. Meanwhile, let the crumbs soak in the scalding—*not* boiling—milk. Beat these to a smooth paste, and spread a layer in a buttered pudding-dish. Strew with raisins and spice, and put on more of the crumb-paste. Fill the dish within half an inch of the top in this order; set in the oven, covered by a tin plate or pail-top while you whip the eggs *very* light with the creamed butter. Draw the pudding—just heated through—to the oven-door, pour on this mixture, cover again and bake twenty minutes, then brown.

Eat warm without sauce.

Boiled Bread Pudding.

2 cups of crumbs.
2 full cups of milk.
3 eggs.
½ cupful of suet, powdered and freed from strings.
½ cup seeded and cut raisins, well dredged with flour.
4 tablespoonfuls of sugar.
½ teaspoonful of salt.
1 heaping teaspoonful of corn-starch rubbed into the butter.

Heat the milk to scalding, stir in the butter and corn-starch; cook one minute, and pour upon the crumbs. Let them soak while you beat the eggs very light. This done, whip in the sugar, and, by degrees, the soaked crumbs. Cover the bottom of a buttered tin mould, with a tightly fitting cover (or a tin pail), with a layer of this, scatter suet, raisins, and spice over it, and go on in this order until the ingredients are used up. Fit on the top, set in a pot of boiling water—not so full as to overflow the top in cooking—and boil an hour and a half. Dip the mould into cold water, and invert upon a hot dish, to turn it out.

Eat hot, with or without sauce.

Lemon Bread Pudding.

2 cups of fine crumbs.
3 cups of milk.
1 tablespoonful of butter.
1 small cupful of sugar.
Juice and grated peel of a lemon.
3 eggs.

Rub butter and sugar well together. Beat the eggs light, then the sugar and butter into these. Meantime, the crumbs should be soaking in the milk. Beat all together faithfully before adding the lemon-juice and peel, turn immediately into a buttered pudding-dish and bake quickly before the milk has time to curdle.

Eat warm—not hot—or cold, without sauce.

Tapioca Pudding (No. 1).

1 cup of tapioca.
4 cups of lukewarm milk.
1 cup of sugar.
3 eggs.
Nutmeg.
Bit of soda the size of a pea in the milk.

Soak the tapioca in the milk four hours—for two of these at one side of the range, where it cannot get more than blood-warm. If it really heats before softening, it is ruined. Then set the vessel containing it in one of warm water, and bring very slowly to a gentle simmer. Stir up the tapioca from the bottom often after the first hour's soaking. When it is thoroughly dissolved, increase the heat, until it is quite thick and very hot. Take from the fire and turn upon the beaten eggs and sugar. Beat well, season, pour into a buttered dish and bake until a light-brown crust forms on the top.

There is no more delightful tapioca pudding than this.

Tapioca Pudding (No. 2).

1 cup of tapioca.
1 quart of milk.
2 eggs.
2 tablespoonfuls of sugar.
1 tablespoonful of melted butter.
Nutmeg.
½ teaspoonful of salt.
Bit of soda the size of a pea in the milk.

Cover the tapioca with two cupfuls of cold water and soak three hours. Stir into the milk and soak an hour longer. Put into a tin pail or inner compartment of a farina-kettle, surround with boiling water and heat until the tapioca is very soft. Cream butter and sugar, beat very light with the eggs, pour the tapioca over this; stir up well, and bake in a buttered dish.

Eat warm with sauce.

Cracker Pudding.

1 full cup of powdered cracker.
1 cup of boiling water.
3 cups of milk.
3 eggs.
1 tablespoonful—a liberal one—of butter.
½ teaspoonful of soda dissolved in the water.
½ teaspoonful of salt.

Scald the salted crumbs with the boiling water and stir in the butter. Let them stand while you whip the eggs light. Mix the milk with the cracker-paste, then the eggs. Whip all together well, and bake in a buttered pudding-dish. Eat with sauce.

Suet Pudding (No. 1).

1 heaping cup of crumbs.
2 tablespoonfuls of sugar.
1 even cupful of suet, freed from strings and powdered.
3 cups of milk.
3 eggs.
1 teaspoonful of salt.
¼ teaspoonful of soda, dissolved in a tablespoonful of hot water.

Mix as directed in last receipt, and bake about an hour. Eat hot, with sauce. It is nice boiled in a mould, and will require an hour and a half to cook.

Suet Pudding (No. 2).

1 cup of suet, minced to powder.
½ cupful of raisins, seeded and chopped.
1 cup of molasses.
1 cup of milk.
1½ cup of flour.
1 teaspoonful of soda.
1 teaspoonful of salt.

Mix milk and molasses together. Sift salt and soda three times through the flour, then chop the suet into it until it is fairly "shortened" by it; pour in the milk and molasses, mix and beat up thoroughly before adding the raisins dredged with flour. Pour into a buttered mould or pail with a top, and boil steadily three hours. The water must boil when it goes in. Eat with hard sauce.

Marmalade Pudding.

⅔ of a cup of cracker-crumbs.
½ cup of sugar.
1 full cup of milk.
1 tablespoonful of butter.
2 eggs.
½ cup of marmalade or jam.

Cream butter and sugar, and soak the crumbs in the milk. Beat the eggs light, add creamed butter and sugar, finally the soaked crumbs. Put the marmalade in a buttered bake-dish. It should be quite firm, so as not to float when the rest of the ingredients go in. Press it hard, to make it hold well to the bottom, and put in the cracker mixture by the spoonful. Bake forty minutes, or until set and nicely browned. Eat cold.

Baked Corn-starch Pudding.

4 cups of milk.
4 tablespoonfuls of corn-starch.
3 eggs.
½ cup of sugar.
1 teaspoonful of butter.
Nutmeg to taste.
1 saltspoonful of salt.

Heat three cups of milk to scalding; dissolve the corn-starch in the other cup and add, stirring and cooking until it thickens well. Stir in the butter and salt, and set away for several hours to get cold and stiff. Then beat the eggs light, whip in the sugar and nutmeg, and beat up with the corn-starch little by little to a smooth batter. Bake half an hour in a buttered dish. Eat cold.

Corn-starch Minute Pudding.

1 quart of fresh milk, heated to scalding in a farina-kettle. Wet up with cold water 4 tablespoonfuls of corn-starch and a teaspoonful of salt, and stir into the milk until it has boiled ten minutes. Add a tablespoonful of butter; let the pudding stand, without boiling, in hot water for three minutes before turning it into an open dish.

Sauce for Pudding.

2 eggs.
1 cup of powdered sugar.
$\frac{1}{4}$ cup of boiling milk.
Season with nutmeg, lemon, vanilla, or bitter-almond essence.

Beat whites and yolks separately, very light, then the sugar into the yolks. Pour upon yolks and sugar the boiling milk. Set in very hot, but not boiling water, stirring now and then until just before it is wanted; when beat in lightly the frothed whites, and flavor to taste.

Graham Minute Pudding.

1 cup of Graham flour.
1 large cup of boiling water and same of hot milk, with a pinch of soda stirred in.
Salt to taste.

Wet up the flour with cold water, slightly salted, and stir into the boiling. Cook in a double vessel, the outer one being full of hot water. Boil and stir fifteen minutes. Add the milk gradually, beating out lumps, and cook after the boil begins again ten minutes longer. Turn out into a deep, open dish, and eat with powdered sugar and milk, or with butter and sugar.

Rice Hasty Pudding.

1 cup of raw rice.
1 cup of milk.
1 egg.
A little salt.

Boil the rice soft in salted water, breaking as little as possible. It should be almost dry, but not hard, or "pasty." Heat the milk in another vessel to scalding, stir in the egg, beaten light; cook one minute, and mix up well with the rice just before removing the latter from the fire.

Baked Rice Pudding.

½ cup of raw rice.
4 cups of milk.
4 tablespoonfuls of sugar.
½ teaspoonful of salt.
1 tablespoonful of butter, melted.
Mace and cinnamon to taste.

Soak the washed rice in the milk two hours, stir in butter, spice, sugar, and salt, and bake in a *moderate* oven more than an hour, until nicely browned on top, and like custard throughout. Eat very cold.

Tapioca Rice Pudding.

Make precisely as above, but soak equal quantities of rice and tapioca three hours—then cook as directed.

Rice Custard Pudding.

1 cup of boiled *warm* rice, well drained.
3 cups of milk.
2 eggs, beaten light.

2 teaspoonfuls of butter.
1 saltspoonful of salt.
Nutmeg to taste.

Cream butter and sugar and add to the beaten eggs, then the milk, lastly the rice. Beat thoroughly and bake half an hour, or until set and browned. Eat warm (not hot) or cold, as you prefer.

Batter Pudding.

2 full cups of flour (prepared).
2 cups of milk.
3 eggs.
1 teaspoonful of salt (scant).
Bit of soda the size of a pea.

Sift soda and salt three times through the flour. Beat the yolks of the eggs until thick and smooth, add to the milk, stir in the flour, beat one minute steadily; stir in the whipped whites quickly, and bake in a buttered pudding-dish in a brisk oven. Serve in the bake-dish before it has time to fall. Eat *very* hot, with sauce.

Cottage Pudding.

2 eggs.
1 scant cup of sugar.
1 cup of milk.
1 tablespoonful of butter.
2 full cups of prepared flour.
½ teaspoonful of salt.

Cream butter and sugar. Beat the yolks smooth, and whip in the buttered sugar, then the milk, salt, and the whites—whipped to a froth; at last, and lightly, the flour. Bake in a buttered cake-mould until a straw comes up clean from the thickest part, turn out upon a plate, and send in hot. Cut in slices in helping, and pour sweet sauce over each piece.

This is the most elegant pudding—for one so simple and inexpensive—in this collection, and has the added virtue of always "coming out right." If you use plain flour, stir in a half-teaspoonful of soda and twice as much cream of tartar, or a heaping teaspoonful of Royal Baking Powder, and sift all three times.

Lemon Pudding.

3 eggs.
1 scant cup of sugar.
2 liberal tablespoonfuls of corn-starch.
1 lemon, juice and rind.
2 cups of milk.
1 heaping teaspoonful of butter.

Scald the milk and stir in the corn-starch wet up in four tablespoonfuls of cold water. Cook—stirring all the time—until it thickens well; add the butter, and set aside until perfectly cold. Then beat the eggs light, add the sugar, the lemon, juice and grated peel, and whip in, a great spoonful at a time, the stiffened corn-starch milk. Bake in a buttered dish, and eat cold.

Macaroni Pudding (*plain*).

1 cup of macaroni, broken into short pieces of uniform length.
3 cups of milk, with a tiny bit of soda stirred in.
1 tablespoonful of butter.
½ teaspoonful of salt.

Boil the macaroni twenty minutes in plenty of slightly salted water. Have ready the milk scalded in another vessel, stir in salt, soda, and butter; drain the macaroni in a colander and drop into the hot milk. Simmer in a saucepan or pail set in boiling water ten minutes, covered; turn out, and eat with butter and sugar.

It will be found very good.

Baked Macaroni Pudding.

1 cup of macaroni, broken into inch lengths.
2 eggs.
3 full cups of milk.
1 tablespoonful of butter.
½ cup of sugar.
½ teaspoonful of salt.
Nutmeg and cinnamon mixed, ½ teaspoonful.

Boil the macaroni twenty minutes in salted hot water. Drain and put into the milk, which should stand ready, scalding hot and salted, in another vessel; cover and leave in hot water while you cream butter and sugar, and beat the eggs very light. Turn the macaroni and milk into a bowl, stir in creamed butter and sugar, then the eggs and spice. Mix well, but not hard enough to break the macaroni, and bake in a buttered pudding-dish until browned.

Eat warm, without sauce.

Berry Pudding.

1 pint of flour.
1 saltspoonful of salt.
1 egg.
1 cup of milk.
½ teaspoonful of soda, sifted twice with the flour.
3 full tablespoonfuls of yeast.
2 cups of huckleberries, blackberries or "black-caps," or the same quantity of cherries (stoned), well dredged with flour.

Beat the egg light, add the milk and salt, then the yeast, and pour into a hole in the middle of the flour. Beat to a good batter and stir in the dredged berries. Set to rise until light in a buttered dish, and bake in the same, or boil in a well-greased mould or tin pail with a close top, set in a pot of boiling water. It will bake in forty minutes, boil in double the time. (It should be light in four or five hours, if set to rise in a tolerably warm corner.)

Serve in the dish if baked, turn out if boiled. Eat at once, with sweet sauce.

You may omit the egg, yet have an excellent pudding.

Roley-poley Pudding.

Make a paste as for apple dumplings (see page 170); roll out evenly into a sheet twice as long as wide and spread with fruit—sliced apples, or peaches, or berries, or cherries; sprinkle with sugar lightly, and roll up closely into a short, compact cylinder. Sew a stout cotton or linen cloth about it, leaving room for swelling, and "felling" the seams at side and ends to keep out the water. The cloth should be floured on the inside before the roley-poley goes in. Plunge into a pot of boiling water, and keep at a steady bubble one hour and a half.

Turn out and eat hot, with sauce.

Corn Meal Pudding.

2 cups of milk.
2 cups of boiling water.
2 even cups of Indian meal.
2 eggs.
½ cup of suet, powdered.
3 tablespoonfuls of brown sugar or molasses.
½ teaspoonful of salt.
¼ teaspoonful of ginger, and same of mace.

Scald the meal, salted, in the water; stir in the suet while hot, and let it get perfectly cold. Then beat the eggs light, put in the sugar and spice and stir to a cream, before adding the milk, at the last the corn meal paste. Beat all hard and faithfully, and bake in a buttered dish an hour, or boil two hours in a floured cloth or buttered mould, leaving plenty of room for swelling.

Corn Meal Hasty Pudding.

1 cupful of Indian meal, a teaspoonful of salt stirred in.

1 quart of boiling water and 1 cup of cold.

Put the water over the fire, and when it boils hard stir in the meal, wet up with the cold water. Cook half an hour at least, stirring often. Serve in an open bowl or deep dish.

Eat with butter and sugar, or with milk and sugar.

Fried Hasty Pudding.

Set corn meal hasty pudding made as above in small patty-pans, to get cold and firm. Next day, roll these over and over in dry meal and fry in hot lard or *nice* dripping. Eat hot, with sugar or syrup.

PUDDING SAUCES.

Hard Sauce.

1 cup of powdered sugar.

1 good tablespoonful of butter.

Nutmeg or cinnamon, about $\frac{1}{2}$ teaspoonful.

Warm the butter slightly and cream with the sugar.

Season, beat hard for three minutes, and mound or shape into a "pat" on a plate. Set in a cold place to get firm.

Liquid Sauce.

1 large spoonful of butter.
1 cupful brown sugar.
½ cupful of boiling water.
1 heaping teaspoonful of corn-starch.
Nutmeg or mace to taste.

Rub the butter in the sugar and moisten with a little boiling water until you can whip it to a cream. Beat very light; add the rest of the water and heat to a brisk boil, stirring all the while. Put in the corn-starch wet with cold water and stir smooth. Season and set in hot water until needed.

Lemon Sauce.

Make as you do hard sauce, but, instead of spice, beat in the juice and half the rind of a lemon.

Jelly Sauce.

3 good teaspoonfuls of currant or other fruit jelly.
1 tablespoonful of melted butter.
1 heaping tablespoonful of powdered sugar.
1 cup of boiling water.
1 teaspoonful of flour.

Set the water over the fire, stir in the flour wet up in a little cold water, cook two minutes, and add the rest of the ingredients. Boil up well, and set in hot water until needed.

Custard Pudding Sauce.

1 cup of milk.
3 tablespoonfuls of sugar.
1 teaspoonful of butter.
1 egg.
Nutmeg.

Heat the milk and stir in the butter creamed with the sugar. Season; pour over the beaten egg, whip up well, return to the saucepan, and stir until it begins to thicken well. Serve hot. It is nice for corn-starch hasty pudding.

FAMILIAR TALK.

"KITCHENLY KIND."

LET the phrase stand. If there were more of the active virtue of which it is the clumsy representative, a better-born and more euphonious term would long since have been invented to express it.

Yet there are sections of our country where the grace of kitchen-neighborliness has been understood and practised from time immemorial. In that lively little book, "The Colonel's Opera Cloak," we have an illustration of it that is pathetic in its ludicrousness. The decayed Southern gentlepeople send a breakfast of corn pone and fried bacon to their Northern benefactors, whose intense amusement in the receipt of the untempting offering is the best proof of the non-existence of like customs in their latitude. In this region we have suffered the genius of machinery to invade our hearts and our home-habits, as well as our workshops and kitchens. We keep a debit and credit account of calls with our nearest neighbors, and discharge social debts by giving wholesale "crushes" payable semi-annually. We no longer "run" or "drop in" upon one another as leisure permits and inclination prompts. We entertain in due form and at stated seasons. At Homes and Receptions are announced to let our world know that in the matter of hospitality we have not suspended payment.

The principle has struck root in cottage as in mansion. It was not from the latter that the *enfant terrible* took the invitation to a neighbor to "come in for a sociable cup of tea" on a certain evening.

"Did your mother say at what hour she would expect us?" asked the bidden guest.

"No, ma'am! She only told father that she would ask you, and get the bother off her mind."

To borrow a saying of a former generation—the latch-string no longer hangs outside of the door. Sometimes the bolt is shot on the inside.

I shall never lose the memory of an experience that taught me this in one sharp lesson. One afternoon in early spring I alighted at the door of a city friend, after a drive of twenty miles over rough, dusty roads. I was not strong; the day was unseasonably sultry. My head ached, and with my parched throat craved a cup of tea as importunately as the Lanesboro' "thirsty pilgrim" "some cooling stream at hand." My escort had an engagement to lecture down town, and drove off, leaving me upon the steps of the dwelling where we expected to pass the night. We had been invited repeatedly to "make this our home" on such occasions, and had every reason to believe that we would give offence if we went elsewhere. The house was deliciously cool, the easy-chair set for me by my hostess luxurious. The family were going to the lecture in half an hour, and a minute's talk brought out the fact that my note heralding our visit had not been received. I was pressed to wash off the dust of my drive, and at my request a glass of water was brought. Then the ladies assumed hats and gloves, and I put on mine again. Not a hint of tea, nor so much as a crust or cracker was tendered to the hungry guest who, they knew, could have had no refreshment since an early luncheon.

I was faint, exhausted, intolerant. A factitious energy possessed me when sweetly reminded that "we must be going, if we would be in time at the Hall." In passing through the entry, I picked up the *sac de nuit* I had set down there when I came in.

"I shall not take this car," I said, civilly, as my companions signalled one at the corner. "May I trouble you to see Dr. —— after the lecture, and tell him he will find me at Mrs. ——'s? Good-evening!"

I bore myself bravely, but a hot band tightened steadily about my throat as, after a ride of fifteen minutes in another car, I was set down at a second but not handsomer house. The mistress of the house saw me from the parlor-window, and met me in the hall.

"This is very good of you!" she said.

Were ever words more apt and welcome? I, and not she, was the giver of the benefit.

"*Very* good and kind!" she continued, leading me onward to the quiet library. She untied my hat, and forced me gently to lie down on the lounge. "By-and-by you shall go to your room. Just now you are too tired to mount the stairs. A cup of tea is the first thing. Lie still and rest while I order it."

She was absent ten minutes—a blessed interval that gave me time to dry the foolish drops welling up with the sudden loosening of the strangling throat-latch. Then with her own hands she set on a stand beside me the longed-for beverage, a servant following with more substantial refreshment, and a dessert of strawberries and cream.

The true and loving woman who thus received her who was ready to faint by inhospitable ways, will smile no more into my grateful eyes on earth. I hope—I believe that the angels met her at heaven's door as she met me, and feasted her on fruits of paradise.

I cherish no resentment against her to whom I first went. She was a notable housekeeper, a disciple of system and punctuality. She had not counted my visit among the possible events of the day. The fireless order of her kitchen must not be disarranged for so slight an occasion as the coming of a belated and thirsty guest. The principle is as old as the Christian era. "Trouble me not! The door is now shut, and my children are, with me, in bed. I cannot rise and give thee," said he of whom the neighbor would borrow three loaves.

The hospitality of the drawing-room, always in array for company, and that of the kitchen—the warm, pulsing heart of the home—are very dissimilar virtues. In no way can neighborly good-will testify of itself more truthfully than in the informal interchange of the products of the culinary care and skill of those who think kindly and often of each other. What housekeeper does not weary into appetiteless disgust of an unbroken series of dishes ordered, and often cooked by herself? Whose wan face does not brighten at the unexpected cover sent in at breakfast, dinner, or tea-time "with love" from the friend across the way? It may be only a plate of biscuits, just drawn from the oven, differing in nothing except the grace of sending from those on your own table, or a bowl of soup exquisitely seasoned by the good-will that brought it over to you, or a saucer of pudding with the dainty flavor of unaccustomedness commending it to eye and palate. Homelier fare than your daily food is manna to your jaded taste in such circumstances.

"I tried it once with my pastor's wife," said a lady to me, the other day. "I sent her a chicken-pie at Thanksgiving, and she did not understand it at all. She hoped—so she told a friend who told *me*—that I did not imagine they were too poor to buy chickens for themselves."

"Poor pastor's wife!" commented L. "That suspicion was the fruit of a neglected neighborly education."

Each of us owes it to her friends, to herself, and to humanity, to do all in her power to bring her kitchen into familiar communication and harmony with those to the right and left of her. Minute dots of pleasantness such offices may be, but the succession weaves patterns of beauty and brightness into a web that is apt to be tiresomely monotonous and often sad-colored.

Of neighborly duties to invalids, I would fain hope that I might take up Paul's words and say, "Ye need not that I should write unto you." I could tell, did time and space permit, many stories commemorative of tender fidelity, long-continued, to the sick and suffering of other households than those with which the ministrants were connected by ties of blood and law. Of a consumptive girl, fed from day to day and month to month by the thought-taking of one who, on being thanked by the weeping mother when the need of such care had ceased, said simply, "*Did* I send something every day? I can hardly believe it. I merely took some trifle from our own table when I fancied the dear child might be longing for a change of diet. It is a part of invalidism to have fancies, you know."

Of another—a wife and housekeeper—who during an illness and convalescence that lasted three months, ate literally nothing that was not sent in by neighbors who remembered her in deeds as in prayers. This is—with reverence we say it—a form of Christ-likeness to which she that occupieth the room of the unlearned may attain by the exercise of such gifts as are already hers.

We are in danger of looking too far for opportunities of

doing good and communicating. In reaching for rhododendrons we trample down the daisies.

STEWED AND BAKED FRUITS.

Baked Apples.

Pare and core ripe juicy apples, and pack in a pudding-dish. Fill the holes left by the cores with sugar, and put a clove in each. Pour in a cupful of cold water, cover closely, and bake until the apples are tender and clear. Do not take the cover from the dish before the apples are perfectly cold.

Stewed Apples.

Prepare as above, but pack in a tin pail with a tight cover, putting with them a cupful of cold water, and set in a vessel of water also cold. Bring to a boil, and keep this up for an hour. Peep in to see if the apples are tender. If not, put on the top again and cook longer. When done, set the vessel—still closed—in very cold water, and do not open for some hours. They will be very delightful.

Baked Sweet Apples.

The New Jersey Campfields, pound sweets, and really sound, sweet harvest apples are best for this purpose.

Cut out the blossom-end and dig well down toward the core with a penknife, to make sure there are not worms in them. Wash, but do not peel them, fill a large bake-dish or pan with them, pour in about two inches of cold water; cover as closely as possible and bake tender. Take up the apples and pack in a bowl. Cover with a plate and set in hot water, to keep warm. Add half a cupful of brown sugar (for a dozen apples) to the juice, put into a saucepan, boil fast fifteen minutes, strain through a cloth over the apples, and cover until next day. Eat without or with sugar and cream.

You may leave out the sugar altogether, straining the clear liquid over the fruit. In this case, sugar and eat with milk, if you cannot get cream. You will not soon tire of this healthful and delicious dish.

Baked Sweet Pears.

May be cooked in the same way.

Stewed Pears.

If large, cut in half; if small, gouge out the blossom-end. Do not peel them. Cover with cold water in a saucepan, and stew until a straw will penetrate them; now put in a tablespoonful of sugar for every three large pears, and for every dozen a half-teaspoonful of ginger. Cover and simmer ten minutes; take up the fruit, pack in a covered bowl and set in hot water, while you boil the syrup for half an hour. Strain over the pears and set aside, closely covered, until next day.

You may substitute molasses for sugar, if you like.

Stewed Quinces.

Prepare as you would pears, leaving out the ginger. Either peel the fruit or rub hard with a coarse cloth. Quarter and take out the seeds. Save these and add to the syrup when the fruit has been taken out. Boil forty-five minutes and strain—pressing hard—over the quinces. Cover for eight or ten hours.

Stewed Cherries.

Pack in a "bean-jar," or wide-mouthed stone crock, strewing each layer of a cupful with two tablespoonfuls of sugar. When all are in, set *covered* in a pot of cold water, and cook slowly but steadily three hours after the water begins to boil. Drain off the juice, put the fruit into airtight jars, cover and set in hot water, while you boil the syrup half an hour *hard*. Fill up the jars very full, and screw on the tops immediately.

Fruit thus put up is good to eat on the second day, but will keep all winter, and not only costs less but tastes better than sweeter preserves.

Stewed Plums and Berries.

Put up in like manner as the above.

STEWED DRIED FRUITS.

Peaches.

Wash with great care in cold water, then soak for one hour in the water in which they are to be cooked. At the end of that time put them over the fire, covering the saucepan closely, and bring to a gentle simmer. Keep this up for half an hour, or until the peaches are very tender, almost like jelly. Transfer, with care not to break them, to a bowl or deep dish, and sweeten liberally while hot. Cover, and set where they will cool speedily.

Dried fruit heated in this manner is better worth eating than *cheap* canned peaches, pears, and the like. If dried apples are ever good, it is when prepared thus, and spiced with mace and allspice. Peaches are really palatable cooked as above. Pears and cherries ditto.

Stewed Rhubarb or Pie-Plant.

Scrape the stalks well and cut into inch lengths. Put a layer in a tin saucepan or pail, sprinkle with a tablespoonful of sugar, cover with rhubarb, this with more sugar, and so on until all the materials are in. Put on the lid, set in cold water and bring to a boil. Cook half an hour after the boil begins, or until there is a plentiful supply of juice in the pail; set on the stove, take the top from the saucepan and stew until the rhubarb is very tender. A few raisins, scattered among the stalks and stewed with them, improve the flavor. Eat cold.

JAMS AND MARMALADES.

Berry Jams.

Allow three-quarters of a pound of sugar to every pound of fruit. After weighing, put the fruit on the stove in a preserve-kettle, mash well with a wooden spoon and heat rather rapidly—not, however, allowing the fire to come directly in contact with the kettle-bottom, for fear of scorching. Stir up often and well from the depths. When the berries have boiled half an hour, dip out all the juice you can extract with skimmer and ladle. You can make berry cordial or vinegar with it, or fruit jelly. Add the sugar, and in five minutes you would scarcely miss the juice you have taken out. Cook twenty minutes rapidly, and put boiling hot into jars. Dip each jar before filling it in hot water and set on a folded wet towel, and the scalding jam will not break it. Jam put up in this way will keep for years, and is much nicer than if all the juice be left in.

Red Raspberry Jam is particularly good if a gill of currant-juice be added to every three pounds of fruit. This goes in with the sugar after the raspberry-juice is dipped out.

Gooseberries must be topped and tailed, and boiled one hour before the sugar is added, one hour afterward. They should be ripe when put up.

Strawberries are very much improved by currant-juice. In some sections of our country the seasons of the two fruits overlap. If currants cannot be obtained, put the juice of a lemon to every two pounds of fruit, after the berries are stewed and the juice dipped out.

Peach Marmalade.

Pare and chop the fruit. Crack a dozen of the peach-pits for every three pounds of peaches, and shave with a knife into the kettle with the fruit, which should be put over the fire the moment it is chopped. It darkens with standing. Cook half an hour; dip out the juice and put in three-quarters of a pound of sugar to each pound of peaches. Boil fast half an hour, and seal up in air-tight jars.

Unless they are very ripe, it is a good plan to rub the stewed peaches through a colander, after taking out the juice and before adding the sugar.

Apple Marmalade.

Pare, core, and chop, then treat as above. Use tart, juicy fruit for this purpose. Add a very little water to the raw apples, and heat slowly until the juice flows.

Quince Marmalade.

Pare and core, then chop quite fine. Add a very little water to prevent burning before the quinces soften and break. Proceed then as with peach marmalade.

Set by the juice taken from the kettle until it is cold; put in the parings and cores, which should be carefully saved for this purpose, cook half an hour; strain hard through coarse, stout cloth, and you have an excellent basis for quince jelly.

FRUIT JELLIES.

Currant Jelly.

Put the fruit, freed from stems and leaves, over the fire in a stone jar set in cold water, and covered closely. Boil until the fruit is broken and soft, and, when convenient, leave in the water all night to cool. Strain—putting in a little at a time—through a *strong*, coarse bag, pressing and wringing until nothing but seeds and skins remain in the cloth. Empty this carefully between each "squeeze" and the replenishment of the bag, and wash out often in warm water. Measure and put on the stove in a preserve-kettle, bring rapidly to a boil, stirring frequently, and cook twenty minutes from the time the boil really sets in.

Meantime, weigh the sugar, allowing a pound for every pint of juice, turn it, dry, into a clean dripping-pan or other shallow vessel, and set in the oven to heat. Stir now and then to prevent burning. When the juice has fulfilled its time of boiling, take off the scum from the top, "dump" in the hot sugar, stir until it is dissolved, boil *one minute* and take off the kettle. Have your jelly-glasses all ready, roll each in hot water, and fill while wet inside and out. When the jelly is firm, press tissue-paper closely on the top, working out all the air from beneath, and paste stout papers over the glasses. Should mould form on the tissue-papers it will not injure the taste of the jelly. Indeed, it will help to exclude the air, and when the papers are removed, the surface of the jelly will appear bright and clear. A teaspoonful of brandy on the tissue-paper is said to assist in preserving the jelly.

Blackberry and Raspberry Jelly

Are made in the same way as currant, but may have to be set in uncovered glasses in the sun for a day or two, to form well. Each glassful will shrink perceptibly in the process. Fill up one from another as the shrinkage goes on.

Quince and Crab-Apple Jelly.

Cut up small, without peeling or coring, and treat as you would berries, leaving the fruit overnight in the covered inner jar to cool gradually with the water in the outer vessel. Squeeze out all the juice—not the coarser pulp—measure and heat as already directed.

Grape Jelly.

Make as you do currant. Wild, or "fox-grapes" are especially flavorous for this purpose, and may be had for the gathering. They should be perfectly ripe.

PICKLES.

Green, or Tart Pickles.

These include cucumbers, mangoes, gherkins, onions, young beans, nasturtium-seed (an excellent substitute for capers), etc., and are put up, with trifling variations, in one and the same way.

Wash, pick over carefully to select those that are sound

and firm, pack in a stone jar and cover well with strong brine. A scant pint of salt to a gallon of cold water is a good rule in mixing this. Stir until the salt is dissolved. Leave in this four days, pour off the brine and examine the pickles well, rejecting those that have soft spots in them. Wash in cold water and return to the cleansed jar. Drown deep in very cold water, and soak in this twenty-four hours. Wash again, put into a preserving-kettle and cover with water in which has dissolved a scant tablespoonful of alum for every quart. If you are pickling cucumbers, tiny mangoes (muskmelons), gherkins, beans, or anything else you would have green, line the kettle with grape-leaves, put layers of the same between the cucumbers, etc., and cover the top thickly with them. Fit a lid on the kettle when you have poured in the alum-water, and heat slowly until you cannot bear your hand in the liquid, but *not* until it boils, if you would have the pickles plump and crisp. Remove the kettle from the fire, without uncovering, and let the contents cool gradually. To insure this, throw a thick cloth over lid, kettle, and all, and leave it four or five hours, until the pickles are a little more than blood-warm. Take them out, a few at a time, and drop into a large vessel of *very cold*—ice-water, if you have it. Let them freshen and grow firm in this all night. Next day, prepare the vinegar in the following proportions:

    1 gallon of vinegar (cider vinegar and very sharp).
    3 dozen whole black peppers, as many cloves.
    1 dozen allspice.
    1 dozen blades of mace.
    4 tablespoonfuls of brown sugar.

Boil ten minutes, covered, while you drain and wipe the pickles. When all are ready, and also the vinegar,

PICKLES.

throw in the pickles, and let them get *scalding* hot. They must on no account be allowed to boil. Have a jar heated, that it may not crack at contact with the hot liquid; pour in the pickles, cover closely, and set away.

In three days drain off and scald the vinegar, pour back into the jar, and cover tightly. Repeat this once a week, for a month, the last time adding another tablespoonful of sugar for every gallon of vinegar. Keep in a dry, cool place. Should the vinegar shrink in re-heating add more, properly seasoned.

In soaking the pickles in brine and in fresh water, lay a clean round board or a stout plate on top, with a light weight on it, to keep them covered by the liquid.

Pickled Walnuts or Butternuts.

These must be gathered young. If a needle or pin cannot pierce them easily they are too old for pickling. Soak in brine prepared as for green pickles, a week. Drain, wipe, and "jab" a stout needle—a No. 1—through each, cover with cold water and leave overnight. Then drain, wipe, and plunge into hot spiced vinegar, such as I have directed for green pickles. Boil five minutes, and repeat this process twice a week for a fortnight, adding sugar the last time. They will be "ripe" and fit for use in a month, but improve with keeping.

Green Tomato Pickle.

1 gallon green tomatoes.
6 onions.
1 quart of cider vinegar.
2 cups of sugar.
1 tablespoonful each of ground mustard, black pepper and salt.
2 teaspoonfuls each of allspice and cloves (ground).

Slice the tomatoes without peeling; peel and chop or slice the onions very thin. Put a layer of tomatoes into a preserve-kettle, sprinkle with onion, sugar, and spices; more tomatoes, etc., until all are in. Heat slowly and stew gently about forty-five minutes after they begin to boil. Put up in small jars, as it does not keep well after it is opened.

A most delicious pickle, and a useful sauce for meat and fish.

Sweet Pickles

Are a pleasant medium between sour pickles and preserves, rather more expensive than the former, and universally popular.

Pickled Plums.

Choose those which are ripe but not soft, pick them over, rejecting the specked and unsound, wash, and prick each three or four times with a large needle. For every four pounds of fruit weigh out two pounds of sugar, and pack in the kettle in alternate layers. Heat *slowly*, keeping the kettle covered. Prepare the vinegar by allowing a large coffee-cupful of vinegar to four pounds of fruit, a dozen blades of mace, two sticks of cinnamon as long as your finger, broken into short bits, and one dozen whole cloves. When the fruit fairly boils all over, stir gently, put in the spiced vinegar, boil three minutes, take out the plums with a split or pierced skimmer and lay on broad pans or dishes to cool. As the syrup exudes from them return to the kettle with the rest. When no more runs, pack the fruit tenderly in jars, boil the syrup *hard* for forty-five minutes, and fill up the jars. Seal tightly. Should they show signs of working, within a few weeks, drain off the vinegar into a kettle, bring to a boil, drop in the plums, heat five minutes, and return to the glasses.

Pickled Peaches

May be put up as are plums, except that they are first pared carefully.

Or,

To every 4 pounds of fruit (peeled), allow 1¾ pound of sugar, and rather less than 2 cups of vinegar, 12 blades of mace, and 6 inch-lengths of stick cinnamon.

Put into a bowl the peaches in alternate layers with the sugar, cover and leave them two hours. Then drain off all the juice that will drip from them through a colander, and stir in a kettle over the fire until the sugar melts. Let it boil up once sharply and skim thoroughly. Drop in the fruit, boil five minutes *gently*, take up the peaches with a split spoon or perforated ladle, draining each patiently, and pack in jars. As the liquid collects in the bottom of these, drain back into the kettle. Add the spiced vinegar to the syrup, boil *hard* half an hour. The jar-covers should be on all this while to keep in the steam. When the syrup is ready, fill up the jars with it boiling hot and seal.

How to Use the Surplus Syrup.

There *is* always a surplus if the peaches are juicy—as Bridget Mahony says of the sugar, flour, and butter ordered by her mistress from the grocer—"more nor will go convayniently intil the jars." Strain this through a cloth, boil ten minutes, and seal up hot in jars for pudding-syrup. It needs only to be heated to be ready for table-use, and is very good.

Pickled Cabbage.

1 white, firm cabbage, chopped.
6 onions, medium-sized, chopped.
1 pint of vinegar.
1 cup of sugar.
1 teaspoonful each of ground mustard, black pepper, cinnamon, turmeric, mace, allspice, and the same of celery-seed.
Salt.

Pack the cabbage alternately with the onion in a jar, sprinkling them with salt, and leave overnight. Next day, scald vinegar and spices and put in cabbage and onions. Boil gently half an hour, and put up. It is fit for use in twenty-four hours.

Blackberry or Raspberry Vinegar.

3 quarts of berry-juice.
1 quart of cider vinegar.
4 cups of sugar.

Put sugar and juice together over the fire; bring quickly to a boil, stirring until the sugar is dissolved. Boil hard half an hour, add the vinegar, boil up once, skim well and strain into bottles, rolled in hot water. Cork tightly and seal with sealing-wax, or dip the head of each corked bottle into a mixture of three parts beeswax, one part resin. Lay the bottles on their sides in a cool, dark place. This is a healthful and refreshing beverage when mixed with two-thirds water.

CAKES.

Cream Short Cake.

2 cups of prepared flour.
1 tablespoonful lard and as much butter.
½ cup milk.
3 tablespoonfuls white sugar.
1 saltspoonful of salt.

Rub the shortening into the salted flour, and wet up with the milk in which has been dissolved the sugar. Roll out half an inch thick and bake in two jelly-cake tins. The dough should be soft and handled very little. Bake to a nice brown, and when cold lay between the cakes the following mixture:

½ cup of milk.
1 even teaspoonful of corn-starch.
1 egg.
½ teaspoonful vanilla or other essence.
2 tablespoonfuls of sugar.

Heat the milk and thicken with the corn-starch wet in a *little* cold milk. Beat up the egg, stir in the sugar, and both into the hot, thickened milk. Cook one minute, stirring all the time, take from fire, and when cold, flavor. Sift powdered sugar on the top of the cake, and eat while fresh, cutting into triangles.

Berry Short Cake.

Mix the cake as in last receipt, but in place of the cream filling, when cold, spread between the layers one quart of strawberries, black or red raspberries, mashed in a bowl and sweetened to taste, *just before* the cake goes to table. Sift sugar over the top and eat with milk—or cream.

Peach Short Cake.

Make in the same way, peeling the peaches, and cutting them up small before mashing.

Breakfast Berry Short Cake.

1 quart of sifted flour.
2 cups of buttermilk, or of sour or loppered milk.
½ cup of sugar.
Yolk of egg.
1 teaspoonful of salt and the same of soda sifted three times with the flour.
1 quart huckleberries, blackberries, red or black raspberries.
1 tablespoonful of lard and the same of butter.

Chop the shortening into the salted flour, and wet up with the milk in which has been stirred the beaten yolk. Roll with light, swift strokes into a sheet half an inch thick. Cut a piece to fit a greased baking-pan; lay neatly in the bottom, cover with the berries, sift sugar over them, and lay another sheet, a trifle thinner than the lower, over all. Bake in a steady oven to a good brown; cut into squares and pile on a warmed dish. Split and eat with sugar, hot.

Foundation for Jelly or Cream Cake.

3 eggs.
1 good tablespoonful of butter.
1 cup of sugar.
1 cup of prepared flour.
1 tablespoonful of milk.

Cream butter and sugar. Beat yolks and whites separately. Put the beaten yolks into a bowl, whip in butter and sugar, then milk, the frothed whites, and flour alternately, quickly and thoroughly, bringing up a great spoonful of batter from the bottom of the bowl at every sweep.

Butter three jelly-cake tins, put an equal portion of batter in each, and bake in a tolerably quick oven.

If you have not the prepared flour, make it by sifting three times with plain flour half a teaspoonful of soda and twice as much cream of tartar.

One of the best housekeepers I know always makes this mixture the vehicle of many varieties of jelly, cream, and méringue cakes. It is easy, inexpensive, and very good for this purpose, although not rich enough to "go alone."

Spread jelly between the layers, or a cream made according to directions found below.

Cream for Cake Filling.

1 cup of milk.
1 beaten egg.
½ cup of sugar.
2 teaspoonfuls of corn-starch.
1 teaspoonful of essence—vanilla or lemon.

Heat the milk, stir in the corn-starch until it thickens well; pour gradually upon the egg whipped light with the sugar, return to the saucepan and stir five minutes. It should be like a good batter. Season when cold and spread between the cakes.

Old-fashioned Cup Cake.

1 cup of milk.
1 cup of butter.
2 cups of sugar.
3 cups of *prepared* flour.
4 eggs.

Mix as directed in receipt for Jelly Cake, but bake in a

buttered cake-mould, or in small tins. It is very delightful baked in jelly-cake tins with cream filling, or with a méringue, made thus:

Méringue Filling for Cake.

White of 2 eggs, beaten very stiff, with 1 cup of powdered sugar (heaping). Stir *all* the sugar into the whites before you begin to beat. Then lay aside the spoon and put in the Dover egg-beater, working it steadily until it is very snowy and smooth. Now add the juice and half the grated rind of a lemon, or the juice and half the grated peel of an orange. Whip in well, spread between the cakes, adding more powdered sugar to the portion left for the top if you would frost the cake.

Marble Cake.

Mix in accordance with the rules given for Old-fashioned Cup Cake, but when ready for the pans take out a cupful of batter and beat into it two tablespoonfuls of grated chocolate, rubbed hard in a bowl, with a tablespoonful of milk. Put a few spoonfuls of the plain cake-batter into a buttered mould, and drop on it a spoonful of the chocolate mixture. Stir *lightly* and carelessly, spreading upon the lower layer as irregularly as you can. Then more yellow, and variegate it in the same way, until all is in.

When baked and cut it will be found to be prettily mottled.

Mamie's Cake.

3 eggs.
½ cup of butter.
½ cup of milk.
1 cup of sugar.
2½ cups of prepared flour.

Cream butter and sugar, beat whites and yolks in separate bowls; whip the creamed butter and sugar into the yolks, the milk, lastly, whites and flour by turns, and lightly. Stir well, and bake in one large, or several small tins.

Cocoanut Cake.

3 eggs.
2 cups of sugar.
1 cup of milk.
3 cups of prepared flour.

Mix and bake as for jelly-cake.

Filling.

White of 1 egg beaten light with 1 cup of powdered sugar. (Stir all together before you begin to beat to a méringue.) 1 grated cocoanut.

When the egg and sugar are ready, stir in half the cocoanut. Mix two tablespoonfuls of powdered sugar with the rest and strew on the topmost layer of the cake, when the méringue has been spread between the others.

Nut Cake.

2 eggs.
½ cup of butter.
1 cup of sugar.
½ cup of cold water.
1½ cup of prepared flour.
1 cupful of nut-kernels freed from bits of shell, and rolled in flour.

If almonds are used, blanch them, *i.e.*, take off the skins by soaking them in boiling water; let them get cold and cut small with a sharp knife. White or "English" walnuts must be cut each into several pieces.

Mix as with cup cake, the water taking the place of

milk, and the nuts going in last. Bake in small tins or in one loaf in a steady oven.

Huckleberry Cake.

3 eggs.
½ cup of butter.
1 cup of sugar.
½ cup of milk.
2 scant cups of prepared flour.
2 cups sound, ripe berries, dredged well with flour. Wash and pick them over carefully, and drain dry before dredging.
½ teaspoonful of mixed nutmeg and cinnamon.

Cream butter and sugar; beat in the yolks, the milk, spice, flour, and whipped whites alternately; finally, the berries. Mix them in thoroughly but cautiously. They should not be mashed or broken. Bake longer than you would plain cake, covering with clean paper should it rise too fast. Test with a straw to see if it is done.

Wrap in a clean, thick cloth, and do not cut it until perfectly cold. It is better not to use it the day it is baked.

This is a Virginia receipt, and the product is worthy of its origin. Try it!

Sponge Cake.

6 eggs. Weigh them with care, and take of sugar just their weight—of flour, half the weight.
1 lemon, juice and grated rind.
Use prepared flour.

Beat yolks and whites in different vessels; the powdered sugar into the yolks, whipping long and steadily; the lemon, juice and peel; the whites, and finally the flour, with just as few strokes as will incorporate it with the other ingredients. Butter small tins, or one larger one

CAKES. 209

well, and bake in a steady, rather brisk oven. Cover the cakes with white paper when risen, as they scorch soon.

A safe and easy receipt.

Apple Cake.

Mix and bake as directed in Foundation for Jelly Cake (page 204), and when cold spread with the following mixture:

Apple Filling.

3 juicy, well-flavored apples, peeled, cored, and grated.
1 egg, beaten well.
1 cup of sugar.
1 teaspoonful of butter.
Nutmeg and cinnamon to taste.

Beat the sugar into the egg, and into the bowl containing them grate the apple, stirring it in as you grate. Put into a tin vessel, set in a saucepan of boiling water, and stir to a boil. Cook one minute after this sets in, to make sure the egg is done; while still smoking hot, add butter and spice; beat hard two minutes, let it cool, and spread on the cakes.

Baker's Cake Transformed.

When you have not time to make cake, buy a sponge or plain cup-cake, slice horizontally into three or four divisions, spread with fruit-jelly or made cream, as for cream cake, or with apple-filling. Stir up the white of two eggs with one heaping cup of powdered sugar, then whip stiff, add the juice of a lemon or of a sour orange, and cover the cake, top and sides. Dry in an open oven, or in the sunshine and air, and you have a pretty and really nice dessert.

Soft Gingerbread.

2½ cups of flour.
½ cup of molasses.
½ cup of brown sugar.
¾ of a cup of loppered milk.
1 teaspoonful of soda sifted three times with the flour.
1 teaspoonful of ground ginger.
½ teaspoonful of cinnamon.
1 tablespoonful of butter.

Mix sugar, butter, molasses, and spice together; set in the oven, or other warm place until lukewarm. Then beat hard five minutes, until the contents of the bowl are light and foamy; put in milk and soda; beat two minutes longer, and bake in patty-pans, muffin-tins, or in two large "cards."

This gingerbread is best when warm, although it will keep fresh for a day or two. Eat as a dessert with cheese and chocolate. It is far preferable to the average (or super-average) pie, costs less, and is easier of digestion.

Currant Cakes.

3 eggs.
3 cups of prepared flour.
2 cups of sugar.
1 scant cup of butter.
½ cup of milk.
1 teaspoonful of grated nutmeg.
1 cup of currants, washed, dried in the sun or oven, and dredged well with flour.

Mix as you do other cup-cake, stir in the fruit at the last, beat up one minute, and bake in buttered patty-pans or shapes.

Cream-Puffs.

½ pound of butter.
¾ pound of prepared flour.
6 eggs.
2 cups of warm water.

Stir the butter into the warm water; set over the fire and stir to a slow boil. When it boils, put in the flour. Cook one minute, stirring constantly. Turn into a deep dish to cool. Beat the egg light—yolks and whites separately—and whip into the cooled paste, the whites last. Drop in great spoonfuls upon buttered paper, not so near as to touch, or run into each other. Bake *about* ten minutes in a quick oven, until they are of a golden brown.

Filling.

4 cups of milk.
4 tablespoonfuls of corn-starch.
2 eggs.
2 cups of sugar.
1 full teaspoonful of lemon or vanilla essence.

Wet the corn-starch to a smooth paste with a little of the milk; boil the rest of the milk. Add to the beaten eggs the sugar and corn-starch. Pour gradually upon these the hot milk; mix well; return to the fire, and stir to a thick custard. Let it get cold before flavoring it. Pass a sharp knife carefully around the puffs — which should also be cold—split dexterously, and fill with the mixture. They are best when eaten fresh.

Frankly—this is not a cheap receipt. But it is so good and so safe that I cannot resist the temptation to insert it here. It is especially commended to the country housewife, as the chief expense is in the butter and eggs used.

Cookies (No. 1).

½ cup of butter.
1 cup of sugar.
1 egg.
½ cup loppered milk or of buttermilk.
½ teaspoonful of soda, sifted three times through 2 cups of flour.
¼ teaspoonful of nutmeg.
A handful of raisins.

Rub butter and sugar to a cream. Use powdered sugar, if you can get it. Beat up this cream well with the egg, add milk and spice, finally the salted flour. Roll into a thin sheet, cut into round cakes and bake in a quick oven, burying a raisin in the centre of each cooky.

Cookies (No. 2).

½ cup of butter.
2 cups of sugar.
1 cup of sour milk, buttermilk, or "clabber."
2 eggs.
1 heaping tablespoonful of anise, caraway, or coriander seed. If the latter, pound them quite fine.
1 teaspoonful of soda sifted into *about* 4 cups of flour.

Mix as above directed, stirring in the seed last of all.

Ginger Cookies.

½ cup of butter.
1 cup of molasses.
½ teaspoonful of cinnamon.
2 teaspoonfuls of ground ginger.
¼ teaspoonful of soda *well* sifted into the flour.
Enough flour to enable you to handle the dough—and just enough.

Warm butter, molasses, and spice together, and beat to a yellow cream. Work in the flour gradually until you can mould it with floured hands. Pull off a bit of the batter, and roll in your palms to a little ball. Lay this in a greased pan, and pat gently into a flattened cake. When the pan is full of such, none of them touching his neighbors, bake quickly.

Molasses cakes are liable to burn, and need more vigilant watching than those in the manufacture of which sugar alone is used.

Ginger Snaps (*good*).

- 2½ cups of flour.
- ½ cup of lard.
- ¼ cup of butter.
- 1 cup of sugar.
- ½ cup of molasses.
- ½ cup of water.
- 1 even tablespoonful of ginger, and half as much cinnamon.
- 1 even teaspoonful of soda sifted three times with the flour.

Warm sugar, butter, and lard until you can whip them to a light-brown cream; beat in spices, water, at last the flour. If the dough is not stiff enough to roll out, add flour cautiously. Roll into a thin sheet, cut into small cakes, and bake quickly. They keep well and long.

Jumbles, or Drop Cakes.

- 1 cup of sugar.
- ½ cup of butter.
- ½ cup of loppered milk.
- 1 egg.
- 1 even teaspoonful of soda sifted three times through 1½ cup of flour.
- ½ teaspoonful of nutmeg or mace.

Cream butter and sugar, beat in the whipped egg, the milk, spice, and work in the flour to a *soft* dough. Drop by the tablespoonful on well-greased writing-paper laid in a baking-pan, or with a spoon make small rings of dough on the same. These will broaden in baking. The oven should be very quick, and the cakes so far apart that they will not run together as they warm.

Crullers.

1 cup of sugar.
½ cup of butter.
1 egg.
1 cup of loppered or buttermilk.
½ teaspoonful of soda sifted three times with the flour.
2 cups of flour.

Mix as you would cookies, roll out thin, cut into shapes, rings, rounds, etc., and fry in boiling lard. Put this over the fire in a cold frying-pan and heat gradually. There should be five or six spoonfuls of it. Have the crullers all cut out before you begin. Test the heat with a bit of dough. It should rise almost immediately to the top. Put a *small* peeled potato in the lard with the crullers, and leave it there until the frying is over. Turn each cruller once, and as soon as it is puffy and delicately browned take up with a split spoon and put into a hot colander. Sift powdered sugar over them while hot.

Doughnuts.

1 heaping cup of sugar, brown and dry.
½ teaspoonful of salt.
¼ teaspoonful each of ground cinnamon and mace.
As much allspice as will lie easily on a silver half-dime.
3 cups of flour.
1¼ cup of warm (not hot) milk.
3 good tablespoonfuls of yeast.

Sift the salt twice through the flour, and make a hole in the middle. Put sugar, spice, and milk together, and stir until the sugar dissolves, pour into the hollow, and stir the flour down into it with a chopping-knife. When the flour is all wet, hollow the dough, put in the yeast and, still using the chopper, mix and work it throughout the mass. It should be a soft dough *just* fit to handle. Lay it on the floured pastry-board, roll it over gently several times and put into a floured tray or bowl to rise. Cover and set in a moderately warm place. It should be light in six hours. When well risen, turn it out on the pastry-board, work up lightly into a ball, and give it a second rising of two hours. Roll into a sheet half an inch thick, cut into strips and twist into fantastic shapes, or into circles, the hole in the middle made with a smaller cutter, and the pieces thus extracted forming a "nut." Fry as you would crullers, in plenty of boiling lard. Drain in a sieve or colander as fast as they are done.

Corn-starch Cakes.

2 eggs.
1 cup of sugar.
½ cup of milk.
1 cup of flour (prepared).
2 tablespoonfuls of corn-starch.
A little nutmeg.

If you have only barrel flour, prepare it by stirring in ½ teaspoonful of soda and twice as much cream of tartar and sifting three times. The corn-starch should be mixed with the flour and all sifted together.

Cream butter and sugar, whip in the beaten yolks, the milk, nutmeg, lastly, the mingled corn-starch and flour.

Bake in small tins. They should be eaten the day they are baked, and are then really nice.

Unity Gingerbread.

1 even quart of sifted flour.
1 even cup of butter and lard mixed.
1 cup of molasses.
1 cup of sugar.
1 tablespoonful of ginger.
1 teaspoonful of mixed cinnamon and allspice.
1 *small* cup of cold water, and the same of chopped and seeded raisins.
1 teaspoonful of soda, sifted with the flour three times.

Warm together butter, lard, molasses, sugar, and spice, until you can beat them up with an egg-whip. Beat five minutes, steadily, to a creamy froth; add the water, then the flour; lastly, the raisins dredged well with flour.

Stir faithfully and bake in greased patty-pans. They are extremely good.

CUSTARDS.

Boiled Custard.

This is the base of so many delicious desserts that it is worth while to learn the art of preparing it successfully.

4 cups of milk.
4 eggs (5 are better, if you can spare them, but 4 will make a tolerable custard).
1 cup of sugar.
1 saltspoonful of salt.
2 teaspoonfuls of vanilla, or other essence.

Heat the milk to scalding, add the salt and sugar, and stir over the fire until they dissolve. Beat yolks and eggs in a bowl, very thick and smooth; pour on them, by degrees, the boiling milk, stirring with the other hand all the time. Put the custard into a tin pail or saucepan and set in boiling water. The water in the outer vessel should be at least two-thirds of the way to the level of the custard. Stir steadily ten minutes, then watch, as for hid treasure, for signs of thickening. The raw-egg color will have gone by now, and a creamy consistency will be apparent to eye and taste in the compound. A minute too long will curdle it, two minutes too early will leave a crude flavor. When you have once detected the just mean, you will not be likely to mistake it afterward. Remember that it thickens after it leaves the fire, and allow for this. Pour from the kettle the instant it is removed from the stove, and set in a cold place. Nobody in this day—not even a London alderman—eats hot custard. There is a tradition that it was a favorite dish with these city magnates some centuries ago. An old rhyme tells us—

"They gather, they gather,
Hot custards in spoons."

Do not weary of the repetition of the caution to drop a tiny bit of soda into milk that is to be boiled. It arrests the acidification which is hastened by heat. Season when cold.

Floating Island.

4 cups of milk.
4 eggs.
4 heaping tablespoonfuls of sugar.
2 tablespoonfuls currant or other fruit-jelly.
1 teaspoonful of vanilla.
A good pinch of salt, and one of soda stirred in the milk.

Heat the milk to scalding, and pour upon the beaten *yolks* of the eggs. Add the sugar, return to the fire and stir until it begins to thicken, which should be in about ten minutes. Take from the fire, and let it get cold before you flavor with vanilla or other essence. Pour into a glass or china bowl. Beat the whites up to a standing froth, whipping in, a little at a time, the jelly or preserve. This last should sweeten the méringue sufficiently. Pile the froth upon the surface of the custard in great spoonfuls, and in helping it out see that some of the méringue goes on the top of each saucer.

A pleasant variation of floating islands is cup-custards. Small cups or glasses are filled almost to the top with the custard, and a spoonful of méringue, or "whip," crowns each. If you have nice cookies or light cake, send these around with the custard.

Baked Custard.

1 quart of milk.
4 eggs.
4 tablespoonfuls of sugar.
Vanilla, or other seasoning.
A pinch of salt and the same of soda.

Scald the milk; beat the eggs light, alone, then with the sugar. Pour over these the boiling milk, and having mixed well, turn into a buttered bake-dish. Season, and set the dish in a dripping-pan of boiling water within a steady oven. There is no danger of scorched custard while there is water enough in the outer vessel. Bake until well set in the middle, but no longer. When a knife makes a *cut*, and not a fast-closing dent in the centre, the custard is done. Eat cold.

Tapioca Custard.

1 small cup of tapioca.
4 cups of milk.

2 cups of water.
1 cup of sugar.
3 eggs.
¼ teaspoonful of salt.
A pinch of soda.
1 teaspoonful of vanilla.

Soak the tapioca overnight in the cold water. Scald the milk with the soda and salt. Stir in the soaked tapioca, and do not withdraw the spoon until it is dissolved. Take from the fire, and pour upon the yolks and sugar, beaten light in a bowl. Return to the fire and stir ten minutes, or until it thickens well. Pour out and mix in lightly the whites of the eggs, whipped to a standing froth. Flavor, put into a glass bowl, and set on ice or in a very cold place. It is delicious. Always cook in an inner vessel set in hot water.

Rice Custard.

Soak a cupful of rice five hours, the last two in warm water; put over the fire in four cups of milk, with a pinch of soda and a quarter teaspoonful of salt. Set in a vessel of cold water and bring slowly to a boil, shaking up the inner vessel now and then. When the rice is very soft, add a cupful of sugar, stir until dissolved; pour upon the beaten yolks of three eggs, and thenceforward follow the directions given for tapioca custard.

Sago Custard.

See directions for tapioca custard.

Cocoanut Custard.

Make a good boiled custard, flavor with one teaspoonful of bitter almond essence, grate a cocoanut, and when the custard is quite cold (it should be poured while warm into a glass bowl) strew the cocoanut on top. Sift white sugar over this.

Snow Pudding.

½ package of *Cooper's* Gelatine. It costs half as much as Coxe's, and is even better for blanc-mange and similar preparations where transparency is not a desideratum.

3 eggs.
2 cups of milk.
2 cups of sugar.
A pinch of soda and one of salt.
Juice of a lemon, strained.
1 cup of cold water, and 2 cups of boiling.

Soak the gelatine two hours in the cold water. Then turn in the boiling, and stir until the gelatine is melted. Add the lemon-juice and two-thirds of the sugar, and set in a cold place until it begins to congeal. The whites of the eggs should all this while have been on the ice. Now whip to a standing froth, and beat in the gelatine, little by little, whipping three or four minutes on each spoonful until you have a white sponge. The process is facilitated if the bowl containing the mixture be set in ice-water while you beat. Wet a mould with cold water and put in the sponge. It will be ready to turn out in a few hours.

Of the yolks, milk, and one-third of the sugar make a good custard, flavor with vanilla, and let it get cold. Turn the snow-sponge into a glass dish, and pour this around the base.

"The Dover" will bring solidity and lightness out of the materials specified for this pudding with from twenty to thirty minutes' beating. I know of no other egg-whip of which the same can be asserted with truth.

This is an elegant dessert.

FAMILIAR TALK.

PECULIARLY APPROPRIATE WHEN SANDWICHED
BETWEEN TWO CHAPTERS ON SWEETS.

Flies.

FROM a gossipy private letter I extract a paragraph :

"Our friend M—— lives the same fidgety life as of old; has the same unsparing eye for grease-spots; is as intolerant of finger-marks on paint, and spends as many hours a day chasing the one audacious fly that has strayed into her house in spite of her closed blinds and screen-doors. She tells me that she believes *flies* will shorten her life by twenty years."

The tight, trim little woman is plainly present to my mental sight as I read. She is a dweller in a cottage where even the suspicion of dirt is actual transgression. Some day we may, perhaps, examine somewhat minutely her kind—the *genus* coarsely but aptly characterized as the "nasty-particular housekeeper."

But, throughout the country, every moderately neat housewife will sympathize in her last-named antipathy. There is hardly one of us who has not read with full appreciation of the impatient loathing that moved the outcry— Pharaoh's mandate to Moses, hastily summoned to the palace by reason of the "grievous swarm of flies" that "corrupted the land"—"*I will let you go! Entreat for me!*"

The domestic fly is a necessary accompaniment of civilization, say natural historians—a beneficent scavenger; a cleanly insect that spends much of his brief existence in dusting his plumage and polishing his legs; a friendly little creature whose beauty under the microscope justifies the spider's praise of his "diamond eyes" and "gauzy wings." With nerves worn to the quick by his teasing buzz and eyes continually offended by be-specked windows, pictures, chandeliers, and hangings, we reject scientific prattle and write down the *musca* tribe as "vermin" and "unclean." In the desperation of disgust we do not consider it an unwarrantable use of Holy Writ when we speak of them as "spots in our feasts of charity, when they feast with us, feeding themselves without fear."

I say "desperation," for the moods and habits of the pests vary with times and seasons, baffling experience and prophecy. One summer, we organize forces and conduct operations according to the most approved methods of defensive warfare. By six o'clock each morning,

"All the windows of the *house*
We open to the day."

By eight o'clock we brush out all the flies that have not been lured into the out-door world by the sunlight, and shut Venetian blinds upon the morning coolness we have imprisoned for our daily need. When breakfast is over, soiled dishes, cups, etc., are removed to the kitchen or pantry sink, scraped, rinsed, and left under water until some one is ready to wash them. A piece of mosquito-netting kept for the purpose is thrown over the table when the crumbs have been swept off and the cloth relaid for the next meal. In ten minutes after we rise from the board, not a scrap of food is left in the dining-room or kitchen to tempt a "scavenger" or a gluttonous fly. If we can live without air as well as without sunshine, we fit wire nettings in windows and doors, and rest in flyless respectability from morning until night, possessing body and soul in Pharisaic tranquillity.

The next summer is neither colder nor hotter, neither drier nor wetter, than the preceding, nor is one precaution omitted. But within a week after the "cleanly" insects make their first friendly call, our warfare becomes aggressive. We tack fly-paper on the walls of our chambers, set traps of soap-suds-and-treacle in the kitchen and in the eating-room concealed from general view, the latest patented snare for the unwary among the "grievous swarm" that tickle our noses while asleep, ramp over cooking utensils and promenade greedily upon dishes, plates, cups, and spoons—into our very mouths unless we beat them away, a "plague" that drives temper and almost reason out of the most patient household saint. We cease to respect ourselves, and expect condemnation of our housewifery from others when we do not succeed in abating the nuisance, while conscious that we have done our very best.

Thus much of discouraging confession of the perplexities of the Fly Question—the most serious of the minor problems with which our housekeeper has to deal. She would not be human did she not abhor the officious torments naturalists class as harmless. More grace is required to overcome the irritation they engender, than to wage open, honest combat with wasps and hornets. The largest gift this "Talk" holds for their victim is sympathy. But a suggestion or two growing out of practical acquaintanceship with the subject may be of value.

First: Repel the temptation to use fly-poison in any

shape in or near dining-room or kitchen. It is not appetizing to behold the struggles of a drowning fly in cream-jug or soup-plate. The added impression that he dropped there in death-agony from poison is nauseating, and the chances of such accidents are multiplied a hundred-fold by insect-powder, "Sure Death," and fly-paper. It is almost impossible to protect food while in process of cooking or consumption from sickened, reeling vermin.

Second: Cool darkness and vigilant cleanliness *must* be in some degree effectual in banishing the pertinacious creatures that revel in heat and filth. Our misery is measurably less than if we had not resisted the raid. If hundreds have stolen in past our defences, thousands have been kept out. By the help of judicious appliances, the infliction has been mitigated into tolerableness. The virtue of neatness, of watchfulness against all imaginable sources of discomfort from this cause is, likewise, vigilance against provocatives to disease, the prime blessing, in this case, depending upon the secondary. The uncovered drain, the uncleansed swill-pail that "draws flies," as surely sends up *infusoria* that breed pestilence. In so far as the annoying hum of the eager swarm sounds this alarm their agency is beneficial.

Third: It is a groundless if plausible superstition that it does no good to kill flies, that "for every one slain ten come to the funeral." Fly-traps, the contents of which are scalded or burnt to death, not only lessen the present nuisance, but damage the prospects of a future supply, for which there is assuredly, to our way of thinking, no demand. I know a notable housekeeper who is reaping the reward of patient and continued experiment with one of these inventions—the "Clockwork Fly-trap," manufactured at Pittsfield, Mass. It is wound up every day. A slowly revolving cylinder is smeared with molasses, and carries the flies under a grating from which they cannot escape. Every night this cage is detached from the rest of the apparatus, and set in a hot oven. When all the flies are dead they are thrown into the fire, the cage is washed and ready for another day's work.

"I have used it for four years," said the owner, when my remark upon the scarcity of flies in her house led to the exhibition of the treasure. "Our family is very large, and screen-doors do little good where there are so many young people running in and out. The first summer I caught and burnt nearly a pint a day; the next not half so many, the third fewer still. This year, while my neighbors are terribly annoyed by flies, the cool weather driving them in-doors, the trap seems to catch all that come to us. Yet I have not taken a quart in all in three months. I account for this by supposing that the germs die with the flies that would deposit them for another year."

For the sake of my fellow-sufferers from a common plague, I give this account and the title of the valuable "catcher." My informant is a woman of intelligence and veracity; her house is charmingly clean throughout; her dining-room is kept dark between meals, and the fresh air admitted freely to all parts of the farmstead. Her machine is needed nowhere now except in the kitchen, where the cooking for twenty people is done, and here it does, as she affirms, "seem to catch all that come."

JELLIES AND BLANC-MANGE.

Cider Jelly.

1½ cup of sugar.
½ package of Coxe's Gelatine.
Juice and half the grated peel of a lemon.
⅓ cup of cold water.
2 cups of boiling water.
A pinch of cinnamon.
1 cup of clear sweet cider.

Put the gelatine in a large bowl, pour the cold water over it, and soak one hour. Then put in with it the sugar, lemon-juice and rind, the spice, and covering the bowl leave for an hour longer. This will extract the full flavor of the lemon and further soften the gelatine. Next, pour in the boiling water and stir until the gelatine is entirely dissolved. Add the cider, and strain through a double flannel cloth, not shaking or squeezing, but letting the jelly drip at its own will into a vessel set beneath. Wet a mould with cold water, without wiping it, pour in the jelly, and let it form in a cold place.

When you wish to turn it out, dip for a second—hardly more—in warm water, and invert on a dish or glass bowl.

If jelly is not clear after the first straining, put it through the bag again and yet again.

Lemon Jelly.

½ package of Coxe's Gelatine.
1 cup of cold water.
2 lemons—the juice of both and grated rind of one.
1 heaping cup of sugar.
2 large cups of boiling water.
Pinch of nutmeg.

Make as directed in foregoing receipt, leaving out the cider.

Orange Jelly.

½ package of Coxe's Gelatine.
Juice of 1 lemon and half the peel.
Juice of 2 oranges, and grated peel of one.
1 cup of cold water.
1 cup of sugar.
2 cups of boiling water (large ones).
Pinch of cinnamon.

Put the ingredients together as directed in receipt for Cider Jelly.

Jelly in Oranges.

You may produce a very pretty dessert-dish with comparatively little trouble by making orange-jelly as above, and instead of setting it in moulds, use for this purpose the emptied rinds of oranges. Cut a small piece from the top of each, tearing out pulp and fibres cautiously until you leave the inner walls smooth and clean. Fill with and lay in very cold water while you make the jelly with the juice squeezed from the extracted pulp. If there is much of it, lessen somewhat the quantity of water. When the jelly is cool—*not* congealed—empty the rinds of water and fill with jelly. Set in a cold place until very firm, and when you wish to use them, divide each orange in half with a sharp knife, and lay as you would the ripe fruit on a glass salver or dish. Send around spoons with them.

Ribbon Jelly.

1 package of Coxe's Gelatine.
1 cup of cold water.
4 cups of boiling water.
Pinch of cinnamon.
2 cups of sugar.
1 cup of milk.

Soak the gelatine in cold water three hours. Add a cup and a half of sugar and the cinnamon to two-thirds of it; stir well and pour on the boiling water. When perfectly dissolved, strain through double flannel, not pressing or shaking it. While it cools, make blanc-mange of the reserved third of the soaked gelatine by heating a cup of milk, putting in half a cup of sugar, then the gelatine. Stir until melted, and strain into a bowl. Wet a mould with cold water, pour in a little of the plain jelly and set on ice, or in a very cold place, to form quickly. Color half the plain jelly with a little pulverized cochineal, rubbed up in a tablespoonful of water, then the deep red dye squeezed hard through fine muslin. A teaspoonful will color a cupful of jelly. When the moulded, pale yellow jelly is pretty firm, put on with a spoon enough red to make a neat stripe; set back on the ice, and when this stratum can bear the weight of another, drop in carefully some of the white blanc-mange. Use up your ingredients in this order, having a rather broad band of white at the top, which will be the base when turned out.

Let all get very firm before you loosen the contents of the mould by light, persuasive finger-touches, and dip for a second in warm water.

Understand that this mould of ribbon jelly is really very little more trouble than a much plainer dish. While the strata are hardening, other work can go on without interruption, and the real expenditure of time and care upon the ornamental part of the dessert be scarcely appreciable.

Apple Jelly.

½ package of Coxe's Gelatine.
1 heaping cup of sugar.
6 large, finely flavored juicy apples.
1 lemon—the juice and half the grated rind.

> A good pinch of cinnamon. (This spice, when combined with lemon-peel and juice, makes a peculiarly pleasant flavor, resembling the aroma of lemon, verbena, or "citron aloes.")
>
> 1 cup of cold water.

Peel and, at once, slice each apple into very cold water. Before they can change color, pack closely in a glass or stone jar, *just* cover with cold water, put on a loose lid that the steam may not crack the jar, set in cold water almost up to the neck, bring to a boil, and cook until the apples are clear and very tender.

Soak the gelatine two hours in a cupful of cold water, add the lemon-juice and peel, sugar and cinnamon. Strain and squeeze the apples over them, boiling hot, stir to dissolve the gelatine, and pour into a three-fold thickness of flannel. Let it drip slowly, without pressing or shaking, and put into a wet mould.

Eat with milk—or cream—or with a nice cold custard, poured about the base of the mould when turned into a bowl.

Peach Jelly

Is delicious when made in the same way. Crack a few kernels and mix with the fruit before stewing it.

Jelly and Custard.

Make apple, or peach, or orange jelly; dip jelly-glasses in cold water, half fill with the jelly. Let it get cold, and fill up with cold custard (boiled). If you make this of the yolks of eggs and a méringue of the whites, heaping this latter on the surface of the custard, you will have a really elegant dessert. Send to table in the glasses, accompanied by sponge-cake.

Arrow-root Jelly (*for invalids*).

3 full tablespoonfuls Bermuda arrow-root.
1 cup of boiling water.
2 tablespoonfuls of cold water.
2 teaspoonfuls of white sugar.
Juice of half a lemon.
A pinch of salt.

Have ready the boiling water in a clean saucepan. Wet up the arrow-root with the cold water and stir into the boiling, *slightly* salted, and the sugar dissolved in it before the arrow-root goes in. Stir clear, and when the last trace of cloudiness disappears, add lemon-juice, and pour into a wet mould or glasses.

When firm, eat with powdered sugar and cream.

I hardly know how sick children (and grown people) could be nourished in cases of feverish colds without this jelly. When the bowels and gastric organs are attacked, leave out the lemon-juice. Where weakness from these causes is extreme a tablespoonful of brandy may be added. Arrow-root thus prepared is singularly soothing and healing to weak or inflamed bowels; always strengthening and palatable.

Sago Jelly.

3 tablespoonfuls of sago. The "pearl" sago is best.
1 cupful of cold water.
2 full teaspoonfuls of white sugar.
Juice of half a lemon.
Pinch of salt.

Soak the sago in cold water two hours. Set the vessel containing it then in another of cold water; bring slowly to a boil, stirring up from time to time. When it is warm, add the sugar and a very little salt, to take off the flat taste. If it gets too thick in heating, thin with boiling water from the kettle. Cook until clear and about as thick as custard. Put in the lemon-juice after taking it from the fire. Form in wet glasses, and eat with sugar and cream.

Never take too large a quantity of food into a sick-room. The sight discourages, instead of tempting appetite.

Tapioca Jelly.

Make as you would sago.

Blanc-Mange (*plain*).

1 package of Cooper's Gelatine.
1 cup of cold water.
1 scant cup of sugar.
Pinch of salt.
3 *pints* of milk.
Bit of soda the size of a pea dissolved with the salt in the milk.
2 teaspoonfuls of vanilla-essence, stirred into the blanc-mange while it is lukewarm.

Soak the gelatine two or three hours in the water. When it is soft and clear, put the milk over the fire, with soda and salt, in a vessel set in boiling water. When the milk is scalding, take the thin skin from the surface, put in the sugar, and when this is melted the gelatine. Stir five minutes, or until the contents of the vessel are boiling hot, strain through a coarse cloth, and set to form in a mould wet with cold water, not forgetting to flavor it.

Eat with or without milk or cream.

Blanc-mange is a popular dessert, and so simple, so easily and quickly made, it is surprising that in some of its attractive variations it has not driven the national pie clean out of the field.

Corn-starch Blanc-Mange.

4 heaping tablespoonfuls of corn-starch wet up in 2 tablespoonfuls of milk.
2 eggs, whipped light.
1 quart of milk.
1 cup of sugar.
¼ teaspoonful of salt.
Bit of soda the size of a pea dissolved with the salt in the milk.
2 teaspoonfuls of vanilla or bitter almond.

Scald the milk, with salt and soda stirred in; add the sugar; when this is melted, the wet corn-starch; stir until thick; dip out a cupful and beat into the whipped eggs; return this to the saucepan, cook one minute longer, stirring all the time, and set to form in wet moulds. Eat with milk or cream. You can make it without eggs, if you cannot spare these.

Arrow-root Blanc-Mange.

Make as you do arrow-root jelly, omitting the water entirely, substituting milk.

Tapioca Blanc-Mange.

1 scant cup of tapioca.
1 large cup of cold water.
2 cups of milk.
1 cup of sugar.
2 teaspoonfuls of vanilla.
Pinch of salt and the same of soda in the milk.

Soak the tapioca four or five hours—overnight if you

can remember it. Scald the milk, stir in the sugar, then the soft, clear tapioca. Cook and stir fifteen minutes; take from the fire, pour into a bowl, put in your egg-beater and whip two minutes to get out the lumps. Flavor, and mould in cups or bowls wet with cold water. When firm, turn out and eat with cream. It is very good, especially for sick people.

Farina Blanc-Mange.

- 4 tablespoonfuls of farina, soaked one hour in a cupful of cold water.
- 1 egg.
- 4 cups of milk.
- 5 tablespoonfuls of sugar.
- ¼ teaspoonful of salt.
- 2 teaspoonfuls of vanilla or other essence.
- Pinch of soda.

Scald the milk, add salt and soda, sugar, and when this is dissolved the soaked farina. Stir and cook twelve minutes; take out a cupful, and beat the whipped egg into this. Return to the saucepan and stir two minutes. Form in moulds wet with cold water.

Eat with sweetened cream or with custard.

Chocolate Blanc-Mange.

- ½ package of Cooper's Gelatine.
- ½ cup of cold water.
- 2 good tablespoonfuls of chocolate, grated, and wet up with 1 tablespoonful of milk.
- ½ cup of sugar.
- 2 cups of milk.
- Bit of soda no larger than a pea in the milk.
- 1 teaspoonful essence of vanilla.

Soak the gelatine two hours in the water. Heat the milk, add soda and sugar, stir in the gelatine and chocolate, until well dissolved, and cook two minutes. Strain through a thick cloth into a wet mould. Flavor when cooler.

Medley Blanc-Mange.

2 heaping tablespoonfuls of corn-starch.
2 cups of milk.
Pinch of soda.
½ cup of sugar.
1 heaping tablespoonful of grated chocolate.
1 teaspoonful of vanilla essence.
½ of a grated cocoanut.

Scald the milk, wet the corn-starch into a paste with a little cold milk. Add the sugar, soda, and, when these are dissolved, the corn-starch to the hot milk in the saucepan, and stir five minutes to thicken, and cook it well. Turn out half into a bowl and set in a cold place, while you mix in the chocolate with that on the fire, and cook one minute. Wet a mould with cold water and pour in a third of the chocolate mixture. Set where it will soon form. Flavor with vanilla. When the uncolored blanc-mange is perfectly cold, but not hardened, beat in half of a grated cocoanut, and when the brown mixture is firm enough to bear the weight, put a third of the cocoanut blanc-mange on it. Let this get firm on the ice, or other very cold place, keeping the reserves of both kinds in a warm room. So soon as the cocoanut layer is congealed, put in another of chocolate, and wait until it will support more of the white. Use up your ingredients in this order, and when all are firm—say, in five or six hours—turn out upon a flat dish, pour cold custard around the base, and serve.

This is a nice dessert for Sunday when made on Saturday, and is neither dear nor difficult. The alternate brown-and-white stripes are very pretty.

Coffee Blanc-Mange.

½ package of gelatine.
2 scant cups of milk.
1 cup *strong* clear coffee.
½ cup of sugar.
Pinch of soda in the milk.
½ cup of cold water.

Soak the gelatine two hours in the water. Scald the milk, stir in soda and sugar until dissolved, add the gelatine, and, this melted, the coffee, hot and freshly made. Boil all together two minutes, and strain through a thick cloth into a wet mould.

Tea Blanc-Mange

Is made as above, substituting a cup of *strong* mixed tea for the coffee.

A Pretty Dish.

Divide a soaked package of Cooper's Gelatine into three equal parts. Make one into chocolate blanc-mange, a second into coffee, a third into tea, in accordance with the receipts just given. Form in wet wine-glasses or egg-cups, and turn out on a flat dish when you are ready to use them. Give your guests their choice of flavoring. Strew powdered sugar and pour a little milk—if you have not cream—over each portion in serving.

Jaune Mange.

½ package Cooper's Gelatine.
½ cup of cold water.
Yolks of 2 eggs.
½ cup of sugar.
3 cups of milk.
Pinch of soda in the milk.
1 teaspoonful of vanilla or other essence.

Soak the gelatine two hours in the water. Heat the milk, stir in soda and sugar, then the gelatine, and cook five minutes. Pour upon the beaten yolks by degrees; return to the saucepan, and stir for two minutes steadily, to cook, but not curdle the eggs. Pour out into a wet mould, flavor as it cools, and set in a cold place.

An Easter Dessert.

1 package Cooper's Gelatine.
1 cup of cold water.
2 cups of sugar.
4 cups of milk.
2 tablespoonfuls of grated chocolate.
Yolks of 2 eggs.
1 teaspoonful of pulverized cochineal.
12 empty egg-shells.
Vanilla or other essence—2 teaspoonfuls.
Pinch of soda in the milk.

Soak the gelatine three hours in the water. Heat the milk, stir in soda and sugar, then the gelatine, for three minutes after it is boiling hot again. When you take it up, flavor and divide into three parts; color one-third yellow with the beaten yolks, return this to the fire and cook one minute. Into a second portion stir the grated chocolate,

JELLIES AND BLANC-MANGE.

rinse out the saucepan, and cook this one minute. The third should be colored with the cochineal, rubbed into a tablespoonful of water, squeezed through a bit of muslin, and added, drop by drop, to the white blanc-mange until you have the desired shade of red. It needs no more cooking.

In anticipation of this dessert save up egg-shells for several days, emptying them through holes in the small end. Now, wash and soak well in cold water, leaving them filled with this for an hour or more, to get all the albumen out. Fill them with the three mixtures, four of each color, and set carefully upright in a pan of meal or bran, to keep them from spilling or tipping. Next day, break the shells away, bit by bit, cracking each all over by tapping it gently with a knife or spoon. Lay them in a dish and pour a cupful of clear jelly—cold, but not yet firm—over them. Set in a cold place to harden the jelly.

This dish may seem elaborate at the first glance, but it is really a very simple affair, and beyond the fifteen cents paid for the gelatine, and five or six cents for the sugar, involves but a trifling outlay.

You can, if you like, divide the blanc-mange into four parts, leaving one white. It is a beautiful dessert.

A Bird's Nest.

Make plain white blanc-mange, flavored with vanilla, mould in egg-shells and set to form. Shred the yellow rind of two oranges into slender lengths like straws; put over the fire in cold water, and bring to a boil. Drain and drop the shreds into another saucepan in which you have boiled for half an hour three tablespoonfuls of sugar in a *scant* cup of hot water. Simmer gently half an hour longer, and set away syrup and peel to cool together.

On the next day, drain *every drop* of syrup from the shreds and arrange them, nestwise, in a glass dish. Dispose the eggs (when the shells have been removed) tastefully upon the "straw," and the dish is ready.

Or,

Make a custard, allowing three eggs and half a cup of sugar to two cups of milk, a pinch of soda, and one teaspoonful of vanilla, and cooking into a fair thickness. Let it get very cold in a glass dish, and as the eggs are freed from the shells, lay gently in the yellow bed.

Or, again,

Arrange the blanc-mange eggs on a bed of grated cocoanut lightly sprinkled with powdered sugar, and pour a little custard into the saucers in which an egg and a spoonful of cocoanut are passed to each person at the table.

All of these combinations are pleasing, and will repay the thought and ingenuity expended upon them.

BEVERAGES.

Coffee.

1 quart of boiling water.
1 even cup of freshly ground coffee, wet up with half a cup of cold water.
White and shell of 1 egg or the freshly broken shells of two.

Stir into the wet coffee the white and shell, the latter broken up small. If you cannot afford to break an egg every morning just for this purpose, save the shells of those used for muffins, cakes, or omelette, and clear the coffee with them. Put the mixture into the coffee-pot, shake up and down six or seven times hard, to insure thorough incorporation of the ingredients, and pour in the *boiling* water. Boil steadily from twelve to fifteen minutes, pour in half a cup of cold water, and remove instantly to the side of the stove where it cannot boil. Leave it there five minutes; lift and pour off the clear liquor *gently* into the table-urn or coffee-pot, not to disturb the grounds.

This will make a quart of *strong* coffee. Never make weak. It is better to take half the quantity of water and coffee and dilute their product with hot water or milk in the cups, than to pour out the wishy-washy decoction misnamed "good coffee" by housewives whose families "don't take it so strong as some people like it." Every expert coffee-maker will agree with me that the genuine article — clear, fragrant, and red-brown as the toasted berry that has yielded up its strength to give it body and beauty—when diluted with half its weight of boiling water or scalding milk in the cup, is infinitely preferable to coffee that was *made* weak in the boil. The taste and look and smell of the two beverages are entirely different, as unlike as the temporary enfeeblement of a robust constitution, and the debility of one that has always been fragile.

Black Coffee

Is an excellent stomachic. Physicians are fast settling into the belief that it is the most wholesome preparation of coffee. Many can drink it clear, *i.e.*, without cream or sugar, who dare not use it with these modifications. It is a pleasant and graceful *sequitur* to dinner, and most "Johns" like to take it in sitting-room or parlor, seated at ease, with liberty to chat while they sip it slowly.

Make as you would breakfast coffee, but heap the cup with ground coffee for the quart of water, boil fast fifteen minutes, and pour out as soon as it is settled. The beauty of black coffee is to be fresh and hot. Serve in small cups, and put no sugar in the coffee. Lay, instead, a lump in each saucer, to be used as the drinker likes. I have seen excellent judges and true lovers of coffee eat a lump of sugar after emptying the cup of clear liquid.

Café au Lait.

½ cup of ground coffee wet with three tablespoonfuls of cold water.
2 cups of boiling water. Cold water for settling.
1½ cup of fresh milk.

Make the coffee in the usual way, boiling it fifteen minutes. Rinse out your table coffee-pot very clean, or use a pitcher instead. Pour in the milk, scalding hot, add the cleared coffee, cover closely, and set for five minutes in a pot of boiling water. It is very good.

Tea.

As an appreciative lover of good tea, I have to guard pen, tongue, and countenance when thinking of the unconscionable murder of the Chinese plant going on, daily and tri-daily, in homes where a blessing is made to be a curse. The saddest feature of the wrong is that those who drink most tea understand least how to make it. The Irish servant-girl "couldn't live without it," nor the pale seamstress who "feels as if she would break in two" if her supply is withheld for a single meal. Good tea is costly, so the twice-steeped and dried herb, mixed with others of native growth and colored with blueing, is bought at half-price and boiled to extort all the bitterness of strength left in the wretched imitation. The teapot stands on the range all day, and the topers find a "power of comfort" in it. Our grandmothers invented the phrase "tea-cross" to express the reaction consequent upon the comfort aforesaid. Young girls and growing lads should use neither tea nor coffee habitually. Their complexions and nerves would be the better for total abstinence from even these milder stimulants. Their elders would do well to follow their example, unless they can afford to buy good tea and real coffee, and know how to prepare both properly for table-consumption.

First and pre-eminent in importance, let your kettle be on the boil, actual and hard, before you begin to make tea. Scald out the teapot, allow for four cups of boiling water three *full* teaspoonfuls of tea. Put this dry into the pot, wet with half a cup of boiling water, and cover. If you have no "cosy," make or improvise one. It is a wadded cap set down over the pot, fitting it tolerably close, and keeping in all the aroma and heat. In five minutes, lift it, and pour in as much boiling water as you need for those who are to take tea with you. Fit on the cosy again, and in three minutes more pour out into the cups.

The prettiest and most satisfactory method of tea-making is to prepare it on the table. A spirit-lamp keeps the boiling water brought from the kitchen hot until the "maceration" or steeping prepares the leaves for the larger supply. The flame may then be extinguished. Those who are accustomed to tea made thus, revolt at the poor infusions in unboiled water and the as abhorrent rankness of boiled tea.

Chocolate.

5 heaping tablespoonfuls of chocolate. Baker's is perhaps the best.
3 cups of boiling water.
2 cups of boiling milk.
Sugar at discretion.

Rub the chocolate smooth in a little cold water, and stir into the boiling water over the fire. Boil twenty minutes; put in the milk, which has been heated in another vessel, and simmer ten minutes longer, stirring often. Sweeten on the fire, or in the cups, as you prefer.

Shells or Cocoa "Nibs."

1 quart of boiling water.
2 ozs. of cocoa shells.
2 cups of milk.

Wet the shells with cold water and let them steep an hour. Stir this into the boiling water and cook gently one hour. Strain through a coarse cloth, pressing hard, add the boiling milk, sweeten to taste; set in a pan of hot water ten minutes and pour out.

These "shells" are cheap, and it is worth while to keep a small supply on hand. The drink made from them is more pleasant to the taste, less heavy than chocolate, and better for people of weak nerves than tea or coffee.

Lemonade.

4 lemons.
4 tablespoonfuls of sugar.
1 quart of water.

Peel, roll, and slice the lemons into a pitcher; add the sugar, and leave until just before you want to use the lemonade. Pour in the water then, stir well, crushing the lemons to get out all the juice, and it is ready.

Lemon-peel should never be put into this beverage. It imparts a bitter, and if it stands long, a pungent flavor.

Put ice in each glass.

Tea à la Russe.

Make tea in the usual way; let it get cold on the leaves; then strain off into a pitcher, and slice two or three *peeled* lemons into each quart. The slices should be thin. Put sugar and ice into tumblers and fill up with the tea.

Great bowls of this, ice-cold and well-sweetened, are popular at fairs, church-receptions, and picnics, and have become a fashion at evening-parties where wines and punch are not served.

Iced Coffee.

Make *café au lait*, let it get cold, and serve, sweetened and iced, at lunches and boating or gipsying parties.

Crust Coffee, or Toast-water.

6 slices of toasted bread, stale, and well browned, but not scorched. Dry them in the oven before toasting.
1 quart of boiling water.
Sweeten to taste.

Break the toast into a pitcher; cover with the water, lay a thick cloth over all, and let it get cold. Then strain, ice, and sweeten. It is often prescribed for invalids—especially for teething children.

Apple Tea.

2 finely flavored pippins.
1 quart of cold water.
As much ginger as will lie on a silver dime.
Sugar to taste.

Pare and slice the apples, leaving the seeds in. Pack with the ginger in a glass or stone jar, pour in the water, put on the top loosely, and set in a kettle of cold water. Let it boil until the apple is broken to pieces. Strain while hot, squeezing hard. Strain again through flannel without pressing, and let it get cold. Sweeten and ice. It is recommended for fever patients.

Flax-seed Lemonade.

5 tablespoonfuls whole flax-seed.
Juice of 2 lemons.
1 quart of boiling water.
Sugar to taste.

Steep the flax-seed two hours in the water. Add lemon-juice and sugar. For heavy colds, take it warm, keeping the pitcher containing it covered in a vessel of hot water.

Iceland-Moss Lemonade.

1 handful (dry) Iceland or Irish moss.
2 quarts boiling water.
2 lemons—the juice only.
Sugar to taste.

Wash the moss over and over in several waters, picking out bits of stick and sand, until it is white and clear. Rinse once more and shake off the wet before putting it into a pitcher with the juice and four tablespoonfuls of sugar. Leave for ten minutes, then pour on the water boiling hot, and, covering the pitcher, set it in hot water for one hour. It is best very cold. Keep it in a cool place, and let the sufferer from hoarse cold, sore throat, or cough, drink very freely of it by day and night.

PICNIC DISHES.

There is no more wholesome or satisfactory method of entertainment—cheap or dear—than an afternoon tea or noon-day lunch in the woods in fine summer weather. If the dwellers in American cottages would expend half the sum per season in this kind of merry-making that goes to the getting-up of a single high tea or evening party served in a crowded room to people who are not hungry, the race would be happier and healthier. A "basket-picnic" served in a grove accessible by a short walk from railway station or street-car terminus needs only a summer sky, chosen friends, and good spirits to make it a social success. Whatever tempts to such holidays for our overworked, over-anxious men and women, is an experiment in active benevolence we do well to try. In the hope of encouraging our young housekeeper to do her part in the good work, I append some practical hints that may simplify the process of preparing and serving her woodland fête.

Pack one basket with spoons, forks, one or two knives, Japanese napkins, wooden plates—such as grocers use for butter—common tumblers, two or three towels, a bit of toilet soap, a table-cloth, and a pitcher or tin pail. Put in as few heavy articles as possible, out of regard to the carrier's arm. In another have sandwiches, cold meats, cake, etc., the "body" of the feast, not forgetting pepper and salt, each done up in a sealed envelope. A third should contain the cold tea or coffee in tightly corked bottles, the sliced lemons and sugar in a glass jar with a screw-top, and pickles or olives. If you have fruit, give it a small hamper by itself, an ornamental one if convenient, which may be lined with fresh leaves on the picnic ground and passed from guest to guest. Take care to pitch your sylvan tent in contiguity to well, spring, or brook, from which you can get water for filling up lemonade-jar and water-pail. Carry a lump of ice, wrapped tightly in newspapers and bound with packthread. Unless the distance is great, it may then be folded in a gossamer rubber cloak and done up in a shawl-strap, or in a hand-basket. Ask your guests to take shawls and waterproofs. In the driest weather it is never prudent to sit on the ground without such protection.

Arrived at the appointed place, serve your little feast while daylight lasts, postponing strolls, boating, and games until it is over. Make a frolic of setting the table. Young and old will enter zestfully into the business of the hour. Appoint committees, if you will, upon substantials, cake, fruit, lemonade-making, water-bearing, and the like. If you have salad, prepare the dressing at home and take it out in a sealed jar or bottle, the salad itself, cut up and ready for dressing, in a bowl tied about in a napkin. Dress it altogether in the bowl when everything else is ready. Cut the sandwiches of uniform size, and wrap in packages of a dozen each in white tissue-paper. Devilled, or stuffed eggs, should be enveloped singly in squares of tissue-paper fringed at two ends and twisted lightly about the eggs. Berries must have a bowl or fancy basket of their own. Take sugar for them in a tumbler, tied up securely, and small saucers. The ice should be unpacked, washed, cracked, and a piece put into each tumbler. Pass sugar with coffee, tea, and lemonade for those who like these very sweet. There should be no carving done on the ground. Fowls should be jointed, tongue and other meats carved at home and wrapped in close piles, in thick white paper. Use printed paper for nothing except ice.

The ladies should be seated alternately with attendants of the other sex, and the waiting, replenishing glasses and plates, etc., be done by the latter. Have a certain easy decorum in the appointment and conduct of the collation, holding the direction of this in your own hands. Impress by your example and bearing what gay young people are prone to forget under the influence of out-door air and scenes, to wit, that informality and lawlessness are not interchangeable terms. Stand as pleasantly upon the order of your feast as you will, but do not let it degenerate into a scramble.

Boiled Ham.

Soak all night in cold water. In the morning wash and scrub it well, put it over the fire in plenty of cold water, and boil fifteen minutes to the pound. Run a skewer or knitting-needle into the thickest part, and if it goes in easily, take off the pot and let the ham get cold in the water.

Strip off the skin then, and slice as much as you need for your picnic, using a sharp knife and cutting the slices very thin.

For sandwiches, butter the end of the loaf after removing the crust, and cut into thin, uniform slices, buttering the loaf between the removal of each piece and the next. This is a neater and easier way of spreading bread than slicing the bread and then applying the butter. If you put the slices of ham in whole, do it smoothly, trimming each to fit the bread, and leaving but a narrow margin of fat on the lean. If you spread a little made mustard on the meat, divide the sandwiches containing this seasoning from the others, and give your guests the choice between them and the plain slices.

Chopped ham is much preferred by many to the whole slices in making sandwiches. Mince it in a chopping-tray, season with pepper, work in a *little* melted butter to make a slightly-coherent paste, and spread between the buttered slices of bread.

Boiled Tongue.

Soak overnight in cold water. In the morning scrape off the grease and dust, put over the fire in plenty of cold water, and boil four hours if the tongue is of fair size. Take out of the water, peel away the skin, and return the tongue to the water until cold. Slice and pack in a close parcel, buttering bread to pass with it, or make into sandwiches, slicing thin and lengthwise—that is, from the tip to the root, which, of course, cannot be used. The advantages of cutting it thus, instead of in the usual way, is, first, in superior tenderness, then in the facility offered for dividing the tongue-slices evenly and impartially to fit the bread.

Sweetbread Sandwiches.

Boil two sweetbreads twenty minutes in salted hot water. Take them out and plunge into *very cold*, leaving them there for an hour. Wipe them dry, mince, season with pepper and salt, work in a tablespoonful of melted butter, and spread between buttered bread.

The two sweetbreads will fill perhaps six sandwiches. Mixed with an equal quantity of chopped ham they will suffice for a dozen. This is the best sandwich mixture I know of.

Chicken-and-Ham Sandwiches.

If chickens are dear and scarce, buy for sixty cents a can of boned chicken; mince and mix with a like quantity of chopped ham, seasoning with pepper, and adding a little melted butter.

This will fill two dozen large sandwiches, thirty small ones.

Sardine Sandwiches.

Open a half-box of sandwiches, take out the fish and drain off every drop of oil by leaving them in a colander for an hour, then spreading on thick, soft paper. Remove the backbones, and one by one scrape them into bits with a knife and fork. Work into the picked fish a little cayenne pepper, a tablespoonful of melted butter, and the juice of two lemons. Spread the paste between buttered slices of bread.

Egg Sandwiches.

Boil six eggs hard, drop them into cold water and leave for half an hour. Peel and chop *very* fine, rub to a paste with a tablespoonful of melted butter, salt and pepper to taste, and spread on the bread.

Or,

Slice the hard-boiled eggs when they are cold with a keen, clean knife, butter, pepper, and salt each slice, and lay closely together between buttered bread.

Cheese Sandwiches.

Grate dry, mild cheese, work in cayenne pepper and salt to taste, then a little melted butter, and spread in the usual way.

Beef Loaf.

1½ lb. of raw beef, cut into small dice.
⅛ lb. of fat salt pork, minced.
½ cup of crushed cracker—very fine.
1 egg.
1 teaspoonful of salt, and the same of pepper.
1 small tablespoonful of butter.

Season to taste with minced or powdered sage, parsley, or summer savory.

Work the mixture up well in a chopping-tray and pack in a buttered bowl or mould. Cover very closely, set in a dripping-pan of hot water, and cook one hour and a quarter, replenishing the pan with boiling water as it evaporates. When done, take from the oven, press a closely fitting plate or saucer down upon the surface of the loaf, and set a flat-iron on this. Let it stand thus all night. When you are ready for it, turn out and slice with a sharp knife.

FAMILIAR TALK.

DISH-WASHING.

AKIN in absurdity to the belief prevalent with men that all women take naturally to the use of the needle, is the impression, not confined to the sterner sex, that all varieties of household work are equally agreeable to her whose turn of mind and taste is "domestic." In no other department of duty and labor are specialties more distinctly defined, or the liking for one and aversion for another occupation more decided.

I think that I hardly hazard contradiction in asserting that next to washing the soiled linen of a family—work now almost universally committed to hired laundresses—the least popular branch of household employment is the cleansing of vessels used in the preparation of food, those in which it goes to the table, and in which it is served to the consumers. The arbitrary term "dish-washing" is supposed to cover the ground, and is varied in some mouths by the still less descriptive definition, "washing up *the things*"—a sigh of patient wearriness or impatient contempt often supplying the emphasis. I recall, now, the flush that suffused the wan face of a city missionary's wife when detailing to me the nature and amount of the exactions that had worn her down from a pretty accomplished girl to a hollowed-eyed drudge, who "had no time to keep up reading, study, or music." She had five children, a parish, and one servant, did most of the family sewing, helped with the fine ironing, and had no one to assist her, in turn, with nursery and chamber work.

"I have never stood at the wash-tub," she concluded. "And I will *not* wash dishes! *That* form of degradation has, up to this time, been spared me."

In the depth of my compassion I did make to her a confession I hesitate to utter in the hearing of certain very exemplary women who look well to the ways of their household, and do not know so much as the taste of the bread of idleness. I like to wash dishes! I am secretly pleased when domestic exigencies in the form of illness, absence, and "change" indicate the expediency of my assumption of this part of the family service for the day. I enjoy getting hold of the china, that cannot be to any one what it is to the house-mistress; like to rub the silver bright with soft linen as it is drawn from the scalding suds; to dry, with a dexterous twist of the glass towel, crystal almost too hot to handle, and hold it up to the light to be sure no cloud remains to mar its sparkle and clearness. The taste may be plebeian, but it is ineradicable.

Bear with me, contemptuous reader, while I relate in partial justification of the idiosyncrasy the manner in which the friend who taught me dish-washing as a fine art conducts the process.

She has two pans—large and of the same size—set on a table in the light closet adjoining the dining-room.

"The sink of a butler's pantry would be more convenient," she says, blithely, "but, you see, I haven't a butler's pantry!"

One pan contains clean *hot* suds, in which she dips, as soon as the table is cleared, first the silver, then emptied cups and saucers, next, the scraped plates, lastly, the dishes; putting in several pieces at a time, giving each a swirl with a mop, to rid it of grease or sweets, and setting it, dripping wet, on a broad tray. When all have been rinsed, she throws away the much-abhorred "dishwater," once and forever. With it go reek and scum, and all that could offend even my poor "born lady," who shrank from this form of degradation. If my friend is not ready to finish the task, she returns the china—not glass and silver—to the rinsing-pan, when she has scalded this, and pours clean warm water over the pile, to await her convenience. If the business is to be got out of hand forthwith, she lays her "Dover Soap-shaker" clasped fast over a piece of hard yellow soap in the bottom of the second pan, and sends a jet of scalding water directly from the teakettle upon the wire cup. A miniature geyser arises, foaming and seething, until, when the pan is two-thirds full of water, the snowy lather, the very essence and type of purification, heaves upward to the brim. The glasses go in first, each being dipped deftly full of hot water as soon as it touches the surface. There is no danger of breaking when this is done. Each is fished up with a second mop (that used for rinsing being kept for that purpose only), and wiped quickly with the finest of the cup towels. When the last glass is drawn out, the silver takes its turn. Every article is rubbed fast and hard in the drying. Usually, the strong, scalding suds suffice, with this friction, to polish it. If a spoon or fork is tarnished, a tooth-brush kept for this office, rubbed on Indexical Silver Soap or dipped in "Electro-Silicon," sets all right. Next comes the china; lastly, what coarser ware may need attention—bowls, pitchers, and the like. Nothing is *drained*. That process of the slow and easy hireling or ignorant housewife our artist repudiates with fine scorn. She takes out and wipes her treasures, piece by piece.

The pile disposed of in shining rows, ready for table or cupboard, the pans are washed, emptied, wiped, and hung up, the mops wrung hard, shaken well, and returned to their nails; and the satisfied housewife takes off her bib-apron and her gloves. That dish-washing may be done with gloves on, she demonstrates triumphantly, thus avoiding chapped hands in winter, and red, sodden fingers at all seasons. Her gauntlets are a pair of old wash-leather gloves discarded by her husband, and fitting her hands loosely. She cut off the finger-tips, tacked each seam at the top to prevent ripping, and sewed elastic ribbon at the wrists, to keep them close and firm. When they get wet, she stretches them in the sun to dry.

"I never dreamed there could be invented a *toney* way of washing dishes," cried a gay collegian, who chanced to witness the operation. "I believe you could dignify a scrubbing-brush!"

He touched the secret without unfolding it. No species of honest labor is in itself degrading. Every task, performed because it is duty and for others' good, is dignified and ennobling.

Hired servants do not, unless tutored and watched, wash dishes in the manner above described. Nor yet coarse-natured, hard-handed women whose "best things" are kept for high-days and city company, and who eschew as "finical" napkins and butter-knives. But she whose genuine ladyhood subordinates her cheap surroundings who, faithfully making the best of herself, brings circumstances up to her level—or the well-to-do matron who winces at the sight of what a wondering masculine householder once called in my hearing "*fringed* china," yet cannot drill her servants into tenderness of touch and dainty method—may with propriety and profit follow this lesson in "Dish-washing made easy."

NEST-BUILDING.

"THAT is the key-note," said a celebrated painter, dashing what looked like a broad charcoal scrawl on a sheet of drawing-paper. " Now we will work up to it!"

The youthful pair, bent upon the conversion of the enchanting abstraction—" our home "—into the concrete of "our house," may take a hint from the anecdote. The inharmonious interior of many households results from inattention to the cardinal law of consistency in design and tone. A pernicious custom, more in vogue formerly than now, ordained the postponement of the furnishment of "the parlor" until the family finances warranted the execution of the task in "handsome" style. When the auspicious period arrived, the effect of new cloth upon an old garment had the added element of garishness. The spick-and-span splendor of the state apartment agreed as well with the rest of the house as a figure cut from a Japanese screen would consort with the environments, if pasted upon one of Raphael's age-mellow cartoons.

The bride of our day is apt to blunder to the other extreme of making her parlor the key-note and working other rooms up to it. There can be no question as to the comparative taste of the two methods—and none as to the comparative economy.

To descend to details and practical talk: In beginning house-keeping, first get your house. Avoid the error of choosing too large a shell. The pains and expense that would suffice to make a small house pretty would diffuse scant desolateness throughout a large one. The Darby and Joan in whose behalf this sketch is penned, desire to house, not establish, themselves. We assume, furthermore, that they are not yet able or ready to build. They have hired, at a nominally moderate rate, one of a block of brick tenements, two-and-a-half stories high and two rooms deep. Every house-hunter knows the stereotyped topography of such. Being a cheap construction, there is not even the relief of a bay-window in the front elevation. If Joan would introduce nookiness as an element of home comfort she must make it after the fashion of the Israelites' bricks. Darby whistles softly and not merrily as they tramp up and down the uncarpeted stairs; the bare rectangles of the walls give back their young voices in unsympathetic echoes.

"I suppose it will look different when the furniture—and you—are in it," he says.

The honest affection which is his best substitute for tact transforms the dreary scene for the brave little wife.

"It begins to feel like home already!" she cries. "We can't make it grand, dear, and if we could, grandeur does not go well with youth. But we can and we will make it cosy!"

She uses the first person plural in loving compliment. But it is she who spends succeeding weeks in examinations many and purchases not a few. The pleasant face is more sober than her husband could wish, and the smile of welcome that greets his return at evening does not efface the thought-lines which he dreads may deepen into care-furrows by-and-by. Once he wonders aloud "if the game is worth the candle."

Joan's start has the energy of surprise.

"I never enjoyed anything more! And it is such fun keeping within our means."

He does not understand the fact or the fun when the spirit of manly incaution leads him to enter a fashionable carpet emporium and ask the price of parlor carpets. The cheapest and tawdriest Brussels exhibited to him is $1.50 per yard. At his low-spirited mention of the size of the front parlor, he is told that at least twenty-four yards will be required for that room alone.

"If you would like to look at a good body-Brussels, now?" insinuates the salesman.

"Is that less expensive?"

It takes more than the modicum of moral courage possessed by the average masculine customer to say "cheaper," in such a presence and place.

"Not less expensive in one sense, perhaps, sir"—with a smile of compassionate patronage—"but in the end, the best."

Darby does not look at the body-Brussels. He murmurs that he may call again. In sad truth he knows that he will not. It is Joan's affair, not his, he discovers, and with a wretched chuckle born of pity and discouragement, he wonders what she will say when she comes to parlor carpets. She says nothing on the subject. If she has struck the reef she hoists no signal of distress. Her eye is brighter, her silent smile more significant as "opening-day" approaches. Papa, as is the duty and privilege of fathers who can do it, has given her a sum for furnishing. It is all that he can spare, and, as he thinks, all she ought to expend. Darby knows him too well to suspect that he has added to it, and Joan too well to dream that she may have asked for more. Expeditions and consultations with mamma mean only that the latter is liberal with advice and such manual aid as nobody but a mother can lend.

The important day has arrived. Darby has not been admitted to the house since their first visit in company, but takes a half-holiday now, ostensibly for "moving."

"We will begin at the bottom," chirps his conductor, unlocking the basement-door.

The floor of the tiny entry is covered with linoleum, in a block pattern, buff-and-white, with sparse cubes of red.

"It is prettier than oil-cloth, and cheaper," says Joan. The word has no terrors for her. "Moreover, the smell is not so disagreeable."

The strip of gay Venetian carpeting on the stairs is woven in the same colors.

"It is not easy to make a basement dining-room cheerful," continues the little mistress, warningly, her hand on the knob of that door. "I did think of using the back-parlor as an eating-room. But there was no dumb-waiter, and no china-closet on that floor, and, as mamma says, food will attract flies, do what you will, and in warm weather the room would have to be kept so dark on that account that we could not sit in it except at meal-times. And it is a convenience to have eating-room and kitchen on the same floor. So I did my best."

It is a seemly best in Darby's eyes. Fortunately, the room is well lighted by two front windows of good size. So much of the floor as is visible—that is, a strip eighteen inches wide next to the walls—is stained Spanish brown. A large rug in a warmer shade of red-brown covers the middle of the floor. Darby stoops to examine what looks to him like Turkish towelling, the deep fringe at two ends corroborating the impression.

"Such a 'find'!" Joan relapses into girlish slang in her glee. "Of course we could not think of velvet or Brussels for any room." Darby pinches a corner of the rug in his wince. "And tapestries are so gaudy, as a rule!

So I asked boldly for ingrain! I told mamma we had resolved that our life should be even-threaded all through. No veneer, no shams, and no sophistries. I explained frankly to the carpet-merchant that we must furnish economically and wanted to furnish prettily. Like the duck he is, he brought out this. It is ingrain in one color, and unfigured, a yard wide, alike on both sides, wears forever, cost one dollar and ten cents a yard, and needs no making up. He told me how to do it. I sewed the breadths together, fringed out and "serged" the raw ends, and left the selvage sides just as they were. The rug can be lifted and shaken every day, and should be turned often to make it wear evenly and prevent the edges from curling. Ten yards will go as far as twelve of Brussels or tapestry, that has but one wearable side."

The table in the middle of the room is spread with a buff-and-white tea-cloth. The recess on each side of the mantel is filled with shelves of yellow pine rubbed with oil to a fine polish. They are breast-high, and the uppermost of each set projects an inch or more beyond the others. The shelves nearest the window hold Joan's small acquisitions of ornamental china. A felt curtain, in color like the rug, with bands of buff laid on with feather-stitch, and hung from a ringed pole, is partly withdrawn.

"That gilt rod is a bit of gas-pipe," twitters Joan. "I bought it from a plumber and gilded it myself. The curtain-poles on the next floor I had turned roughly, and covered them with black velvet, that sets off the brass rings finely. Here is another cheap device," lifting the buff cloth. "The wide felting used by rich people for underlying their damask table-cloths is awfully dear. I bought Canton-flannel, sewed it together in the middle, hemmed the ends, and spread it on, the wrong side up. It makes the cloth lie smoothly, look richer, and hinders it from wearing so fast as it would on the naked table, and cost just eighty cents.. I couldn't afford window-curtains here; I think, too, they would darken the room too much. The buff linen shades must do for awhile."

Pine shelves are fitted at the bottom of the sashes. Pots of ivy stand on these, and the flexile stems follow and drape the window-frames.

A head of a setter-dog, done in charcoal and framed in yellow pine polished and varnished, hangs over the mantel; water-color pictures of quail and snipe on the opposite wall.

"You recognize my work?" smiles the exhibitor. "The frames were fifty cents a piece. This," tapping the uncurtained shelves, "is our buffet—our sideboard—meant for holding plates, knives, and forks between the change of courses. This"—she raises the cushioned top of a low, wide box, nearly six feet in length, filling the space between the door by which they entered and the front wall —"is my linen chest. I shall keep here such napery as we have in daily use. I stuffed and covered it!"

It is upholstered with carpeting like the rug. A square, fat pillow of buff-and-red-brown cretonne lies at the wall end.

"A cool place for a nap on hot Sunday afternoons!" says Darby. Joan claps her hands.

"Just what I told mamma you would say! When summer comes I will slip on a buff Holland cover. Doesn't this room look really furnished—considering?"

There are but six chairs, walnut with cane bottoms, besides what we have described, if we except a clock under the picture of the dog, and an ice-pitcher and glasses on the "buffet" top. But Darby's warmth of speech is sincere.

"I don't see what we could do with more furniture!"

"And nobody need know—we would die before we would whisper it," Joan fastens on his arm and grows yet more emphatic, her face and feet restless with mischief and happiness, "but the top of the table is plebeian pine —if the legs *are* genteelly turned—and a lame carpenter in a back street made the chest and shelves and picture-frames, and a German painter's apprentice stained the floor under my direction. I don't mind confiding to you, moreover, that everything in this room—except my scraps of china, of course, that I have been collecting for years— cost just fifty-one dollars, eighty-seven and a half cents."

Between dining-room and kitchen are two doors and a passage five feet long; on the right of this, china shelves behind a sliding glass door, on the left, a blank wall. The kitchen looks out upon a neat backyard. A couple of stationary tubs are one flank of a sink, a copper boiler the other. Under it is a pot-and-kettle closet. The modern improvements are packed into the smallest possible space consistent with availableness. The floor is painted; the range shining clean. Two tables and three wooden chairs —one of them a low rocker—compose the movable furniture.

"A trifle cheerless," Joan admits, blithely; "but when the fire is lighted it will look different. Here is my mixing room!" opening the door of communication with the small apartment cut off from the back hall.

A table is set against the solitary window. Before this a rug knitted of woollen strips, warm, thick, and serviceable, lies on the painted floor. A broad ledge runs along one side of the room. Under it are a covered flour barrel, above which a square section of the ledge is hinged like a trap-door. Several wooden buckets for holding sugar and other dry groceries are ranged in a line with the barrel. From a row of nails over the shelf depend egg-beater, spoons—iron, wire, and wooden—toasting-fork, cake-turner, and a dozen other light implements. Bright tin-ware and kitchen-crockery are in neat array on the shelf, with pastry-board, chopping and bread-trays, etc.

If Joan was content in the dining-room, she is jubilant here.

"The dearest, jolliest, most fascinating little nook!" she avers, perching herself on the coner of the table while she enumerates its charms. "In winter it can be warmed by opening the door. In summer the kitchen door will be shut while I am busy in here; that leading into the hall, and the window, be opened. There need be no litter of materials in the kitchen, and on washing-day, when I must run down to toss up something nice for dinner, I shall not be suffocated by soapy steam. In this corner I hope to be queen. Mamma says no servant would keep it as orderly as I would; that most young housekeepers make the mistake of expecting such work from hirelings as they would do themselves. She told me to be careful always to wash the bowls, spoons, etc., that I have used, and put them back in their places; to brush up the floor and wipe the table clean when I have finished my work. She thinks one reason so many servants dislike to have the 'mistress' in the kitchen is that she makes so much clearing up for them. She is a hinderance rather than a help. 'Our girl' enters upon her duties to-morrow. She is young, and will need training, but mamma says I ought to be able to do that, and it will be better and pleasanter for me to lead and instruct from the beginning than to be tutored by an elderly woman who is 'set' in her way. That mother of mine is a wonderfully wise woman!"

"She has a marvellously sensible daughter," rejoins the three-month-old bridegroom, following her up the stairs.

If he had been told that he would find the parlors laid

with ingrain carpets, his pride as a home-owner and his taste would have revolted together. Yet such is the fact. The figureless fabric here is a rich, tawny tint, like that of a bed of woodland moss on which successive frosts have fallen gently. Joan terms it "dark old-gold," and it is relieved by a border of shaded olive and scarlet. The hall is carpeted to match, as is the mere closet above the mixing room dignified by the title of "library."

The walls throughout the house are "hard-finish."

"We had to put up with it in the other stories," represents the italical little manager, "but I made a stand here, and talked the landlord into agreeing to put a *cheap* paper on the walls. He named the price he was willing to give and graciously permitted me to choose the pattern. With five of the eight dollars I had saved (from the sixty I had allowed for the dining-room) added to his limit, I bought from James C. Munroe, 179 Devonshire Street, Boston—don't laugh—'ingrain paper' for these three rooms and the entry. It comes in plain colors, and has double the weight of ordinary wall-paper. Is not this creamy-brown, or brownish-cream, a luxury to the eye? And it harmonizes perfectly with the carpet, without having a touch of the metallic yellow so trying to the complexion."

A hat-rack with a small mirror set in it is hung in the hall; a spindle-legged table that was Joan's grandmother's beneath it; a bracket covered with birch-bark, on which is painted a thorny bough incrusted with lichens, is fastened on the wall between the front and back parlor doors. A gray trail of Spanish moss floats from it; upon it a benevolently complacent owl stands guard, a crotched branch interwoven by a vireo's nest projects upward. Half-drawn *portieres* of Turkey-red cotton hang in the parlor doors. They are lined with cream-colored silesia, and bands of olive-and-scarlet cretonne are laid near the top and bottom. Similar hangings drape the parlor windows, front and back.

"The lining tempers the red glare, and makes a cheap material look like one that cost twice as much," reports Joan. "When a room is properly papered, curtained, and carpeted, it may be said to be three-quarters furnished. I have long considered a parlor sofa a cumbrous monument to popular prejudice. I could write an essay upon 'The Sofa' longer than Cowper's poem. It is expensive, clumsy, and as inconvenient in a small room as an elephant in a horse's stall. Etiquette forbids men to seat themselves upon it while ladies occupy chairs; yet the youth of the present day delights to establish himself thereupon. People ought not to lounge in reception and drawing-rooms. What is needed there is encouragement to conversation. As a seat, the sofa is like the glutton's turkey—'inconvenient; being too much for two and not enough for three.' Here are my substitutes for the costly monster."

She shows two wicker chairs, painted black and lightly gilded, which she has cushioned in the seats and padded at the backs; also three reception chairs, black-and-gilt, the rush bottoms painted in stripes of white and scarlet. A Japanese stand and an ebonized cabinet were wedding presents, as were three fine engravings. A round table is draped with a cloth embroidered by another friend. There is an easy-chair upholstered in raw silk, old-gold and black; a bamboo easel (price $5) supports the largest of the engravings: a pale blue scarf of soft woollen stuff breaks the sharpness of one corner. Pale blue is repeated in a silken banner screen and a trophy of Japanese fans. On one end of the mantel is a clock; a cluster of thistle balls, white and fluffy, are suspended by a scarlet cord from a gas bracket. Various pretty trifles, such as girls delight in and gather to themselves by unconscious attraction, are arranged on stands and mantel. A few choice books, the kind that suggest thought and discussion, rest on the table; several unframed photographs help to cover and ornament the walls. A foot-cushion, pale blue, appliqué with scarlet, lies before the easy-chair; a square ottoman, stuffed to match the latter, is at the corner of the hearth.

"Home manufacture," Joan remarks. "Except the turned legs."

In the door-way connecting the parlors is a curtain that Darby examines curiously.

"Odd and oriental," is his comment.

"Made of silk strips—cast-off ribbons and the like—sewed together as our grandmothers joined rags for carpets, and woven into magnificence by John Ryan, 83 Bowery!" he is informed. "You will see the same in the door between the library and this"—passing into the back room. "I call this our retreat, the heart of the home, your bower of repose! It is where you and I are to *live* and learn what *home* is! I consider it my *chef d'œuvre*."

She would say "the key-note," if she had ever heard the anecdote with which our sketch began. She made a mental cartoon of it, first of all, in entering upon her work of love, and has wrought the rest up to it. Darby puts out his arm to draw her closer to him as the reposeful hush, the heart-comfort of the place, steal into his soul.

There is a lounge here. Joan had it made to order—half as wide again as the conventional pattern, with a long, easy slope at the head, and with no back—then covered it with cretonne; old-gold and black picked out with scarlet. Pillows of turkey-red heap it into luxuriousness. A folded afghan falls over the head slope. There is a twist of red drapery about the frame of the portrait of Darby's mother over the mantel, a plume of pampas grass behind it.

Screens of trellised ivy hide the view of the clothes-yard. A Shaker rocker is set near a basket work-stand. An ancient arm-chair, an heirloom, has been stuffed into plumpness and comfort, and covered with cretonne like that on the lounge. At the left elbow is a round table. The sweeping cloth repeats the tint of the wall-paper, and is finished at the edges with deep scallops embroidered with scarlet silk. A student's lamp—the porcelain shade of softest, most grateful green—a foot-rest in suggestive proximity to the chair, two or three magazines, a paper-weight, even this morning's newspaper, show without need of spoken hint where the tired master is to be most completely and happily at home. No two chairs in this apartment are alike. Most are low—all are comfortable.

"I picked them up at odd times and places, and made a frolic of rigging them out," says Joan.

She is no artist, but she is thankful for the measure of taste and skill that has enabled her to prepare the charcoal sketches Darby greets as old friends. "It all goes to help make home."

The library bookcases are breast-high, and stocked with her books and her husband's. The shelves, like those below stairs, are of polished yellow pine, and edged with notched strips of red morocco. Joan tacked them on with brass-headed nails, and fastened down with the same the red baize on the topmost shelf. On this are three plaster casts. A baize-covered table, and an office chair, a study-lamp, inkstand, portfolio, and blotting-book, testify that work and not leisure is to bear rule here. A curtain of olive felt, banded with scarlet, shades the one window.

The bedroom floors are stained, and rugs of the invaluable ingrain are laid down. In the guest-chamber are muslin curtains; in Joan's own, cretonne. The floor of the bath-room is covered with linoleum. There is abundant store of sheets, and towels, and white counterpanes, clean, warm blankets, and no comfortables or bed-quilts, if we except a *duvet*, or *couvre-pied*, thrown across the foot of each bed. The furniture is of inexpensive native woods: in one room ash, in the other poplar. In the servant's chamber are an iron bedstead, a good bureau, washstand, and rocking-chair.

In neither of the second-story bedrooms are there many ornament. Mamma's pupil sensibly reasons that the dust of sleeping apartments should be dislodged and expelled every day; that china figures, and vases, picture frames, and plaques, and dried grasses, and Japanese umbrellas collect flying particles which Professor Tyndall warns us contain embryotic bacteria. If undisturbed they breed evil to human lives, and to get rid of so many myriads requires more time than our Joan can spare.

Thoroughness and consistency are the leaven of good housewifery as of stable character. To unite taste and true economy; to be content when the result reached is comfort and prettiness, with no incongruous streakings of splendor; to sound a key-note that shall bring the whole composition within the easy compass of those who are to conduct it—this is to make the true best of one's self and the means at her disposal; to be honest and ingrain throughout.

INDEX.

	PAGE
INTRODUCTORY TALK	1

SOUPS.

	PAGE
Soup and Stock-pots (*Familiar Talk*)	9

Fish Soups 15

	PAGE
Catfish soup	18
Clam "	16
" chowder	17
Cod "	18
Eel soup	20
Fish "	15
Lobster bisque	19
Oyster soup	16

Vegetable Soups.

	PAGE
Bean soup	24
" and corn soup	25
" " tomato soup	25
Canned corn soup	28
Green pea and potato soup	26
Katherine's soup	22
Lenten soup, A	21
Onion "	22
Pea and rice purée	27
Peas, a purée of	26
Potato soup	24

	PAGE
Quick potato purée	26
Tomato soup	28
" and rice broth	27
Turnip purée	29

Meat Soups.

	PAGE
Bone soup	30
Chicken and corn soup	31
Clear sago soup	32
Family soup, A	30
Giblet "	32
Ham "	29
Mutton broth	33
Scotch soup, A	34
Scrap " "	34

MEATS.

	PAGE
FAMILIAR TALK	36
Beef	52
Beef, braised	53
" boiled *with vegetables*	52
" chipped	61
" corned	58
" " , pressed	59
" hash	60
" mode, à la	53

	PAGE		PAGE
Beef, pie	58	Calf's head spiced	51
" " , potato crust for	58	" " stew of	50
" roast	55	Veal, stewed breast of	44
" scalloped	57	" chops	47
" steak	54	" cutlets	47
" " and onions	57	" pie	45
" stew	55	" scallop	45
" stew, *Irish*	56	" savory stew of	46
Mutton	38	**FAMILIAR TALK.**	
Mutton boiled, shoulder of	39	COUNTRY BOARDING	67
" brown stew of	42		
" minced, on toast	43	*Chicken*	73
" mince of	44	Chicken, boiled, and rice	73
" pudding (No. 1)	42	" brown fricassee of	74
" " (No. 2)	43	" pot-pie, old-fashioned	75
" roast, breast of	38	" scallop	76
" stew of	39	" and egg scallop	76
" stewed, with dumplings	40	" smothered	74
" summer stew of	41	" stewed whole	73
		" Virginia stew of	77
Pork	62		
Bacon and apples	65	EGGS	78
Barbecued ham	65	Eggs, baked	78
Pork and beans	62	" boiled	78
Pork chops	63	" breaded	80
Pork pie	64	" cups	80
Pork and pea pudding	64	" devilled	81
" salt, and potato-stew	63	" dropped	82
" stewed	62	" in the nest	81
Sausages	66	" scalloped	78
		" scrambled	82
Veal	44	" " with shad-roes	83
Calf's head	48	" stewed	79
" liver, larded	49	" on toast	79
" " smothered	50		

INDEX.

	PAGE
Omelettes	83
Omelette, baked	83
" aux fines herbes	84
" ham	84
" plain	83
" tomato	84

SALADS...... 84

Salad, beet	87
" cabbage	84
" celery	87
" lettuce	85
" lobster, crab, and halibut	89
" mayonnaise, dressing for	87
" potato	86
" salmon	88
" tomato	87
" tomato and lettuce	89
" water-cress	86

FISH 89

Clam-fritters	92
Codfish, boiled (*fresh*)	89
" " (*salt*)	90
Cod (salt), lunch or supper-dish	95
Cold fish, how to use up	90
Fish, fried	91
Halibut, baked	95
Herrings, Scotch	92
Mackerel, creamed	91
Salmon croquettes	94
" fricassee of	93
" pudding	93
" strips	93

FAMILIAR TALK.

	PAGE
TABLE MANNERS	97

VEGETABLES.... 103

Asparagus	109
Asparagus biscuit	111
" and eggs	110
" pudding	110
" on toast	109

Beans	111
Beans, boiled (*dried*)	112
" buttered	112
" fried	114
" Lima, and other shell	114
" Lyonnaise, à	113
" string (*fresh*)	114
" " (*canned*)	115
" stewed (*dried*)	111
" with white sauce	113

Beets	133
Beets, boiled	133
" Lyonnaise	133

Cabbage	131
Cabbage, boiled plain	131
" scalloped	131

Corn	119
Corn, boiled	119
" (*canned*) fritters	120
" (*canned*) pudding	121
" chopped and potatoes	121
" green, fritters	120
" " pudding	120
Succotash	121

INDEX.

	PAGE
Hominy	122
Hominy, baked	123
" boiled	122
" croquettes	123
" fried	122
Macaroni	124
Macaroni, baked	124
" Bettina's	126
" in Italian style	124
" with onion sauce	125
" moulded	126
Onions	132
Onions, boiled	132
" fricasseed	132
Parsnips	136
Parsnips, boiled	136
" fried	136
" with white sauce	136
Peas	133
Peas, boiled	133
" canned, green	134
" green, pancakes	134
Pea purée on toast	134
Potatoes	103
Potatoes, browned	104
Potato croquettes	106
Potatoes, fried	105
" Lyonnaise	109
" old, boiled	103
" " stewed	103
" puff	106
" scalloped (No. 1)	104
" " (No. 2)	105

	PAGE
Potatoes, soufflé	108
" stewed	107
" " (cold, boiled)	108
" " in gravy	107
" stuffed	107
" whipped	104
Radishes	137
Rice	127
Rice, boiled plain	127
" " and cheese	128
" croquettes	130
" giblet pudding	129
" savory	129
" " pudding	129
" with tomato sauce	128
Spinach	118
Spinach, boiled	118
Squash	118
Squash, boiled	118
" scalloped	119
Tomatoes	115
Tomatoes, baked (canned)	116
" " (fresh, No. 1)	116
" " " No. 2)	117
" scalloped and corn	117
" stewed (canned)	115
" " (fresh)	116
" " and corn	117
Turnips	135
Turnips, boiled	135
" mashed	135
" stewed	135

INDEX.

PORRIDGE OF VARIOUS KINDS 137

Porridge, crumb 139
" Indian meal 138
" Little Boy's 140
" milk 138
Mush-and-milk 138
Porridge, oatmeal 137

FAMILIAR TALK.

MAID-OF-ALL-WORK 141

CHEESE DISHES ... 145

Cheese cups 146
" pot 145
" pudding 146
" sandwiches 147
Welsh rarebit 147

BREAD 148

Bread, Boston brown 153
" Graham 151
" sponge 149
" raised with sponge .. 149
" without sponge 151
Biscuit, bonny-clabber 154
" Graham 154
" quick 153
Light rolls 152
Yeast 148
Crackers, toasted 155

Some ways of using stale bread 155
Toast, buttered 155
" cream 156
" tomato 156
" water 155

Muffins, corn-bread and griddle-cakes 157
Bread-crumb cakes 163
Cakes, buckwheat 161
" buttermilk 164
" flannel, without eggs . 163
" Graham griddle 163
" hominy griddle 162
" Indian meal 162
" mush 164
Corn bread, boiled 160
" " risen 159
Gems, Graham 159
Muffins, hominy 158
" minute 157
" risen, English 157
Sally Lunn, Indian meal ... 160
" " (wheaten) 158
Wafers 161
Waffles 165

Useful Rule for Mixing Dough and Batter.

PUDDINGS 166

Apple dumplings (baked) .. 170
" " (boiled) ... 170
" méringue 167
" bread pudding 168
" tapioca " 167
" scallop 169
" snow 170
Batter pudding 179
Bread pudding (boiled) 172
" and raisin pudding .. 171
" sugarless, " ... 171
" lemon, " ... 173
Berry pudding 181

INDEX.

	PAGE		PAGE
Corn meal pudding	182	Apples stewed	191
" " hasty pudding	183	Cherries, stewed	193
" starch pudding (baked)	176	Pears (sweet) baked	192
" " minute pudding,	177	" stewed	192
sauce for	177	Plums and berries stewed	193
Cottage pudding	179	Quinces, stewed	192
Cracker "	174		
Fried hasty pudding	183	**STEWED DRIED FRUITS.**	193
Graham minute pudding	177		
Lemon "	180	Apples dried, stewed	193
Macaroni (plain) "	180	Cherries " "	193
" (baked) "	181	Peaches " "	193
Marmalade "	176	Pears " "	193
Maude's "	166	Pie-plant "	194
Rice pudding (baked)	178		
" " (custard)	178	**JAMS AND MARMALADE.**	194
" " (hasty)	178		
" " (tapioca)	178	Apple Marmalade	195
Roley-poley pudding	182	Berry jam	194
Suet " (No. 1).	175	Gooseberry jam	195
" " (No. 2).	175	Red Raspberry jam	195
Tapioca " (No. 1).	173	Strawberry "	195
" " (No. 2).	174	Peach marmalade	195
Toad-in-a-hole pudding	168	Quince "	195
PUDDING SAUCES	183	**FRUIT JELLIES**	196
Custard pudding sauce	185		
Hard " "	183	Blackberry and Raspberry jelly	197
Jelly " "	184	Crab apple jelly	197
Lemon " "	184	Currant "	196
Liquid " "	184	Grape "	197
		Quince "	197
FAMILIAR TALK.			
"KITCHENLY-KIND"	186	**PICKLES**	197
STEWED AND BAKED FRUITS	191		
		Cabbage pickle	202
Apples, baked	191	Green "	197
Apples (sweet) baked	191	" Tomato pickle	199

INDEX.

	PAGE
Peaches, pickled	201
Plums, "	200
Sweet pickles	200
Walnuts or butternuts, pickled	199
Vinegar, raspberry	202
Surplus syrup—how to use it	201

CAKES ... 203

	PAGE
Apple cake	209
" filling for cake	209
Berry shortcake	203
" " breakfast	204
Cocoanut cake, with filling	207
Cookies (No. 1)	212
" (No. 2)	212
" ginger	212
Corn starch cakes	215
Cream shortcake	203
" for filling cake	205
Cream puffs	211
Crullers	214
Cup cake, old-fashioned	205
Currant cakes	210
Doughnuts	214
Drop-cakes or Jumbles	213
Foundation for jelly or cream-cake	204
Gingerbread, soft	210
" unity	216
Ginger snaps	213
Huckleberry cake	208
Mamie's cake	206
Marble "	206
Méringue filling for cake	206
Nut-cake	207
Sponge-cake	208
Transformed baker's cake	209

CUSTARDS ... 216

	PAGE
Baked custard	218
Boiled "	216
Cocoanut "	219
Floating Island	217
Rice custard	219
Sago "	219
Snow pudding	220
Tapioca custard	218

FAMILIAR TALK.

FLIES	221

JELLIES AND BLANC-MANGE ... 226

Apple jelly	228
Arrowroot jelly	230
Cider "	226
Jelly and custard	229
" in oranges	227
Lemon jelly	226
Orange "	227
Peach "	229
Ribbon "	227
Sago "	230
Tapioca "	231

Blanc-mange.

Arrowroot blanc-mange	232
Bird's nest	237
Blanc-mange (plain)	231
Chocolate blanc-mange	233
Coffee "	235
Corn-starch "	232
Easter dessert	236
Farina blanc-mange	233
Jaune-mange	236

	PAGE
Medley blanc-mange	234
Pretty dish, A	235
Tapioca blanc-mange	232
Tea "	235

BEVERAGES..... 238

	PAGE
Apple tea	244
Café au lait	240
Chocolate	242
Coffee, breakfast	238
" black	239
" iced	243
Cocoa-nibs or shells	242
Lemonade	242
" flax-seed	244
" Iceland-moss	244
Tea	240
" à la Russe	243

	PAGE
Toast-water, or "crust-coffee"	243

PIC-NIC DISHES... 245

	PAGE
Beef-loaf	250
Cheese sandwiches	249
Chicken-and-ham sandwiches	249
Egg sandwiches	249
Ham, boiled	247
Sardine sandwiches	249
Sweetbread "	248
Tongue, boiled	248

FAMILIAR TALK.

	PAGE
DISH-WASHING	251
NEST-BUILDING	255

"*To those who love a pure diction, a healthful tone, and thought that leads up to the higher and better aims, that gives brighter color to some of the hard, dull phases of life, that awakens the mind to renewed activity, and makes one mentally better, the prose and poetical works of Dr. Holland will prove an ever new, ever welcome source from which to draw.*"—NEW HAVEN PALLADIUM.

Complete Writings of Dr. J. G. Holland

WITH THE AUTHOR'S REVISION.

Each one vol., 16mo, (sold separately,) Price, $1.25.

Messrs. CHARLES SCRIBNER'S SONS have now completed the issue of a New Edition of Dr. Holland's Writings, printed from new plates, in a very attractive style, in artistic binding, and at a greatly reduced price.

It is believed that the aggregate sale of Dr. Holland's Books, amounting as it does to half a million volumes, exceeds the circulation of the writings of any other American author. There is not a single book of his which has not had an unquestionable success, and most of them have been in such constant and increasing demand that the plates were actually worn out.

ESSAYS.
TITCOMB'S LETTERS, GOLD FOIL, THE JONES FAMILY,
LESSONS IN LIFE, PLAIN TALKS,
EVERY-DAY TOPICS, First Series,
EVERY-DAY TOPICS, Second Series. A New Volume.

POEMS.
BITTERSWEET, MISTRESS OF THE MANSE, KATHRINA,
PURITAN'S GUEST, AND OTHER POEMS.

NOVELS.
ARTHUR BONNICASTLE, BAY PATH, NICHOLAS MINTURN
MISS GILBERT'S CAREER, SEVENOAKS.

16 Volumes, in a Box, per set, - - $20.00.

Complete Poetical Writings of Dr. J. G. Holland.

With Illustrations by Reinhart, Griswold, and Mary Hallock Foote, and Portrait by Wyatt Eaton. Printed from New Stereotyped Plates, Prepared expressly for this Edition.

One Volume, 8vo. Extra Cloth, - - - $5.00.

"*Dr. Holland will always find a congenial audience in the homes of culture and refinement. He does not affect the play of the darker and fiercer passions, but delights in the sweet images that cluster around the domestic hearth. He cherishes a strong fellow-feeling with the pure and tranquil life in the modest social circles of the American people, and has thus won his way to the companionship of many friendly hearts.*"—N. Y. TRIBUNE.

⁎ *For sale by all booksellers, or sent post-paid upon receipt of price by*

CHARLES SCRIBNER'S SONS,
743 AND 745 BROADWAY, NEW YORK

"Externally and internally the book is a book of beauty."—
NEW YORK EVENING POST.

The House Beautiful.

BY CLARENCE COOK.

WITH OVER ONE HUNDRED ILLUSTRATIONS FROM ORIGINAL DRAWINGS BY FRANCIS LATHROP, MISS MARIA R. OAKEY, A. SANDIER, J. S. INGLIS, AND OTHERS; ENGRAVED BY HENRY MARSH, F. S. KING, AND OTHERS.

A NEW EDITION. PRICE REDUCED FROM $7.50 TO $4.00.

One vol. small 4to, superbly printed on superfine paper, cloth extra (design by Cottier), gilt top, $4.00.

"The air of elegance and taste which first breathes upon us from the cover, and comes as with a spicy aroma from the title-page, pervades every feature of the book—paper and type, text and illustration—from beginning to end; indeed, no work of the kind, which has yet appeared in this country, quite equals it in a certain combination of richness and simplicity."—*The N. Y. Tribune.*

"The text and illustrations have also the unmistakable stamp of original investigation and independent feeling for the tasteful and refined in household decoration."—*The N. Y. Times.*

"The charm of it lies deeper than in paper surface and letter-press and graver's lines; and wherever it goes it will educate, inspire and refine."—*The Literary World.*

"It is one of the most practical and useful books of its kind, and hits exactly the wants of to-day."—*Hartford Courant.*

"Mr. Cook's book—it seems as if any dwelling, no matter how humble, might make itself to blossom with touches of real beauty by the following of some of his wise suggestions."—*The Congregationalist.*

"The book is a beautiful one, and it will be a treasure in the hands of all who can appreciate the beautiful, and are asking the important question—'How shall we furnish our homes?'"—*Christian at Work.*

"Mr. Cook is not a slave to any one style of furniture or furnishing."—*Cincinnati Gazette.*

"In the simple adoption of the means to the end to be reached will be found the true artistic elegance and comfort. We commend this volume to the perusal of all who are interested in making home-life beautiful."—*Baltimore Gazette.*

*** *For sale by all booksellers, or sent, post-paid, upon receipt of price, by*

CHARLES SCRIBNER'S SONS, PUBLISHERS,
743 AND 745 BROADWAY, NEW YORK.

WOMAN'S HANDIWORK IN MODERN HOMES.

BY

CONSTANCE CARY HARRISON.

One Volume, 8vo, Richly Bound in Illuminated Cloth, with numerous Illustrations and Five Colored Plates from designs by SAMUEL COLMAN, ROSINA EMMET, GEORGE GIBSON, and others.

Price, $2.00.

Mrs. Harrison's book combines a discussion of the principles of design and decoration, practical chapters on embroidery, painting on silk and china, etc., with most helpful hints as to the domestic manufacture of many objects of use and beauty in house-furnishing, and also suggestions for the arrangement and decoration of rooms in the details of screens, portieres, the mantel-piece, etc.

CRITICAL NOTICES.

"A volume quite the most comprehensive of its kind ever published."—*The Art Interchange.*

"It is, indeed, the most comprehensive and practical guide to the amateur decorative arts that has yet appeared."—*Art Amateur.*

"The work supplies a current need of the day, which nothing else has met."—*Boston Traveller.*

"Unquestionably one of the very best of its class that we have."—*N. Y. Evening Post.*

"Mrs. Harrison has grouped together in her book about as much useful information as it is possible to get together in the same number of pages."—*Baltimore Gazette.*

"Mrs. Harrison's book is one of the very few books on household art which can be unreservedly commended."—*The World.*

"Mrs. Harrison's suggestions are within the reach of the most limited means."—*The Critic.*

"Full of suggestions, descriptions, and illustrations, of the kind that fascinate all those whose chief joy is in making home beautiful and happy."—*N. Y. Observer.*

"Everything important that relates to the furnishing and ornamentation of houses will be found in this work, which is rich in important information, and noticeable for its good taste, sound judgment, and practical wisdom."—*Boston Saturday Eve. Gazette.*

"Mrs. Harrison seems to have included in her work instructions for every æsthetic emergency that can arise in a household."—*Providence Journal.*

** *For sale by all booksellers, or sent, post-paid, upon receipt of price, by*

CHARLES SCRIBNER'S SONS, PUBLISHERS,

743 AND 745 BROADWAY, NEW YORK.

A NEW BOOK BY MARION HARLAND.

Loiterings in Pleasant Paths.

One volume, 12mo, - - - - - $1.75

Books of travel have multiplied of late years almost in a direct ratio to the increased facilities for journeying, and it may be said that the quality has also proportionately improved. We have works profusely adorned with superb illustrations, and others without pictorial embellishments, relying for their attractiveness on the charm of a skilled pen and the freshness of first impressions. Such a book is LOITERINGS IN PLEASANT PATHS, by "Marion Harland," whose *Common Sense* books have made her name a household word in every part of the land.

"These 'familiar talks from afar' are no fancy sketches, but actual experiences and impressions of a shrewd observer, whose mind was enriched and fully prepared to observe accurately and write intelligently and profitably. Marion Harland always writes books with a purpose, and the present volume is no exception to her rule."—*Chicago Inter-Ocean.*

"The observations of so clever a woman, who carries her head with her upon her travels and ventures to make use of all her faculties, are worth writing about and reading about, and this particular traveller has the good gift of so writing about them that the reading is a constant and unfailing source of pleasure."—*Evangelist.*

"Those who are going abroad will find this volume a delightful companion by the way; while those who are compelled to stay at home will find it the best possible substitute for the pleasure of foreign travel, as proved by actual experience."—*N. Y. Evening Post.*

⁎ *For sale by all booksellers, or sent post-paid upon receipt of price, by*

CHARLES SCRIBNER'S SONS,

743 AND 745 BROADWAY, NEW YORK.